THE SINGING CHURCH

THE
SINGING CHURCH

an outline history
of the music sung by choir
and people

by

C. HENRY PHILLIPS

New Edition prepared by
ARTHUR HUTCHINGS

ARCHON BOOKS
Hamden, Connecticut

*First edition published
in the United States*

1969

© *C. Henry Phillips 1969*

SBN: 208 00976 0

Printed in Great Britain

FOREWORD

Writing before the last war, Dr. Phillips voiced some of the desires for changes and exchanges in religious thought which have since affected the worship of most Christian denominations. In an age of ecumenism the continued demand for his book may be thought remarkable, since it was primarily concerned with one denomination; and although churches in Australia, Canada, America and elsewhere are in communion with the anglican church, from whose missions many of them grew, that church is still politically established and insular; her organisation is even less than insular now that the Scottish and Welsh episcopal churches are disestablished. Yet episcopal reformed churches, including those that were once daughters of the anglican church, use similar patterns of worship; and just as one may find much of the Lutheran legacy of choral, congregational and organ music in a German Roman Catholic church so one may find in a non-episcopal church an awareness of the anglican treasury of music such could shame many an anglican church. Moreover much that is loved by anglicans, especially much congregational hymnody, is of non-anglican provenance.

Dr. Phillips lived long enough to know that this book, by a staunch high anglican, was valued by non-anglican clergy and musicians; he died, however, before knowing the extent to which they would use the courses and publications of the college now known as the Royal School of Church Music. In its beginnings as the College of S. Nicolas he was probably its most valued teacher after the actual founder, Sir Sydney Nicholson. Dr. Phillips' was a merry temperament, and the few occasions when I met him were those of short respite for him between meetings or teaching periods or other duties; it did not occur to me, therefore, to ask him how he envisaged the future expansion of the work then done by the College of S. Nicolas. During that time the shadow of war was looming over us, but certain it is that even his optimistic imagination has been more than fulfilled by the royal charter granted to the college, the magnificent headquarters it now

7

occupies at Addington Palace and the breadth of its services to church musicians and clergy from villages near Croydon to those of the antipodes.

The foreword to the original issue of this book declares it to be 'the outcome of lectures . . . at the College of S. Nicolas, Chislehurst, Kent, during the years preceding 1939'. It did not purport to be a complete short history of music and liturgy, nor a comprehensive practical manual for organists and choirmasters, but a 'first text-book' to supply what was missing in the curriculum of clergy training colleges and music institutions. Dr. Phillips paid due tribute to the scope of diplomas of the Royal College of Organists and the high standards of its examinations; but the R.C.O. was not specifically a religious institution and Dr. Phillips was therefore happy to record, just before sending his book to press, that it had met the request of the 'School of English Church Music' to institute the Archbishop of Canterbury's Diploma in Church Music, and he hoped that diplomas of the R.C.O., together with the A.D.C.M., would be 'the norm of attainment for every serious-minded church musician'.

The slight alterations in this reprinting of his book avoid any deliberate suppression of his opinions, however much they differ from mine. Most alterations are the result of the very advances the book advocates. In 1939 he could write: 'Dunstable, Fayrfax and Taverner have but a line or two, not so much as Attwood and Stainer . . . but they are sung and Dunstable is not.' In 1968 two pieces by Dunstable and three by Taverner are in the repertory of my provincial parish church. In 1939 there was no *Musica Britannica*, and Dr. Phillips had more sense than to lecture about music which his hearers had little chance of examining for themselves. In 1968 it is no longer necessary to include in the bibliography his lists of publications of well-known anthems and settings. If one is too indolent to search the catalogues one can use the R.S.C.M. 'Recommended Lists', but it is no more the policy of the R.S.C.M. than it was of Dr. Phillips to encourage the church musician in reliance on second-hand recommendations alone.

Let it not be thought, then, that Dr. Phillips' deliberately restricted range of musical references (at a time when many classics of church music were not available in cheap reprints) represents the limit of his scholarship. He would have held a university chair if he had not died suddenly in middle age. He had an unusual knowledge of medieval French literature and music, none of which is mentioned in this book, for 'swank' was utterly foreign to his nature. His modesty as much as his geniality and drive made him an inspiring teacher.

'Like all other *Gebrauchsmusik*', he wrote, 'church music must be judged by its fitness in the service. . . . Separated from its ballet *Petrouchka* makes, most of the time, pointless nonsense. And if one cannot judge a church composition from the printed copy, neither can one assess it with a mind out of sympathy with the church service. . . . The litany looks bald in the music copy. Sung in procession with cross and candles in the half-light of some cathedral it comes to new life. The litany is more than the words, more than the music; it is a piece of corporate expression, a liturgical act.' Those words reveal the imagination of an author whose 'first text-book' was intended to help the church musician to 'discover the principles underlying his work'.

Durham, 1968   ARTHUR HUTCHINGS

CONTENTS

Part IV. From Croft to Wesley

Part V. Since 1871

PART VI. AN ESSAY ON PRINCIPLES AND PRACTICE

ILLUSTRATIONS

ILLUSTRATION TO PSALM 150 IN THE CANTERBURY
PSALTER *facing page 64*

The magnificent 'Canterbury' Psalter, a volume of 286 leaves
plus fly-leaves, all 18 by 13 inches in size, is the work of one
man, Eadwine, who had finished it at Christ Church, Canterbury, before the death of St. Thomas in 1170. During the
sixteenth century it was bound in leather-covered wooden
boards and furnished with metal bosses representing the Tudor
rose; it was presented to the library of Trinity College, Cambridge, by Thomas Nevile, Master of Trinity, 1593–1615, and
Dean of Canterbury. Besides the psalter and canticles it contains a kalendar and notes on the *Pater Noster* and Apostles'
Creed. These are followed in the medieval manner by a treatise
on palmistry, another on a system of prognostication, a self-
portrait of Eadwine and two plans of the famous water-piping
system of the Canterbury precincts.

Three parallel Latin versions are given of the psalms, (1) the
Hebraicum, Jerome's translation from the Hebrew, never used
in the services, (2) the Romanum, the version brought to
England by Augustine and in use here till 1066, the correction
by Jerome of his Latin version by collation with the Septuagint,
and (3) the Gallicanum, the Vulgate or Authorised Version, a
Latin version of the Septuagint corrected by collation with the
Hebrew text. Philologically the psalter is important, as the
Hebraicum text is interlined with a French version, the earliest
known, the Romanum with a similar Anglo-Saxon version and
the Gallicanum with glosses in Latin.

When drawing his illustrations Eadwine had open before him
a psalter made in the diocese of Rheims in the ninth century and
now known as the 'Utrecht' Psalter: Eadwine then drew his
pictures allowing both the psalm itself and the Utrecht picture
to suggest his subjects. Above the illustration here shown is a
line from the collect after psalm 149, below which, top centre,
is the figure of Christ flanked by six angels. Top left are four
musicians playing respectively from left to right a long-necked

15

'lute', the same, drum (tabret) and harp as mentioned in the following psalm. Of the four figures top right that on the left plays another stringed instrument, while the two inner figures hold unidentifiable instruments shaped like ear-trumpets. The lower groups at the sides show four players of curved, conical instruments no doubt intended to be trumpets or shawms: their strident notes are graphically shown by parallel lines issuing from the bell rather in the manner of a modern cartoon. The trumpeters' neighbours (one with a leg missing!) may possibly be praying or more likely performing some rhythmic movement of the hands as in dancing, which would illustrate the psalm very well. The psalmist's cymbals are not represented. Eadwine's organ seems rather to be a copy of that in the Utrecht Psalter than the result of direct observation, for at this time the Winchester organ had 400 pipes and few were content with his meagre ten, six white and four black (pipes were often painted in England at this time). His 'casework' is merely a rather pointless frame and he leaves much to be desired in the way of mechanism, for the players' fingers merely caress the base of the pipes, the soundboard shows some unaccountable holes (?), and the wind reservoirs seem of an unworkable pattern. But the human interest is there with the bent backs of the blowers and the impatience of the players avid as ever for more wind.

The illustration is reproduced by permission of Messrs. Percy Lund Humphries & Co. Ltd. and the Friends of Canterbury Cathedral from their facsimile of this monumental work. The author tenders his thanks to Messrs. Lund Humphries for facilities to consult the preface of the facsimile.

NEUMES IN THE MOZARABIC PSALTER   *facing page* 65

A corner of a damaged page from the Mozarabic Psalter in the British Museum showing neumes written above the first verse only of Psalm 127 (lines 4–7 of the MS.) reading:

Nisi dns ed
berit do
In uano la
qui edific
Nisi dn
dierit

The full reading would be:

> Nisi d(omi)n(u)s ed(ifica)berit do(mum)
> In uano la(borant) qui edific(ant eam.)
> Nisi d(omi)n(us custo)dierit (ciuitatem).

The first two lines of the MS. are the end of a prayer attached to the previous psalm, the third line being the heading 'CXXVI Canticum' (Psalm 127 in our Prayer Book). The MS., in Visigothic script, was made in the eleventh century and used at the Monastery of St. Sebastian at Silo, 30 miles from Burgos in Old Castile in Spain at the time when its most famous abbot, St. Domingo de Silos, flourished. Over the initial words of the psalms the rising intonation can easily be made out with a capital letter at 'In uano' where the choir joined in after the Cantor had sung the first half-verse. Even if the monks at Silo had known the stave notation they might well not bother to use it for the familiar psalms, the first verses only of which are marked with neumes. Presumably the other verses were pointed from memory. Reproduced by permission, from a photograph supplied by the British Museum.

A PAGE FROM JOHN PLAYFORD'S 'WHOLE BOOK OF PSALMS' *facing page* 80

The title-page of the book from which this page is reproduced by kind courtesy of the owner, Mr. William J. Amherst, shows that the copy is one of the 'Fourteenth Edition Corrected and Amended' in 1717, the original having appeared in 1677. In this edition the music is 'Composed in THREE PARTS, *CANTUS, MEDIUS & BASSUS*: In a more Plain and Useful Method than hath been formerly Published.' The tune here shown is the 'Old 100th', here called 'Proper Tune', the melody and bass of which are given first, then the Medius—with G clef—and lastly the Bassus alone. Note that the key signature is two sharps only (F-sharp being given twice), the necessary G-sharps for the key of A being inserted as accidentals. The *alla breve* time signature is here equal to $\frac{2}{2}$, which if obeyed makes the whole much less heavy than when sung four in a bar. Note the interesting barring of the first half of lines one and three.

CHAMBER ORGAN BY SNETSLER *facing page* 81

A type of instrument used in many private chapels in the

middle of the eighteenth century and still occasionally to be
found in use. At this period most village churches managed the
accompaniments to their hymns and psalms with winch organs
and gallery orchestras. In 1767 no English organ could boast a
set of pedals, even though the larger instruments had two
manuals. The instrument shown, which has a small pedal in the
centre for operating the bellows, is by Snetsler, usually known
as Snetzler, and is now in the Permanent Collection of Antique
Musical Instruments of Messrs. Rushworth & Dreaper, Liverpool, who have generously granted facilities and permission to
reproduce.

THE VILLAGE CHOIR—THOMAS WEBSTER, 1847
facing page 208

The picture shows a 'cello and bassoon playing in unison and
a clarinet—who alone seems to watch the beat—playing the
melody, with four men at the same stand also, presumably,
singing the melody. Allowing for painter's licence it seems
unlikely that any real harmony is being attempted by this
gallery choir of 1847. Webster, whose father intended him for
the musical profession, attended the school of St. George's,
Windsor, and some of the originals of his figures are still
remembered in the village of Bow Brickhill, where the painting
was executed. It may therefore be considered an authentic
document. Further information will be found in the pamphlet
'Bow Brickhill' by the Rev. R. Conyers Morrell (1934). The
original of this painting is in the collection of the Victoria and
Albert Museum who have generously granted permission to
publish. Crown copyright reserved.

MAY MORNING ON MAGDALEN TOWER *facing page* 209

Singing from Magdalen Tower in the early morning of May
1st each year has a romantic and a realistic aspect. The first
plate, from a painting by Holman Hunt (who made two versions between 1888 and 1891), catches the spirit of the occasion
in the manner of its time; the figures are all portraits taken during service time in chapel. The second, from a modern press
photograph, gives the realities. Included in the music sung is
the *Hymnus Eucharisticus* of Benjamin Rogers. The Holman
Hunt picture is reproduced by permission of the Museum and
Art Gallery Committee of the Corporation of Birmingham (the

other version, slightly different, is in the Lady Lever Collection at Port Sunlight), the press photo by courtesy of the *Oxford Mail*.

CHORISTERS AT WORK IN THE CRYPT OF CANTERBURY

facing page 224

Some of the choristers of Canterbury singing carols in the crypt on the site of the first church of Augustine. The boys without surplices are 'probationers' who have not yet attained the status of 'singing boys'. Singing boys later become 'choristers' and are then on the foundation with all its rights and privileges. From a photograph by *The Times*.

THE THREE CHOIRS FESTIVAL *facing page* 224

The picture shows the scene at the opening service of the 217th meeting at Gloucester in 1937, with clergy and civic representatives of the three cities of Gloucester, Hereford and Worcester standing below the orchestra. Beginning as combined services for mutual betterment of the three cathedral choirs about the year 1716, the festival had by 1724 acquired an orchestra for the performance of works by Purcell and Handel and was sponsoring secular evening concerts outside the cathedrals. Boyce was appointed conductor in 1737 and in 1759 *Messiah* was first performed at the festival. In 1869 Sullivan conducted his *The Prodigal Son* and so began the practice of producing native oratorios which resulted in the happy connection of Elgar with the festival. It is perhaps a pity that the original purpose of improving the service music has rather been lost sight of; such a purpose need not exclude the performance of other music. From a photograph by *The Times*.

THE NAVE CONSOLE AT LIVERPOOL CATHEDRAL

facing page 225

To appreciate the ingenuity of this giant console, completed in 1939, from which all the organs of the cathedral are controlled, one must imagine the thousands of hidden electrical connections between the stop-knobs and pallets. The design, by Willis, is an attempt to supply accompaniments, however and wherever needed, in the varied services of a large modern cathedral. We may, in fact, think of such a console as a symbol of the conception of what a cathedral in a great city must do for its many types of congregation. From a photograph kindly supplied by Messrs. Henry Willis & Sons and reproduced by courtesy of the Dean of Liverpool and Messrs. Willis.

Music example 50 is taken by kind permission from an old choir book in the possession of Mr. Wilfrid Norman of Wheddon Cross. The author is indebted to the proprietors of *Hymns Ancient and Modern* for permission to reprint versions of hymns from the *Plainsong Hymn Book*.

PART I

PRE-REFORMATION SERVICES AND MUSIC

1

THE ORIGINS

AUGUSTINE

Little authentic is known of the Christian Church in these islands before the year 600 and still less of its music. Christian church music as we know it was first brought to England, it is supposed, by the missionary Augustine (died 604). Towards the end of his life Augustine was sent by Pope Gregory with forty monks on a mission to England to convert the bulk of the population, who were not Christian, and to take the land under the aegis of the see of Rome. It is said that hearing of the fierceness of the inhabitants the party took fright and wished to turn back, but urged on by the inexorable pope they arrived in Thanet in 597. Augustine succeeded in getting a hearing and ultimately converted King Ethelbert who gave him a centre for his work at Canterbury. Here the missioner rebuilt an old church as Christ Church, now the cathedral. From the results of the mission, we can infer that among Augustine's party were monks skilled in music, perhaps even old members of the pope's Schola Cantorum in Rome. The music they brought with them (in their heads, not written) came to us as an already developed art which was the handmaid of an equally well-organised liturgical art. This importation of two arts used in the service of worship and first established at Canterbury spread rapidly, owing partly no doubt to the zeal of the missioners and musical experts but owing also, we may imagine, to the perennial English genius for absorbing foreign ideas. By 633 'James', Archbishop of York, was introducing the liturgy and chant to Northumbria and a hundred years later both of these Christian arts were established across the length and breadth of Britain.

PLAINSONG TODAY

Some of the music of the Gregorian system is still sung in anglican churches. It is in no sense English, though English forms of it differed later in detail from the original continental importation.

As a result of research by the monks of Solesmes working for the Roman Church and by the Plainsong and Medieval Music Society and private scholars for the Church of England, more of this music is finding its way back into our services, from which it was absent during the seventeenth and eighteenth centuries. It is a matter of regret that the introduction of plainsong has become a matter of 'high' and 'low' church politics.[1] But as plainsong is sung, though with an English text, we must attempt a rapid description of the music; it will, however, be impossible to do this until we have studied briefly the liturgical system which it served. No attempt will be made to give a complete history of liturgiology. Instead, we shall seek to discover the principles underlying the structure of the services of the medieval system, mentioning the history only incidentally.

[1] In the United States low and high churches alike use plainsong. On the other hand chanting the psalms is a sign of definite 'high' tendencies. There is no defence for such unmeaning fashions. Since Dr. Phillips wrote the party associations have receded. Acquaintance with plainsong in universities and colleges, as well as by radio and gramophone, may partly explain the fact that we have heard it in Congregational and Methodist services, and also in those of the Scottish Kirk.

2

THE STRUCTURE OF THE SERVICES

THE MASS: ORIGINS

We can infer that of the people who met in a 'house' on the first Day of Pentecost after the resurrection the greater number were Jews who still attended their synagogues on the Sabbath. As Christians they had almost certainly met before and by written or spoken notice had been convened for this occasion. At subsequent meetings someone would propose an agenda. He would, no doubt, model it on the plan of the familiar synagogue service, but one type of meeting would obviously recall the last supper when Jesus had shown them what they must do. They would break bread in the manner some of them had witnessed and say the words their master had used, trying to mean by them what he had meant. The mass as a service had been born. The meeting would probably start and finish with singing—it had ended with 'an hymn' on the night before the previous Good Friday—and before the breaking of the bread one of the apostles or leaders would doubtless say some form of preparation. The prayers would soon tend to follow certain lines. No formal prayers are known, however, until about the year 200.

THE MASS FORMALISED

In 150 Justin Martyr tells us that the service consisted of a form of preparation based on the synagogue service and made up of:

(*a*) The reading of the scriptures,
(*b*) A sermon,
(*c*) Some prayers,

the second and essential part of the service proceeding as follows:

(*d*) The oblation or offertory of the bread, wine and water,
(*e*) A long prayer of praise,
(*f*) Some responses, i.e. prayers with Amens,
(*g*) The administration.

It was not, however, until fifty years later that Hippolytus of Rome gives a set form of the prayers for the central part of the service—(*e*), (*f*) and (*g*) on the preceeding page. This he gives thus:

(*a*) *Sursum Corda*, as today,
(*b*) A thanksgiving for the incarnation,
(*c*) The narrative of the institution at the last supper,
(*d*) The memorial oblation—'we offer these gifts in memory of the death and passion . . .'
(*e*) The invocation of the Holy Spirit,
(*f*) Some intercessions,
(*g*) A doxology.

We see here the clear twofold form of the service: a first part meditative and preparatory and the second essential, consisting, so far as the spoken words went, of a long, formal prayer during which the words of institution were said.

THE MASS: SUBSEQUENT HISTORY

This general formula has not been radically changed though many systems flourished in various parts of Europe with minor differences. The so-called Gallican Use (North Italy, Milan, Gaul, Spain in early times, Britain, Ireland) and the later Spanish or Mozarabic Use were ultimately supplanted by the Roman Use. The Eastern or Orthodox Use ceased to influence the Western Uses after the Great Schism of 1050 and so the Roman Use was supreme in the west. It has remained virtually the same since the fifth century and was the type of service brought to England by Augustine. In England the Use of the see of Salisbury, called Sarum, tended to oust other local Uses until it became practically universal; it differed only in detail from the Roman imported Use. We can therefore study the form of the Sarum mass as an example of the sort of service which was sung by musicians in England before the Reformation.

THE SARUM MASS

The Sarum mass, then, went as follows:

(*a*) The Preparation, said by the celebrant in the vestry. It consisted of:
    1. *Veni Creator.*

2. A collect.
3. Psalm 43.
4. A litany for purity of intention.
5. *Pater Noster*.

This section was the personal concern of the celebrant.

(*b*) The Introit, sung by the choir as the celebrant proceeded to the altar. During the singing the celebrant and his deacons said the mutual confession and absolution, still used in many churches today, and performed the preliminary censing of the altar.

(*c*) *Kyrie eleison*, sung by the choir antiphonally.

(*d*) *Gloria in excelsis*, sung by the choir and people.

(*e*) The Mutual Salutation (℣. The Lord be with you. ℟. And with thy spirit.) and the collect for the day. Today the collect for the reigning sovereign is inserted here.

(*f*) The Epistle.

(*g*) The Gradual, followed by the Alleluia and Sequence, or in penitential seasons by the Tract. These were sung by the choir.

(*h*) The Gospel.

(*i*) The Offertory, sung by the choir during the offertory of bread, wine, water and alms.

This is the end of the first section of the service. The next part, often called the Anaphora, proceeded thus:

(*j*) *Sursum Corda* and Preface, leading to

(*k*) *Sanctus*, sung by the choir.

(*l*) The Canon, a long prayer consisting of:
    1. The Intercession.
    2. The Consecration, including the words of institution.
    3. The Oblation or offering with alms, of the consecrated elements.
    4. *Pater Noster*, said by all together.

(*m*) *Agnus Dei*, sung by the choir.

(*n*) The Commixture and the giving of the Pax.

(*o*) Prayers at the Reception.

(*p*) The Communio Anthem, sung by the choir.

(*q*) The Post-Communio.

(*r*) The Dismissal (℣. Ite missa est. ℟. Benedicamus Domino.)

(*s*) Closing Prayers and the Last Gospel said on the way back to the vestry.

The musical requirements of this scheme will be noticed later; in passing we may notice the differences between the outline given and the form of service in our modern prayer book. They consist chiefly of:

(*a*) The excision of certain parts, as, for example, the Introit, Gradual, Communio, etc.

(*b*) The transplanting of *Gloria in excelsis* from the first, preparatory part of the service to the end of the second part: this was not done until the issue of the 1552 Prayer Book.

(*c*) The splitting up and redistribution of the Canon, which was one long formal prayer, so that:

    1. The Intercession becomes tacked on to the Offertory as the Prayer for the Church Militant, a sort of litany without responses.

    2. The Oblation is placed partly ('Who made there by his one oblation . . .') before the words of institution, and partly in a collect said after the communion.

    3. The *Pater Noster* is also placed after the communion.

By this redistribution of the Canon the prayer book sought to emphasise the communion aspect of the service rather than the consecration of the elements. Controversy was concerned with the sense in which the service continued the Jewish sacrifice by 're-presenting' or representing the sacrifice of Christ.

THE HOURS OF PRAYER

During the fourth century, a new fashion spread through Christendom, that of the monastic ideal of life. It is evident that in such a way of life frequent prayer and meditation were the objects for which it was undertaken. The monastic system thus sought to bring the monks or nuns together at certain times each day for prayer and arranged for the orderly reading of the bible and psalter. Vigils or night-watches had already been kept, first as a piece of symbolism on the night before Easter, later on Saturday evenings and ultimately every day. Meanwhile this night-watch was shortened into three 'hours'—or periods—of prayer, Vespers at the lighting of the lamps, Nocturns at cock-crow, followed at daybreak by Lauds. Unlike the other services, Nocturns, known later as Mattins, ended with a simple versicle without a collect; it was in practice followed immediately by Lauds so that the two were fused into one service. Vespers and Nocturns with Lauds were known as the *Cursus Nocturnus* and were balanced by the *Cursus Diurnus*, three day 'hours'; they were Terce at the third hour after sunrise, Sext and Nones at the sixth and ninth. To meet the requirements of the monastic programme two further 'hours' arose: Prime, a preliminary to the morning chapter meeting, and Compline, held immediately before retiring.

CONTENTS OF THE 'HOURS'

At Nocturns alone three lessons (readings) from the bible formed the major portion of the service. Only a *Capitulum* or Little Chapter (a very short reading, perhaps only a sentence or two) was read at the day hours. At Nocturns psalms 1 to 110 were sung through 'in course', about five Psalms at each sitting, and at Vespers the remaining psalms were similarly sung. Fixed psalms, as, for example, three portions of Psalm 119 at the three day hours, were sung at all the other services. As an example of an hour, here is the scheme for Compline of the Sarum Use:

(a) Private Prayers and Introduction.
(b) Four fixed psalms with variable antiphons, according to the season.
(c) The *Capitulum*, fixed.
(d) A Respond, fixed except during Lent.
(e) A hymn, variable, with a fixed versicle.
(f) *Nunc dimittis* with variable antiphon.
(g) Suffrages and a fixed collect.

MEDITATIVE SERVICES

These hours from which we derive our modern matins and evensong have no central act like the mass. There are no ceremonies except sitting, kneeling and standing, no sense of drama, something being 'done'. Instead, behind them was the monastic idea of turning the mind at fixed intervals to spiritual matters by means of reading the bible and psalter and reciting set prayers. They are, in fact, purely meditative services.

3

ORIGINS OF THE SERVICE MUSIC

CANTUS RESPONSORIUS

While music is in no sense an essential in public worship (though some sort of concerted act is essential if there is to be any *public* worship) even a cursory knowledge of the psalms will show the important part it played in the services of the Jewish Temple. Many of the psalms which have come down to us are obviously liturgical or arranged with recurring refrains for singing. After the last supper the apostles sang 'an hymn', perhaps one of the psalms we know, and Paul exhorts his converts to sing 'psalms and hymns and spiritual songs'. Later, when Roman law persecuted the Christian church, singing was perhaps less indulged in for services would be held in secret. When in 313 the Edict of Milan made Christianity the religion of the Empire, singing came into its own again. But singing can never have died out completely and the form of music used in Christian worship followed the model of that heard in the synagogues. One of the chief features of synagogue music was the solo melismatic, or ornate, chant, in which a soloist sang a phrase which was repeated verbatim by the people or answered by them with a refrain, as, for instance, in Psalm 136. This refrain might be, as in the psalm mentioned, such a phrase as 'for his mercy endureth for ever', or an Amen or Alleluia, and in Christian times *Gloria Patri*, This twofold method of singing was called *Cantus Responsorius*; it had been used no doubt from ancient times in public worship and was clearly the natural result of having present at the service both skilled and unskilled singers. We see it today in a simplified form in the versicle and response or the litany. The frequency of papal fulminations against the melismatic chant shows that the soloists tended to over-indulge by elaborating their chants; their joy in their skill tended to thrust aside the purpose of public worship. Most of this solo chant disappeared with the publication of the 1549 and 1552 Book of Common Prayer.

CANTUS ANTIPHONARIUS

During the fourth century another method of singing spread, like the monastic ideal, from the east where boys were first used as singers; this was called *Cantus Antiphonarius*. The term was first used to denote singing by boys and men together in octaves as well as antiphonal singing. Later it meant antiphonal singing only –one body of voices answering another. Being peculiarly suitable for the singing of the psalms, with their strophic, parallel structure, it was freely used in the new monastic services and brought with it the hymn, a new type of composition founded on accentual rhythm and possibly of Semitic origin.[1] Though Ephraem Syrus (303–373) and Hilary of Poitiers (died 367) are credited with its introduction into Christian services, it was Ambrose, Bishop of Milan from 374 to 397, who first brought it to the form we know, that of a number of four-lined stanzas in iambic dimeters. The subjects of his hymns are always the fundamentals of the Christian dogma and the language is simple and dignified; the tunes, which may or may not be by Ambrose, are perfect models of directness and sober beauty. Of the many hymns claimed to be from his pen four are generally reckoned as authentic:

1. Aeterna rerum Conditor.
2. Deus Creator omnium.
3. Jam surgit hora tertia.
4. Veni Redemptor gentium.

A stanza of the last with its translation and melody will serve as an example of his art.

Ve-ni, re-demptor gen – – ti – um, Os – – ten-de– port-um– vir-gin-e :
O come,redeem-er of—— the— earth, Show—— to the—world thy— vir-gin birth ;

Mi-re-tur om-ne sae-cu-lum :—— Ta - lis dec - et part-us— De - i.
Let age.to age the wonder tell :—— Such birth;O— God, be-seems Thee—well.

[1] Paul's 'hymn' in the passage quoted above probably meant something like a psalm.

THE MUSICAL GROUNDWORK ESTABLISHED

We see then that by the end of the fourth century three distinct types of chant were used in the now well-established services: *Cantus Responsorius*, consisting of the more ornate solos with less florid refrains, *Cantus Antiphonarius*, antiphonal congregational singing which was usually simple, and the metric Hymns. During the centuries that followed these three types were the groundwork of the service music; derived originally from the synagogue music, this music shows other influences like those of folk-music or the infiltrations of Greek and Byzantine elements during the seventh and eighth centuries. It is also possible to distinguish later between the music for the various rites—Roman, Milanese (Ambrosian), Gallican, Mozarabic (Spanish), and Sarum (English)—but the ground-plan remained clear and is common to all in modality, rhythmic scheme and word treatment.

THE GREGORIAN REVISION

The liturgy and chant introduced by Augustine into Britain in 597 was thus already a well-developed system. The work of Pope Gregory (590–601) was in no sense creative; it took the scattered elements so far achieved and welded them into an ordered whole. It was this newly organised system which survived in England during the middle ages and in essentials it is the same as the system used today in the Roman church. This Gregorian revision, a gathering together and a reform at the same time of the liturgy and its chant, was contained essentially in two books. The so-called Gregorian Sacramentary dealt with four matters: *Proprium de Tempore*, the regulation of the daily services, *Proprium de Sanctis*, that of saints' day services, *Missae*, the ordering of the mass, and *Orationes Communes*, the book of prayers; the musical counterpart to the Sacramentary consisted of two parts, the first concerned with the mass and lesser sacraments, the other with the Divine Offices or hours of prayer. The extent of the labour entailed may be gauged from the fact that the mass portion contained over 600 pieces (introits, graduals, etc.) and that for the hours about 2,000 antiphons besides over 1,000 smaller responds, versicles and responses, etc. As well as collecting it, the musical books simplified and curtailed the music of the soloists and choir so that it should be truly subordinate to the worship; singers then as now were apparently over-eager to display their skill.

THE SCHOLA CANTORUM

To advise him, possibly, on the musical revision and to put into practical use the collected and reformed chant, Gregory founded his famous Schola Cantorum in Rome giving it an income derived from property and two houses in which to work.[1] The boys were recruited from a neighbouring orphanage and their training was undertaken seriously enough for many of them later to hold the highest offices in the church, even the papacy; musical popes indeed abounded during the next hundred years. A *Prior Scholae* or director was appointed with two assistants, the *Quartus Scholae*, having charge of the boys. The music was learnt entirely by ear and is said to have involved a training of ten years. Though primarily founded for the provision of music in the papal chapel, the school became a model and many of its alumni were sent out to direct the reform of the chant and the singing in other parts of Europe; we may imagine that some of its members accompanied Augustine on his mission to Britain. The school's influence helped to effect the penetration of the Gregorian Sacramentary and the approved methods of singing its musical settings to all parts of the church, so that by the year 1000 the system can be said to have spread everywhere to the ultimate exclusion of the Gallican and Mozarabic systems. The only exception was the Milanese or Ambrosian tradition which held out against the prevailing Roman system, becoming a sort of liturgical island. The Milanese tradition was not, in fact, finally broken until about 1500.

[1] Other Song Schools, not so famous, had existed in Rome before this time.

4

THE MUSIC

THE WORK OF RECOVERY

During the nine hundred years from 300 to 1200 when plainsong was the basic music[1] of the church much artistic development must obviously have taken place; but it can be traced only by experts owing to the notation of the manuscripts made previous to the year 1000. The work of Solesmes was therefore that of collating manuscripts to obtain the original or the most artistic text. Between 313 and 600 the chant shows alternate elaboration and simplification of detail, and we have seen that collection, organisation and simplification of the existing music was effected by Gregory. The golden age of plainsong may perhaps be taken as the years between 800 and 1100; unfortunately, however, for modern research the only notation used before the year 1000 was neumatic and it may truthfully be said that the invention and use of the stave for noting down melodies happened only just in time to rescue this music from the baffling oblivion from which, for example, Greek music has never been wrested. The neumatic notation was purely mnemonic, consisting of marks (neumes) placed over or at the side of the text and vaguely diagrammatic of the lie of the melody. They were, in fact, an elaboration of the marks used by the teachers of rhetoric to show the voice inflexions to be used in reading. The neume for a leap of a run down the scale did not tell the singer unfamiliar with the melody the interval of the leap or the note from which the run began, so that no sight-reading of the manuscript was possible. By collation with later stave-notation manuscripts, however, these neumatic manuscripts can give an accurate idea of any melody being studied.

[1] The generic name for all service music was *Cantus*, the Chant. *Cantus Planus*, Plainchant or Plainsong, was used later to distinguish the monodic traditional music from organum and still later from harmonised, mensural music.

STAVE NOTATION

During the ninth and tenth centuries a group of French theoreticians, of whom Abbot Otger is the best known, were writing treatises on notation and many teaching devices were invented which used lines and spaces as a diagram of the notes, to be discarded when the student had learnt his lesson.[1] The stave as we know it, nevertheless, owes its origin to a piece of practical convenience, that of scratching a ruled line across the parchment above the words to guide the scribe in placing his neumes. Later, the line was ruled in red ink and represented F, a second line often being added in yellow to represent middle C a fifth above. From this idea the stave was born and reading at sight as well as composition in the sense of being able to write down one's effusion became possible. Guido of Arezzo (born about 990), an outstanding theoretician and an able teacher, combined the stave notation with a method of naming the notes akin to modern 'tonic sol-fa', which made reading at sight a much more certain business. The Guidonian 'sol-fa' method was arrived at by a typically medieval and ingenious piece of pedagogic subtlety: the hymn for St. John's day could, it was noticed, be divided into phrases each beginning a note higher than the last. Everyone knew it and the students under his direction could always sing it over to remind themselves when they got into difficulties. The syllables under the successive first notes of the phrases were the ones he used in his method; the stanza of the lovely sapphic hymn he used went as follows:

Ex. 2
Version at No. 108, Plainsong Hymn Book.

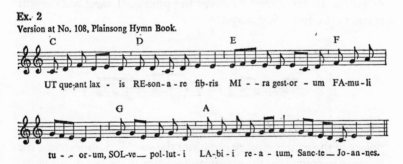

UT que-ant lax - is RE-son-a-re fib-ris MI - - ra gest-or - um FA-mu-li

tu - .- or-um, SOL-ve— pol-lut-i LA-bi-i re-a-tum, Sanc-te— Jo-an-nes.

---

[1] The work of Odo of Cluny and Hucbald (Ubaldus–about 840–930), which was once supposed to have given the lead in this matter of notation, is now reckoned to have been concerned only with the explanation of the gamut (the series of possible notes) and the eight modes.

His system must have revolutionised the teaching, making performance more certain and cutting down the ten years asserted to be necessary to know the whole corpus to a two or three years' course in sight-singing. A four-lined stave usually sufficed for the compass of the melodies, which by 1550 had been enlarged to six lines for instrumental and harmonised music; the modern five-lined staves seem to be an adequate compromise, though it is often found that they are far from useful for large-compassed instrumental music. By 1100, when melodies could be accurately noted down in a form which we can read, the melodies themselves were entering into a period of decadence. The published Solesmes texts are usually followed today, as giving the best form of the melody; in England translation of the texts into the vernacular has made slight alterations sometimes inevitable.

A NOTATION OF PHRASES

The Guidonian notation, written on its four-lined stave and founded on the neumatic system, was not really a notation of single notes in the modern sense. Based, possibly, in the dim past on the principles of rhetoric, the chant itself really showed a construction founded on phrases or melodic inflexions rather than on single notes, and the notation followed similar lines. Even if within the phrases the intervals might differ, most phrases could be divided into characteristic shapes. Thus the *podatus*, two notes ascending (like a question in rhetoric) and the *torculus*, three notes up and down (as an actor might deliver the phrase, 'I *want* to.') might occur in the following ways:

Ex. 3

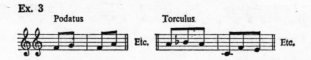

The modern transcription into quavers misses some of the finer points of the contemporary notation: the so-called liquescents, for instance, arranged for the easy pronunciation of certain consonants, chiefly *r*, *l* and *n*. In the following, for example, where the two-note group on the syllable *por-* is called a *cephalicus*, the second note is sung very lightly and takes the consonantal *r*. It has a special contemporary notation different from the *clivis*, the ordinary group

of two descending notes, but in the modern transcription this is
not made clear:

Here we see an interesting refinement showing that the neumatic
groups were the lineal successors of the old rules of rhetoric and
suggesting also that the music and words were thought of as
indivisible. The technique is, indeed, reminiscent of the supposed
methods of classical Greek drama—also a religious art—and of the
methods of recitative used in the seventeenth century. Further
examples of such refinements may also be seen in the *quilisma*,
written as three ascending notes and possibly meaning something
like a turn (though the usual modern rendering burks the suggestion), and the *strophicus*, a kind of shake involving, it is thought,
quarter-tones. They are as follows, though the rendering is not
clearly established:

MODALITY

It is generally supposed that the musical theoreticians in Pope
Gregory's entourage extracted from the existing melodies a system
of fourteen modes of which two—the authentic and plagal versions
of the Locrian, final on B—were purely theoretical. For teaching
purposes in those days and now these modes may be set out dia-
grammatically as on page 90, but modality was, of course, more
than a given arrangement of tones and semitones. The connection
between the words 'mode' and 'mood' is not fortuitous; each mode
had a characteristic atmosphere and melodies in a given mode
showed turns of phrase peculiar to the mode, so that one is immediately aware that a melody is in, say, the Dorian even before it has
come to rest on its final. In Archbishop Parker's hymn-book,

published by Day in 1567, to which Tallis wrote the tunes, the
eight modes are thus described:

> The first is meeke, devout to see,
> The second sad, in majesty,
> The third doth rage and roughly brayth,
> The fourth doth fayne and flattery playth.
> The fifth delight and laugheth the more,
> The sixth bewaileth and weepeth full sore,
> The seventh tredeth stoute in froward race,
> The eyghthe goeth milde in modest pace.

In the later middle ages the following tune was composed to the
words 'Seek ye first the kingdom of God' to show off the characteristics of mode i; the words are a sort of pun in the medieval
manner:[1]

Ex. 6

Typical Phrases of the Dorian Mode

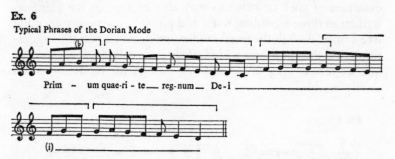

Thus we can describe a melody in the Phrygian as one which
shows the peculiar turns of phrase of that mode, one whose inter-
mediate cadences are on certain notes, called dominants, and one
which comes finally to rest on E.

AUTHENTIC AND PLAGAL MODES

A melody whose compass lay roughly between final and final—
e.g. D to D in the Dorian—was stated as being in the authentic
form of the mode, or in mode i; if the final lay roughly in the
centre of the melodic compass—e.g. A to A in the Dorian—it was
reckoned to be in the plagal form of the mode often called also the
Hypo-Dorian or mode ii. The same distinction was drawn for
other modes, giving a possible twelve in all, if we omit the

[1] Similar phrases for all the modes are given in Grove's *Dictionary* under
the title 'Modes, Ecclesiastical'.

theoretical B or Locrian mode; the distinction was hardly necessary (Ambrose is sometimes reputed to have sorted the melodies into only six modes) and it is perhaps clearer to think of the modes as six in number, those on D, E, F, G, A and C. The difference between the Hypo-Dorian, mode ii, running from A to A and the Aeolian, mode ix, also running from A to A, was seen in their finals: the final of mode ii is D, that of mode ix being A. The B-flat or B were used indiscriminately in every mode during the best period; careful consideration of the use of the B-flat must discount any idea that it was employed to avoid the tritone. The familiar tag:

> Mi contra fa
> Est diabolus in musica,

meaning that B and F sounded unpleasant in close conjunction, was a principle discovered later in the early days of harmonised music. In the chant the choice of B or B-flat depended solely on the emotional effect it was intended to produce.

RHYTHM

The original Solesmes method of editing the texts presupposed that all the notes of a given melody were roughly equal in length, and gramophone recordings show this method in practice. Many, however, consider the point anything but proved and certainly a smoother and more suave effect is got by a more conscious freedom with regard to note lengths. When the chant is sung to English words, which abound in unaccented syllables of short duration and no very definite vowel content, this is certainly the case. Thus in:

Ex. 7

Ad cenam Agni Providi, E.H. 125, A.M.R. 129

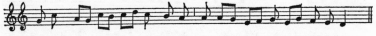

The Lamb's high ban-quet called to share, Ar-rayed in— gar-ments rich and rare

the syllables underlined sound better if sung not only lightly but more quickly than the surrounding accented syllables. No one can finally decide which method was in use in the middle ages, the free or the strict, nor is the point important; it is likely that both methods were used in different places as they are today.

ALTERNATE TWOS AND THREES

Whether the free or strict method is used, it seems clear that in purely melodic phrases unencumbered by words—the Alleluias, for example—the notes can be divided into accentual groups of two and three notes. The principle may first be seen in a text abounding in words, Latin or English; thus, the following hymn would be accented in singing in groups of two (or four) and three in this way:

Ex. 8
E.H. 94, A.M.R. 96

This method makes it perfectly easy to adjust the rhythm of the melody to that of the words when in other stanzas the word-stress occurs at different points from that in the first stanza, an obvious necessity in an English translation. In purely melodic passages the principle would be applied thus:

Ex. 9
Kyrie III from Kyrie 'Splendor Eterne', [Liber Usualis 79]

The music is always contrived so that each melodic phrase (marked off by quarter and half bar-lines) could be sung in one breath. In the hymns strict rhythmic parallelism between the lines of a stanza was, as a rule, carefully avoided. The familiar *Before the ending of the day* is an exception, being an entirely syllabic hymn. The syllabic scheme of the hymns is usually 8.8.8.8, but a welcome change is found in the so-called sapphics where the scheme, which produces some attractive results, is 11.11.11.5.[1] These rigid word schemes are seldom followed by the melody; almost any hymn will show the delightful, artistic unbalance which comes from lengthening out the answering phrase by some graceful melodic embellishment and so holding back the expected cadence. In the more melismatic chant the principle is the same, that of answering phrases which overbalance rather than balance their antecedent.

MELODY

The restrictions placed by later contrapuntal theorists on certain melodic shapes do not find a place in the chant. Leaps are followed by movement in the same direction, the tritone is freely exploited and various other 'inelegancies' are to be found which would not be tolerated in harmonised music. Such passages as the following can be matched anywhere:

Ex. 10

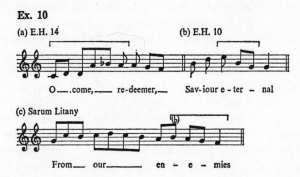

Sung in a resonant building, such passages show the peculiar aptness and beauty of the chant. For the most part the compass is within a ninth, though in some of the longer sequences,[2] intended to be sung by the soloists, certain sections differ so much from the

[1] See as an example the St. John hymn on page 35; a familiar modern example, which, however, does not keep to the rule of having a caesura after the fifth syllable in each line, will be found at *E.H.* 435, *A.M.R.* 253.

[2] See page 52.

general compass of the composition that one can only suppose some division of the choir into tenors and basses, used antiphonally, if both types of voice are not to be landed into difficulties.

UNDERLAYING

In the underlaying a partiality is shown for little melismatic phrases on unaccented syllables,[1] a method which much delighted the Elizabethans; they are essentially of the underlaying technique and when lightly sung, so that the music does not obtrude through the words, have an excellent effect. In the jubilus, where the word *Alleluia* usually constitutes the sole text, and in the longer *Kyries,* breaths were taken in the middle of words, much in the manner of the later 'hocket' (ochetus) and of the more recent Handel arias.

CONTEMPORARY ACCOMPANIMENT

It is assumed that the chant was sung without accompaniment; the Christian church has always been sparing in its admission of instruments into the church. In 811, however, Byzantine musicians were causing wonder, and disapproval, with their organ at the court of Charlemagne at Aachen. If accompaniment was known before 1200 it must supposedly have been a mere doubling of the voices in unison, in the way we imagine the huge Temple orchestra at Jerusalem was used. It has been suggested that couplers on the instruments caused the simultaneous use of pipes an octave or even other intervals above the sung melody; if so, it helps to explain the modern 'mixture' stop and give some inkling, perhaps, of the origin of organum, the name of which sounds suspicious in such a connection. At any rate, where it was installed, the organ would be useful in giving the intonation as nowadays and in helping the singers to keep the pitch constant.

ACCOMPANIMENT TODAY

The modern problem of accompaniment is different. If, in a modern service, plainsong is not sung for its own sake, it has often been used where four-part singing is impracticable—for example, in 'men only' services or at services in monasteries and convents —or where the organ is temporarily not in use. The chant can be

[1] See Ex. 1, page 31.

sung without accompaniment and in a resonant building sounds completely satisfactory even to an ear accustomed to an instrument. With the organ something is added to the effect which, if it is not historically correct, yet may achieve an artistic result.

MODALITY

When accompaniment is used certain principles become clear with regard to the harmony. We may briefly summarise these as follows: the chords allowed are triads and their inversions with a free use of passing notes, anticipatory notes, downward- and upward-moving appoggiaturas, and suspensions. Chromatics and modulations will find no place if we are to keep the modal feeling of the chant, though the B-flat may be used freely. Essentially tonic-and-dominant effects like the perfect cadence give modern associations which are best avoided. The final of the mode is always made the bass of the last chord except in modes iii and iv where it has been suggested by French authors that A and C form allowable basses. The plainsong is, of course, transposed into any suitable key.[1]

ACCENTUAL HARMONY

In the nineteenth century one chord per note was the rule, but as this tends to restrict rhythmic freedom—especially that of the singer—the emphasis nowadays is rightly placed on securing chord-changes at the word-accents. Chords are changed as infrequently as may be and the general rule is followed that the greater the accent the greater the change; if it is realised that the more notes two consecutive chords have in common the less is the stress on the second chord, and that a conjunct bass tends to weaken the accent, the main principles will be clear. The *Plainsong Hymn Book* shows this very adequately: hymn 7, first tune, is successfully accompanied where hymn 27 is not, because of its too frequent chord-changes. A performance of both will convince the hearer which accompaniment interferes less with the singer's freedom. First lines of hymns and intonations, which are usually sung in the medieval way by a soloist or cantor—a necessity then to establish pace and pitch—are never accompanied.

[1] Today the whole practice of accompanying plainchant is questioned but widely condoned as eliciting congregational singing. 'Triads and their inversions', i.e. sixteenth-century practice, has no more authority than harmony of the fifteenth, fourteenth or thirteenth century.

TONAL BACKGROUND

The accompaniment should clearly form an unobtrusive background to the singing. A quiet tone, flute, string or diapason in quality, gives the desired effect. Variety is obtained by using these three types of tone antiphonally, by occasional unison passages, by varying the texture—a three-part texture is an adequate norm —by the sparing use of the pedals, or by placing the melody in an inner part. Only the experienced player will accomplish all this extempore; for most, the workable plan is to write out the accompaniment before playing. Plainsong being a reflective rather than an expressionist art, the accompaniment will keep to the principles enumerated above; loudness of tone is never required, while tampering with the psalmist's trumpets and thunder may be left to the modern expressionist school.

Note added 1968:

However undesirable the accompanying of plainchant seems to scholars, the practice is likely to continue. It is therefore right to emphasise the fact that the association of plainsong with the harmony of the sixteenth or any other century is less objectionable than its association with any kind of accompaniment that fetters the rhythm of brisk singing. Accompaniment should not be attempted by raw apprentices nor by organists who fail to sing the words, actually or mentally, while trying to accompany and assist the singing. An 'unobtrusive background' is still the only tolerable accompaniment for plainsong psalms, but the other liturgical words may not be meditative. Bold unisons, parallel octaves, fifths or fourths may be more congruous than triads for triumphant words, e.g. parts of *Gloria in excelsis* or the hymns *Urbs beata* or *Pange lingua*.

5

TYPES OF SERVICE MUSIC

METHOD OF SINGING THE PSALMS AND CANTICLES

It seems clear that the psalms when not sung throughout by a soloist (*Cantus Tractus*, as when the sub-deacon sings the epistle at the mass) or by everyone (*Cantus Directaneus*) were, from the earliest times, sung either as *Cantus Responsorius*, where the main body sang an unvaried refrain after each verse, or as *Cantus Antiphonarius*, where the performers were divided into two bodies singing verse and verse about. Though at first the two methods existed side by side, the *Cantus Antiphonarius* acquired the refrain methods of responsorial singing, the refrains being called 'antiphons' which usually consisted of a verse of the psalm. By the eighth or ninth century the antiphon was sung only at the beginning and end of the psalm, as now. The Ambrosian methods of chanting have not survived and need not detain us, but we may here fitly summarise the Gregorian system (*Cantilena Romana*) as found in the *Liber Responsalis* or book containing the psalms, antiphons and responds.

THE EIGHT TONES

In this system eight tones or chants were provided, tone i being in mode i, tone ii in mode ii, and so forth. There were no double chants in the modern sense and each half of the tone contained a reciting note—one of the dominants of the mode[1]—which in the first half was preceded by an 'intonation', used only in the first verse (but all through the two gospel canticles, *Magnificat* and *Benedictus*) and followed by a variable 'ending' in the second half. In Palmer's *Sarum Psalter* tone i is given as possessing twelve endings, tone ii having only four; some of the endings were purely local while others were in almost universal use. The last note of the ending, sometimes modified to lead well into the concluding antiphon, was not necessarily the final of the mode so that the use

[1] In Ex. 11 the ending is on the final of the mode. It would not have been so if tone i had been chosen. Because the endings are rarely on the finals of their modes, psalm tones do not always readily suggest their modes.

of an antiphon is really obligatory, the antiphon always ending with the final. If the psalms must be sung today without antiphons—though there seems no reason why they should be—it is therefore necessary to choose an ending whose last note is the final of the mode. To show the method of performance here is a setting of Psalm 23 with antiphon in mode viii; the tone chosen is therefore tone viii. The ending used is the first, but any of the six provided in the *Sarum Psalter* might have been used.

Ex. 11

All, decani (or men only)

3. He shall con-vert my soul   and lead.... righteousness for his name's sake.

All, cantoris (or boys only)

4. Yea, though... death... e – vil   for thou art with me, thy rod and thy staff— comfort me.

All, decani (or men only)

5. Thou shalt.... trou-ble me: thou.... oil and my cup shall be full.

(or an octave lower)

All, cantoris (or boys only)

6. But.... days of my life: and I will.... Lord for ev – er.

Manual

A further tone was often used, chiefly for Psalms 114 and 115, the familiar *Tonus Peregrinus*[1] or irregular tone which was in mode i

[1] Called the 'peregrine' tone because it travels or strays from its first reciting note to the note below, in Ex. 12 from A to G. The example quoted is the simplest form of *Tonus Peregrinus*, of which there are several versions, none established as 'authentic'.

but had an intonation in the second half of the chant as well as in the first, thus:

Ex. 12

Psalm 114, Verse 1 to Tonus Peregrinus

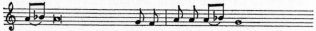

When Israel came out of E-gypt: and the house of Jacob from a-

-mong the strange peo-ple

Its antiphon in the *Sarum Psalter* is in mode viii thus revealing the irregular nature of the tone.

THE CANTICLES

Of the canticles, *Venite*, *Benedicite*, *Quicunque vult* and *Nunc dimittis* were treated as psalms, the last having seasonal antiphons like the short but suave *Veni, Domine* (Come, O Lord) or the equally soothing *Salve nos* (Preserve us, O Lord), while on the third Sunday in Lent it was preceded by a long and involved antiphon, *Media vita* (In the midst of life we are in death) of much power and beauty. *Magnificat* and *Benedictus* were usually sung to elaborate or 'solemn' versions of the tones with highly ornate seasonal antiphons of which the 'Great O' antiphons (*O Sapientia*, *O Adonai*, *O Radix Jesse* and the rest) sung during the week before Christmas are the most famous as well as the most moving and poetical. A special setting of these two canticles to *Tonus Peregrinus* was also provided. *Te Deum* was treated, in the manner of the Nicene Creed, with an elaborate chant-like setting of three chants chiefly in modes iii and iv. The Sarum setting, like the Sarum Litany, is among the noblest of medieval music released to us by modern research; its grandeur makes Merbecke's bald version of it look exceedingly tame and pointless.

THE HYMNS

Since the publication of the *Plainsong Hymn Book* the best of the hymns of the period have been made available in compendious form for choirs and congregations. There is nothing to surpass the melodic beauty of the best of them and the excellent and sensitive

English translations provided match the poetry of the music. Here is a wealth of variety of all kinds: the metres vary as much as those in any collection of an equivalent number of modern hymns, the long metre, sapphic and elegiac mingling with others less common. Over the metre the tune hovers without slavishly following the jog-trot of the words, adding little melodic phrases to break up the regularity. The Englishing of the texts has obviously been done to fit the proper tune, which makes the collection all the more usable. Always intriguing is the melodic form, repetitions and subtle analogies being found between successive or separated lines or within the line itself.

USE TODAY

It seems a pity that the prejudice of the ignorant should prevent these superlative miniatures from finding a hearing anywhere but in a certain type of church. Their objectiveness, their sheer poetry often, as well as the fact that alongside the psalm-tune, the Wesley hymn or the foreign chorale they are part of the church's heritage, should give them an honoured place in the service. Of course, they will not fit into the loud-voiced 'popular' service: they do not treat of the easy religion of the 'missionary', revivalist meeting. But, with their quiet, unclamouring depth, they are eminently suitable as office hymns placed before the psalms or the first canticle at matins and evensong. Thus sung, they cannot be accused of usurping the better-known hymns beloved of singing congregations, and may serve as an introduction to the corpus of plainsong whose idiom would sound least strange if first heard in these tiny gems.

THE ORDINARY OF THE MASS

For *Gloria in excelsis* and the Nicene Creed the settings were originally invariable and based like the Sarum *Te Deum* on the chanting principle.[1] The melody of the creed, known all over Christendom, might well be sung in our churches though at the moment it seems that Merbecke's setting is used more frequently. After the ninth century *Gloria in excelsis* acquired other melodies, but all are simple. *The Ordinary of the Mass*, published by the

---

[1] The Nicene Creed was not in the Roman Use as a regular part of the service until about the year 1000.

Plainsong and Medieval Music Society, gives seven settings, *Sanctus* and *Agnus Dei* being given ten settings each. These latter tended to become more and more ornate but never so elaborate as *Kyrie eleison* whose melodies were lengthened out, words being added to the musical interpolations to help the singer to learn and remember them. Never *à propos*, the new words were presumably sung in church as well as in the practice-room, so that instead of the usual text, *Kyrie eleison*, the following macaronic jumble was sung: Kyrie *rex splendens coeli arce salve jugiter et clemens plebi tuae semper* eleison. Such a medieval hotch-potch was called a 'farced' kyrie, the kyrie being called by the title of its stuffing; the above example, even when the farced text was omitted, was entitled 'Kyrie Rex Splendens'. As a method of identification it was useful: as an idea it was fruitful and gave rise to the proses and sequences. The form of the *Kyrie* was fourfold, the first two limbs (*Kyrie eleison* and *Christe eleison*) being sung three times each, the third (another *Kyrie eleison*) twice; the tenth and last *Kyrie eleison* usually made some melodic allusion to the opening, to please the musical.

THE PROPERS

Of the propers, which were choir music, the introit consisted of a psalm and antiphon, the psalm tending later to disappear: the type of music used is thus antiphon-like with some chanting. An old Hebraic ritual, the singing of a psalm and antiphon after the epistle, was taken over from the synagogue services. In later Christian times the soloists performed more elaborate graduals from the step of the ambo or reading-desk. The further addition of an Alleluia with its jubilus—or in Lent a Tract—made this one of the most musically interesting parts of the service. In our modern Prayer Book the absence of any ceremony or music here is unfortunate. The offertory, like the introit, began as a psalm with antiphon, the psalm being eventually left out and the whole becoming musically more ornate. Some idea may be formed of the large corpus of music available for the choir from the following list of the numbers of settings of propers found in the *Antiphonale Missarum* of the Gregorian revision:

150 introits.
150 communios.

110 gradual responds.
23 tracts.
102 offertories.

This choir music is much the most interesting for the study of
melodic form to the modern musician; it is doubtful, nevertheless,
whether its ornate beauty, fine and moving as it often is, makes
any more vital effect in the service–especially that of today with
its very un-monastic congregation–than the simple chants of the
creed or *Pater Noster*.

TROPES, PROSES, SEQUENCES

Not only the *Kyries* were farced: the method of adding 'tropes'
as they came to be called was applied to *Sanctus* and *Gloria in
excelsis*, though it reached its acme in the jubilus, a long melody
sung on the last syllable of *Alleluia*, itself sung after the gradual.
Here the melody continued untrammelled by words, a singer's
hey-day, and during the ninth century many such melodies were
composed and words were added so that the general scheme was
much like a psalm with parallel strophes in prose, the music
following the general formula, *aa*, *bb*, *cc*, . . . with an occasional
return perhaps to *aa*. One of the first composers of these 'proses' or
'sequences' was a monk of the monastery of St. Gall, Notker (Bal-
bulus, the stammerer) by name, though it is difficult to see how
his work can have had much outside influence with the rudimen-
tary notation used about the year 860; visitors to the famous St.
Gall were, however, frequent, and perhaps came away with a copy
of the words and humming the tunes in their heads. The real
development of the sequence took place later. Examples of later
sequences in prose may be seen at Hymn 18 (*Salus aeterna*) and
Hymn 56 (*Victimae Paschali*) in the *Plainsong Hymn Book*, the
latter by Wipo (about 1030) being doubly interesting as it follows
the dramatic lead of the Palm Sunday and Good Friday gospels in
presenting a *scena* with dialogue on the Easter story. Such work
as this developed gradually into the mystery play which was used
later by the church to drive home to an unlettered people the vivid
drama of the gospel stories. A hundred years after Wipo, the
famous Adam de St. Victor, a canon in Paris about 1150, was
writing the words and music of sequences which had already forgotten their prose origin and used a regular metre in text and tune.

Except that they were not regularly strophic they thus became very much like hymns; an example of his work is seen in *Come, pure hearts in sweetest measure* (*Plainsong Hymn Book* 83). Hymn 134 in the same book is possibly his tune; for it Thomas Aquinas in 1263 wrote his Corpus Christi sequence, the long and fine *Lauda Sion salvatorem* from which we get the modern translation *Lo, the angels' food is given*. Other well-known and fine examples of the metred sequence are the 'Golden' Sequence for Whitsunday, *Veni, sancte Spiritus* (*Come, thou holy Spirit, come*) and the 'Rosy' Sequence, *Jesu, dulcis memoria* (*Jesu, the very thought is sweet*), numbers 67 and 115 in the *Plainsong Hymn Book*. Equally famous are *Dies irae* and *Sponsa Christi*, to be found in most modern hymn-books.

6

HARMONISED MUSIC BEFORE 1500

ORIGINS OF MODERN COUNTERPOINT

Very little harmonised music written before 1500 is in use in the modern service, and it would appear that research has not yet unearthed much usable music of the period; it is only necessary here, for the sake of completeness, to show briefly the origins of the methods of modern composition and especially of the expressive counterpoint brought to the pinnacle of perfection during the sixteenth century.

METHODS OF COMPOSITION

The mainsprings of modern harmonised music are found in three medieval methods of singing, all different in kind from the unisonous performance of the chant. Already in the ninth century adventurous spirits were desecrating the traditional plainsong with 'organum', in which, with one part (the 'tenor') holding on to the plainsong melody, others sang the same tune an octave, a fifth or a fourth below—or later the octave and fourth or fifth simultaneously—and were called 'bassus'. This method would at times, according to the voices available, be varied by singing, similarly above the melody (the 'altus' or high part), while if a third was added above that—especially in the later 'descant'—he would be called 'triplex' or treble, the third voice. The effect of singing in organum of this early type is quite pleasant and must have thrilled its discoverers as it has thrilled many a modern composer. 'Free descant', the name given to the second type of extempore singing, was the practice of improvising a melody above the chant at certain permitted intervals—singing 'seconds', in fact, but according to rules founded on what was supposed to sound well. For these two methods, organum and free descant, no special notation was necessary as the added parts were sung by ear; their historical importance lies in the fact that by means of them men (apparently for the first time ever) learnt that certain intervals were more congenial to the ear than others. In the third method, from which

modern composition really sprang and which was called 'organised descant', the counterpoints had to be written down because
men began to experiment with adding two or more notes against
every one of the chant or 'cantus'; the rules as to permitted intervals were widened to admit thirds and sixths, and the compositions were often in three or even more parts. By the thirteenth and
fourteenth centuries organised descant was of many kinds:
'ochetus' (hocket), so called because it had 'hiccup' rests in the
counterpoint in the middle of words; compositions where all the
parts sang the same words, others where each part sang a different
set of words and still others where only one voice sang the text,
the rest presumably intoning their parts on a vowel or perhaps
being replaced by instruments. All these types are perpetuated in
modern polyphony.

THE RISE OF MODERN POLYPHONY

Ochetus opened the eyes of composers to the expressive power of
rests and re-entries in the parts; the second type, where different
sets of words were used, was used in the motet and created the idea
of independence of parts which was eventually to result in independence of melodic and rhythmic movement; the last type, where
all but one voice sang on a vowel, was the method used in 'conductus'. Conductus has not survived in its original form (except
perhaps in the song), but one of its features was that the melody
or *canto fermo*, round which the other parts wove their counterpoints, was never a traditional ecclesiastical melody; it was usually
original though secular tunes were used, a method surviving into
the sixteenth century in, for example, Taverner's 'Western Wind'
Mass. Conductus is clearly the direct precursor of modern composition.

CANTUS MENSURABILIS

To distinguish it from *Cantus Planus* (Plainchant) this music
was given the name *Cantus Mensurabilis* (Mensural Music) because
the singers had to agree to a time-unit of definite speed before they
could achieve unanimity. The long and intricate history of its
notation, involving the noting not only of relative lengths of notes
but of groupings of accents, need not detain us, though we may
note with interest that following on the first known treatise on the

subject by Franco of Cologne (eleventh or twelfth century) two Englishmen contributed to clearing the way to our modern notation—Odington (thirteenth century) and Robert de Handlo (fourteenth century).

ITS USE TODAY

If none of this music is used in our churches today, two famous English secular songs have survived: 'Sumer is i-cumen in', of 1240, and the 'Agincourt Song', 1415. The first was found at Reading Abbey with an additional 'pious' text in Latin, and is so remarkable a composition for its date—which, according to the exact calculations of palaeography, cannot possibly be put later—that it remains a puzzle to all historians. It might do excellent service still in church if some carol words were added to it. The second has been used successfully as a hymn-tune. Much research had been done on the period, mostly by English scholars, and more remains to be done. It is a long period (say, 1100–1500) to have left no musical legacy, but at no time, so far as we can judge from the available material, did the composers' technique become capable, even in the hands of men like Dunstable, Cornysshe and Fayrfax, of producing 'expressive' work. It needed an extramusical fertilisation to make it live, and this was achieved only in the sixteenth century when a fresh realization of religion and an awakening interest in the new 'popular' national languages urged composers to express themselves through the musical technique acquired during four centuries of struggle.[1]

THE DECAY OF PLAINSONG

During the same period plainsong grew debased and over-ornate, the traditional method of performance was to some extent lost— the composer of *Cantus Mensurabilis* required a very slow *canto fermo* round which to weave his intricate and sometimes incoherent counter-melodies—and by the sixteenth century the

[1] During 1938–9 some of the work of the period 1300–1500 was produced at the meetings of the Plainsong and Medieval Music Society. The performances showed that, while often full of beauty of its own kind, the work was too far removed from modern ideas of length, simplicity and word-significance to be useful in a present-day service. But it is easy to be wrong in our judgment: sixteenth-century music was found dull and ungrammatical by listeners of the eighteenth and nineteenth centuries.

invention of printed texts tempted many to re-edit the traditional melodies with a meagre background of historical knowledge. The resulting official texts of the seventeenth century can be called nothing short of deplorable. Plainsong had, indeed, to wait until the nineteenth century for anyone to be interested enough to want to discover the old unspoilt texts. The Mechlin revision of 1848 and the Ratisbon versions of 1871 achieved some little good, but it was not until the strict principles of modern palaeography were applied to the existing manuscripts by Dom Guéranger, Dom Pothier and Dom Mocquereau that the Solesmes edition gave us a text as near perfect as is possible and opened the eyes of musicians to the real beauties of the chant. In England the compilers of *Hymns Ancient and Modern* published some hymns and mass-music, and later Helmore, Palmer and the Plainsong and Medieval Music Society fostered the growing interest with other important publications.

BOOKS AND MUSIC RECOMMENDED
FOR FURTHER STUDY

LITURGY

Principles of Religious Ceremonial, W. H. Frere (*Mowbray*, 1906–1928)
A History of Christian Worship, Oscar Hardman (*S.P.C.K.*)
The Shape of the Liturgy, Gregory Dix (*Dacre: Black*)

PLAINSONG

The complete treasury of plainsong–all known masses, items of the proper, hymns and offices–is contained in the *Liber Usualis*, with introduction and rubrics in English, edited by the Benedictines of Solesmes. It is available from church shops and the larger bookshops, though published by *Desclée & Cie.*, Tournai, Belgium.

The Elements of Plainsong (*Plainsong and Medieval Music Society*)
Approach to Plainsong through the Office Hymn, J. H. Arnold (*O.U.P.*)

Two excellent and practical first textbooks.

Introduction to the Gregorian Melodies, Part I, Historical, P. Wagner. English translation by *Plainsong and Med. Mus. Soc.*

Grove's *Dictionary* has also many recent and informative articles.

Plainsong Accompaniment, J. H. Arnold (*O.U.P.*)

The standard work for those wishing to write and play their own accompaniments.

Sixteenth Century Polyphony, A. T. Merritt (*O.U.P.*)

Early chapters deal with the forms of plainsong melodies.

MUSIC

THE MASS

The Ordinary of the Mass, adapted from the Sarum Gradual
(*Plainsong and Med. Mus. Soc.*, 1925)
Contains many settings of each number.
Missa ad Libitum, adapted from manuscripts of Xth–XIIth Centuries, ed. G. H. Palmer (*St. Mary's Convent, Wantage,*
1922)

OFFICES

Sarum Psalter, i.e., *The Psalms and Canticles pointed to the Eight*
Gregorian Tones from the Sarum Tonale, ed. G. H. Palmer
(*St. Mary's Convent, Wantage.* New Edition, 1916)
Antiphons for the Psalms, Part I, ferial antiphons (*Plainsong and*
Med. Mus. Soc.)
Antiphons upon Magnificat and Nunc dimittis, ed. G. H. Palmer
from the *Salisbury Antiphoner* (*St. Mary's Convent, Wantage,*
1930)
A Plainsong Hymn Book, ed. S. H. Nicholson (*Clowes,* 1932)
A Liturgical Service for Good Friday, ed. Duncan-Jones and
Arnold (*S.P.C.K.*)

GRAMOPHONE RECORDINGS

The Solesmes monks have made a monumental series of
recordings of all parts of the service.

For various styles of plainchant, organum, descant and other
medieval music the volumes of *A History of Music in Sound* are an
excellent introduction (H.M.V.).

PART II

THE SIXTEENTH CENTURY

7

THE BOOK OF COMMON PRAYER

'ENGLISH' MUSIC

The church music of England previous to 1500 has few English qualities; such music was sung all over Christian Europe, and it would have been difficult in 1500 to assign to any of it a nationality. Christian music did indeed reflect the vision of the Christian community whose object had always been the breaking of barriers and the discouragement, on the whole, of local tradition. A common doctrine, language, liturgy and music assured that local customs were mere excrescences on the parent tree. But by 1600 we can distinguish a 'Lutheran' chorale, a 'Palestrina' mass, a 'Gibbons' anthem and we have now to track down the reasons for this blossoming into nationalism and tell the story of the change.

THE RENAISSANCE

The mainspring of the change was the Renaissance, that new movement in the mind of man to trust his own experience, to draw his own conclusions and, if need be, to jettison authority. Copernicus turned from the Aristotelian books on astronomy to watch the moving stars; Rabelais left his medieval medical treatises to take up dissecting. Both came up against the established authority not only of their own sciences but of the church; they none the less pointed the way to the new experimental attitude in astronomy and medicine. Similarly in religion Erasmus and Luther insisted on thinking about religion instead of blindly accepting the teachings of the church, Coverdale translated the Bible into his mother tongue for all to read and discuss, composers hunted their Bibles and primers for new and appealing texts on which to write their anthems, and reformers of all nations sought to rethink the purpose and forms of the over-complicated church services. 'There was never anything by the wit of man so well devised,' says the Book of Common Prayer, 'or so sure established, which in continuance of time hath not been corrupted'; and, like Luther and Calvin and the rest, the compilers of the Prayer Book attempted to end this corruption by going back to first principles. The spirit of Protestantism was born. It is clear that changes in the forms of service would involve corresponding alterations in the music.

NATIONALISM

Of all possible reforms the most pressing was the replacement of Latin by the vernacular. A new local consciousness was welling all over Europe and great nations were forming. The days of the Holy Roman Empire—in 1500 only a pathetic ideal—were numbered. Even in England, which had always been insular and aloof, the Tudors were reigning over a new and united England and a wave of patriotic feeling was initiated which went eddying through the centuries, especially after the defeat of the Armada in 1588. Spain had become a mighty nation with rich colonial possessions in the New World and France was at last united under the aegis of Paris. The French language crystallised into two main dialects and her modern literature was born with Ronsard, Du Bellay, Marot and Rabelais. The German language was given a fruitful model in the German Bible, while Coverdale translated the Bible into what could justly be called standard English. Taught by the exiled courtier Clément Marot, the reformers taking refuge at Geneva poured out their metrical versions of the psalms in English and French. The nationalist feeling spread to music, so that by the end of the century we can talk of 'English' madrigals, 'German' chorales; 'English' church music begins in the sixteenth century, and it can henceforward be considered as an art product with its own history and traditions.

LITURGICAL REFORM: THE MASS

Certainly 'in continuance of time' the mass had become corrupted: it had, in fact, become little more than a monologue in an unknown language interspersed with singing by a professional choir. Returning to first principles the reformers set out to make it into a congregational service. With this end in view the bishops, after much discussion, issued 'The Order of Communion' to come into force at Easter 1548. An experimental measure, it arranged that the mass should go on in Latin as before, but at the communion time the priest was to turn to the intending communicants and lead them in private devotions consisting of the present exhortation, confession and absolution, together with the com-

Illustration to Psalm 150 in the Canterbury Psalter

Neumes in the Mozarabic Psalter

fortable words and the prayer of humble access, the whole in English. It met with such a poor reception that preaching was strictly curtailed to prevent the clergy—both conservative and left-wing—from influencing the people against it. During the following months the mass was sung in English at St. Paul's and other London churches. Extant choir-books show that many experiments were tried in adapting the traditional plainsong to English words, chiefly by simplifying the music or writing simple four- and five-part settings. From these books it is clear that various translations were tried out, presumably to find the most singable versions. Such efforts to retain the old type of music show that the English reformers were at this time more liberal-minded than those in other countries where everything that smacked of the old traditions was excluded. Here, as everywhere in the 1549 Prayer Book, when it appeared, the spirit shown was one of simplification and cleansing rather than of upheaval and rejection. The experiments went on throughout the summer and autumn of 1548 and ultimately gave us the singable version of the mass as we know it.[1]

LITURGICAL REFORM: THE DIVINE OFFICES

Remaking the mass into a people's service was simple when contrasted with the herculean task of reforming the divine offices. The offices or day hours were not originally intended as services for a congregation of 'men in the street', but were a useful feature of monastic life seeking to turn the minds of the monks at regular times to spiritual matters. Thus, as the Book of Common Prayer points out, the fathers 'so ordered the matter that all the whole Bible . . . should be read over once every year; intending, thereby, that the Clergy . . . should (by often reading, and meditation in God's Word) be stirred up to godliness'. The original intention had long been frustrated; the elaborate system of saints' days, the 'planting in uncertain stories, and legends'—lives and sayings of the saints were often read—the 'multitude of responds,[2]

---

[1] For details of the changes made in the form of the service, see page 28.
[2] The respond at prime goes:
   ℣. Jesu Christ, Son of the living God, have mercy upon us.
   ℟. Jesu Christ, Son of the living God, have mercy upon us.
   ℣. Thou that sittest at the right hand of the Father;
   ℟. Have mercy upon us.

verses,[1] vain repetitions,[2] commemorations' had so complicated the original design that 'commonly when any book of the Bible was begun, after three or four chapters were read out, all the rest were unread'. The question before the reformers was indeed a thorny one and they solved it ruthlessly. Except for the commemorations of the apostles, the saints' days disappeared; only the major church festivals were retained; a calendar of stark simplicity was drawn up; and, 'for this cause be cut off Anthems,[3] Responds, Invitatories[4] and such like things as did break the continual course of the reading of the Scripture'. The psalter was divided into 'days' to ensure its being read in its entirety once a month. Remembering that men going about their daily business attended church only once or twice a week, the reformers cut down the divine offices to two: morning prayer, a fusion of matins and lauds, and evening prayer, similarly made out of vespers and compline.

THE BOKE OF COMMON PRAIER, 1549

This was an uprooting of weeds with a vengeance. But the reformers went further; in the old days the clergy- and choir-stalls must have been littered with books all necessary for the conduct of the service. There were 'missals' or mass-books, 'grailes' containing the graduals sung after the epistles, 'hympnals', 'antiphoners', 'processionals', 'manuals' for the conduct of weddings, etc., 'portuasses' or breviaries containing the priest's private offices, 'primers' or books of private devotion in Latin and English, 'couchers', so called as they were large books to lie on the reading-desk, 'journals' containing the day hours, 'ordinals' for the consecration of priests and bishops, 'epistollers', 'gospellers', 'collectars', 'legends', 'consuetudinaries' and so forth. Here again reform was ruthless. The new service book must be the supplanter of them all, the one and only vade-mecum, a pocket guide for the services of the church. Everything needed must be between its covers and must be readily found. If in previous days the 'number and hardness of the rules called the Pie'—rules for finding out

℣. Glory be to the Father, and to the Son, and to the Holy Ghost.
℞. Jesu Christ, Son of the living God, have mercy upon us.

[1] Versicles.
[2] Antiphons, for example, often repeated between the verses of the psalms.
[3] Antiphons.
[4] See the invitatories to *Venite* in the 1928 Book. They are intended to give the 'key' to the service at the festival seasons.

what was to be sung on saints' days, commemorations, octaves and so forth – 'was the cause, that to turn the book only was so hard and intricate a matter, that many times there was more business to find out what should be read, than to read it when it was found out', it must now be easy for any schoolboy to find his place. Completeness must be sacrificed, even imagination must be strangled, but the book must be compendious and simple. The ancient and imaginative ceremonies connected with the major festivals, and especially with Holy Week, were mercilessly cut down to a few Proper Prefaces. It is unnecessary to point out the obvious merits and disadvantages of such a sweeping reform. Suffice it to say that the 1549 Book was a remarkably sane production for a time when religious temperature was already high. It was faithful to every word of its title, 'The Boke of Common Praier', but was not completed without much discussion and difficulty, made worse by the hurry imposed by the protestant-minded regency of the youthful king, Edward VI. Each for his own reasons, few of the council of bishops expected it to please everyone. On January 21st, 1549, the Boke of Common Praier was given a parliamentary send-off in the first Act of Uniformity. As was to be expected, the subsequent history of the book belied the title of its enabling act. A split appeared within the Church of England which has never been closed. Churchmen of conservative trend interpreted the absence of rubrics as freedom in matters of ceremonial. The more zealous reformers wanted more violent changes and eventually won the day: the second Prayer Book, considerably more protestant than the first, was ordered to be used on and after All Saints' Day, 1552. On that day in St. Paul's Ridley in a rochet and his clergy in surplices celebrated the communion to the new use; the quire of the cathedral had been deprived of its ornaments a week previously and the organ had been – similarly in anticipation – silenced a month before.[1] The reforming spirit had triumphed. The interval during the reactionary reign of Bloody Mary, when the book was repealed, need not detain us, as it had no permanent effect on the music of the church. The Elizabethan Prayer Book of 1559 was substantially the same as that of 1552.[2]

[1] In this matter the reformers mercifully retracted; no doubt a few organ-less services made them think better of it.

[2] Note that no doctrinal questions are discussed in the above brief account of the English Prayer Books. Such questions affected the music only in a general way.

8

MUSICAL PROBLEMS OF THE PRAYER BOOK

ARCHBISHOP CRANMER

The story of English church music can in the sixteenth century boast of two pieces of sheer good luck: one was an archbishop who thought music worth his concern, the other a school of fine musicians to cope with the problems raised by the reform of the services. In the company of music-loving clerics, of Gregory and Ambrose, Archbishop Cranmer deserves honourable mention. He was willing, in the midst of the incessant personal work he did in Englishing the services and supervising the compilation of service books, to give time to caring for the music to be used and the manner of its performance. Like Gregory before him he recognised that once music is admitted as part of worship it must be regulated as to the kind of music used, the use made of it and the manner of its presentation. Thus Cranmer not only translated the Latin litany (1544) to be used in national processions during the war with France, but wrote later to the king: 'If your grace command some devout and solemn note'—that is, music—'to be made thereunto, (as is the procession which your majesty has already set forth in English) I trust it will much excitate, and stir the hearts of all men unto devotion and godliness: But in mine opinion the song, that shall be made thereunto, would not be full of notes, but, as near as may be, for every syllable a note, so that it may be sung distinctly and devoutly.' These words accompanied some drafts of translations which Cranmer was sending to the king, and the words in brackets presumably refer to the already published litany which had appeared in 1544 set to simple music.[1] Later in the letter the archbishop says of the Latin music to *Salve festa dies* that it is 'sober and distinct enough', adding, however, that 'they that be cunning in singing can make a much more solemn note'—festival setting—'thereunto'. Without, in fact,

[1] Note that Cranmer did *not* advocate 'one syllable, one note' as a general principle. 'Syllabic' settings are not necessarily the easiest to learn or sing. Memorability depends on melodic and musical appeal.

suggesting that more ornate settings be discarded, he gives simplicity, dignity and distinctness – clarity of words, perhaps – as the essentials. The ideal was a sensible one, typical of an English churchman, and was unconsciously followed by the composers of the time.[1]

THE TRANSLATIONS

It is clear from the experiments carried out in various London churches[2] that the translations intended to be sung from the Prayer Book are not mere translations but versions compiled to be fitted to music. An obvious example of exact translation yielding to a singable version is Cranmer's English equivalent of *miserere nobis* in his litany. *Miserable sinners* is a rhythmic paraphrase, of which other examples can be found throughout the Prayer Book. The history of the English version of the psalter in the Prayer Book shows a similar principle: the 1549 Book used Coverdale's[3] beautifully sonorous and rhythmic version, which is far from accurate. In the subsequent Prayer Books, though other translations were substituted elsewhere the Coverdale psalter remained; even in the 1928 revision it has been left alone despite the frequent nonsense of its meaning.[4] The reason given in 1662 for retaining it was that the singers had got used to it; in 1928 the reason must have been the same. Its eminently singable qualities can best be appreciated by contrasting it with the more correct Revised Version or with Driver.[5] We must note in passing that all the careful work of

[1] Unconsciously, because Cranmer's letter in which the passages occur was not presumably made public. But Cranmer quite possibly knew many of the composers of the time and we may assume he sometimes discussed the problems with them.

[2] See page 65.

[3] Miles Coverdale (1488–1569). His Bible appeared in 1535.

[4] See, for example, psalm 68, verse 30, a difficult passage. The Prayer Book version:

> *When the company of the spearmen and multitude of the mighty are scattered abroad among the beasts of the people, so that they humbly bring pieces of silver: when he hath scattered the people that delight in war;*

is given by the Revised Version and Driver as:

> *Rebuke the wild beast of the reeds,*
> *the multitude of the (troop of – Driver) bulls, with the calves of the peoples,*
> *trampling under foot the pieces of silver;*
> *he hath scattered the peoples that delight in war.*

[5] 'The Parallel Psalter' – S. R. Driver (*Clarendon Press*).

Cranmer, so far as congregational music goes, amounts to very little. Cranmer's efforts helped the later composers of choir music but did not succeed in establishing a people's song.

THE BOOKE OF COMMON PRAIER NOTED

It is obvious that on the publication of the 1549 Prayer Book an immediate need would arise for some authoritative musical counterpart such as had always existed for the Latin services. Unfortunately no such authoritative book has ever appeared.[1] In 1550, however, John Merbecke,[2] who almost certainly had been working in conjunction with Cranmer during the experimental years before the 1549 Book, published his *Booke of Common Praier Noted*–that is, set to music. His ardent zeal for reform had all but cost him his life when in 1543 he was convicted for writing a concordance to the Bible in English and for uttering blasphemies against the mass. The story runs that he was let off, when three of his fellow singing-men were burnt in front of Windsor Castle for heresy, in order to help with the work of Englishing the services– a possible proof that experiments were being made six years before the appearance of the 1549 Book. Like the Prayer Book to which he added his music, his book was meant for congregations to use; it was not a choir book. Its successful music to the mass and the divine offices is singable and never difficult. Not only does it satisfy Cranmer's ideal of soberness and distinctness but it keeps rigidly–perhaps too rigidly, even though it is intended for the people's use–to the plan of 'for every syllable a note'. The music, however, was neither fish nor fowl; it was a typical English compromise. Though it sounds reminiscent of plainsong, being sometimes, as in the *Te Deum* setting, an adaptation of the traditional Latin melody, it could not be called plainsong. The preface

[1] The *Cathedral Prayer Book*, 1891, was due entirely to private enterprise. A modern 'Prayer Book Noted' drawn up by a joint committee of organists and clergy is long overdue. See page 211.

[2] John Merbecke (dates unknown). The name is spelt in many different ways. Appointed to the Royal Chapel at Windsor, 1541 where he was succeeded by Mundy in 1585. His religious views became so pronounced that he talks of 'playing of Organs, wherein I consumed vainly the greatest part of my life'. Some early Latin music shows him as a composer of considerable ability, but after 1550, though organist of Windsor, he seems to have spent his time writing his concordance and various anti-popery pamphlets. He remained unnoticed in Mary's reign, and was probably humoured as a well-known retainer by Elizabeth.

makes it clear that the composer meant his music to be sung in measured notes with rhythmic mannerisms of the period; the phrase quoted below,[1] *And I look for the resurrection of the dead,* might well be taken from any simple four-part mass of the time. Thus to plant a foot in both worlds was novel, and modern performances of this music show that it is easy to sing even by the uninitiated. At the time, however, in which it was written, no doubt other things crowded out the effort needed to acquire the new style, and there is no evidence of the book's having been used. What chance it may have had of survival was wrecked by the appearance of the 1552 Book where too many alterations were made in the texts for Merbecke's book to be of very practical use. It is a pity that it was not revised and taken up as the authoritative book, for who knows that it might not have been an element in preventing the disuse of the sung mass during the seventeenth and eighteenth centuries; if all the congregations of England had learnt to sing Merbecke's mass they might well have been more loth to let the service drop in esteem as it did. Perhaps owing to his extreme anti-popery (he later wrote a book with the intriguing title, *The Ripping up of the Pope's Fardel*) Merbecke was not willing to help in perpetuating even the traditional plainsong on which his book was in a general way based. The failure of the book to be retained as a singers' handbook was a blow to congregational music and so also a blow to the intentions of the reformers to create a congregational service. From now on only the service without music can be properly described as congregational; the historian of the sixteenth century is thus denied a chapter on the establishment of congregational music. We may note in passing that the book sadly burked the issue in morning and evening prayer by setting the canticles to two plainsong tones apiece; *Venite* and the psalms are dealt with even more cursorily. One verse and an 'etc.' is all they get: it would have been a discouraging prospect to sing the whole psalter year in and year out to tone viii.

MERBECKE TODAY

After three hundred years Merbecke has come into his own as a revival initiated by Stainer's *Cathedral Prayer Book*. But he has not always been sung as he intended, a misfortune for any composer. His note-lengths have been grouped into a square four-in-a-

[1] See Ex. 14, page 78.

bar or ironed out into a series of nothing but minims or quavers; he has been harmonised, even descanted. The accompaniment, if really necessary, interferes least with the composer's felicitous rhythms when done on plainsong lines, though there seems no reason against an occasional accidental in the manner of 1550.

9

CHOIR MUSIC TO THE
DEATH OF GIBBONS

1. GENERAL

The music of the period has been called Sixteenth-century music, Elizabethan music, Tudor music. Much of the most mature work was written when the sixteenth century, Elizabeth and the Tudors were all of the past. The general title is unimportant: the music with which we have chiefly to deal was nearly all written between the appearance of the Book of Common Prayer in 1549 and the death of Gibbons in 1625. Publications begin to crowd after 1570 or so, and this date can fitly mark the beginning of the mature period.

MUSIC FROM 1500-1550[1]

We must first briefly review the music written before 1550. Church music in 1500 was of two kinds, the traditional plainsong, much corrupted, and composed music. The plainsong, apart from a few commonly known melodies such as the music to the Nicene Creed and *Te Deum*, was too ornate to be sung by a congregation; indeed, almost all the singing was delegated to the choir. In the monastic offices the choir would consist of boys and professional singing-men together with such of the monks who could, by dint of long hearing them, sing the psalms and canticles; in the mass the body of professional singers performed the plainsong versions of the ornate propers—introit, gradual, offertory and communion —and supplemented these with elaborate settings in harmony for the other parts of the service. Of this latter music little has remained in the repertory save perhaps a few resurrected faux-bourdons as commonly used at the time in alternate verses of the canticles. The reason is that such music, no doubt reckoned artistically worthy in its day, is seen by us through the glass of the later achievements of

[1] The reader who is surprised by some of Dr. Phillips' comments should consider the amount of sixteenth-century music that has been edited and performed since 1944, as well as the changes in style of performance.

the century, and suffers by comparison. Seen thus, it is stiff and formal both harmonically and emotionally, over-elaborate and lacking in the consummate ease of the best later work. These are, of course, the normal faults of immaturity. Even Taverner, often flattered by the history books and probably a great man, had failed to retain his place in the repertory by the end of the century. His 'Western Wind' mass, founded in the customary manner on a secular theme of that name, has seldom been thought worthy to be tackled by any subsequent choirmaster. As much may be said of such men—one is tempted to call them 'names' – as Cornyshe, Sampson, Fayrfax, Henry VIII. It may well be that, had not the century later produced such a flowering of fine work, the music of these men would have been found of use in the service; the fact remains, however, that no one ever seems interested enough to give them a hearing during an actual service. If, as some think, they are unrecognised geniuses, they were geniuses born at a time when technique was changing and only pioneers were needed. No coherent judgment of their work is, however, possible until they get a hearing.[1]

TYE

Perhaps because he was a pioneer rather than a genius (at least on the showing of his available works) the first composer to be admitted to the modern repertory is Tye[2] who shows signs of throwing off the stiff rhythmic and contrapuntal shackles of the fifteenth century, attaining a new ease in simple music.[3] Of his music only one slight work receives any notice, though it is possible that there are other works which might usefully be recovered. Like other composers of his time he was concerned with the religious questions of the day, and his reformer spirit led him to busy himself with translating, after the manner of Marot, into English

[1] They have now secured a hearing.

[2] Christopher Tye (*c.* 1500–*c.* 1572–3), Mus.B. Cambridge 1536, Mus.D. Cambridge 1545. In 1537 he was lay-clerk at King's College, Cambridge, and was, in 1541 or 1542, appointed Magister Choristarum at Ely Cathedral. He was possibly music master to Henry VIII's children. In 1560 he was ordained deacon and later priested, holding various livings until his death. *The Acts* was his only published work. Works other than those mentioned seem to have been printed but are seldom if ever performed.

[3] Yet his best work is to Latin. His fine *Euge Bone* mass, in English translation, is used by several cathedral choirs.

verses the Acts of the Apostles, not, perhaps, an inspiring theme for true poetry. The fourteen chapters which he thus versified he partly set to simple music in a completely new style, showing that he wished to be sung not only by highly trained choirs. Unlike his contemporaries he often sets his melody in the treble, leaving the tenor to become merely one of the three accompanying voices. For studied and effective simplicity the sober march of *Laudate nomen Domini* (*O come, ye servants of the Lord*)[1] shows a sure touch with its delightful lapse into easy imitation in the middle of each strain, a method followed in the 'fugued' psalm-tunes of a hundred years later; and, even if its block harmony shows a certain lack of free movement, it makes a worthy beginning to the English repertory and can be sung by any village choir today. Tye died too early to be numbered among those great men whose works were produced after 1570, but his easy style pointed the way to the technical felicities of his followers and no doubt earned him the affectionate title of 'the father of the anthem'. The also delightful *Lord, for thy tender mercy's sake*, attributed by the Church Music Society's edition to 'the school of Dr. Tye' and by Fellowes to Hilton, follows a similar formula and shows a similar cheerful lack of emotional feeling.

GENERAL DEVELOPMENT FROM 1550

Dates and biographical details being scanty it is tentative work trying to trace a consecutive evolution in the music of the period. It is, however, possible to contrast Tye and early Tallis with the later Byrd and so find that the emotional content has become more human, while the harmonic and rhythmic range has widened. This was the direct result of setting English words and can thus be attributed on the one hand to the appearance of the Book of Common Prayer and on the other to the general literary awakening. Marlowe, the University Wits, Shakespeare, the Prayer Book, the English Bible, all played their part as much as the individual efforts of the composers in producing the spate of great music—church and secular—after 1570. Music had become the handmaid of words and thus acquired a new freedom. As Elizabeth grew older the reformer outlook of her subjects became more prominent; the minds of composers and churchmen alike turned from the liturgy proper to the engaging excitement of the newly

[1] The published text is an arrangement by a modern editor.

translated Bible. When the chained Bibles were set up in every church in England by order of the king in 1538, so keen was the interest that people in St. Paul's would gather round a reader even during service time. That interest never flagged; indeed, it has never lessened in England where the Bible and pulpit have often been more the focal point of churchgoing than the altar. Englishmen of the sixteenth century made a glorious discovery—their own language. The thrill of it has run like a life-giving stream from the heaped pastures of Spenser and Shakespeare to the trim beauty of Shaw and the lavish wordy panoramas of Joyce. English composers are but men and their muse has come speaking English. So the anthems of Byrd have a human warmth fired by the vivid vernacular which is lacking in the more chill perfection of Tallis' Latin works[1] and the emotionless simplicity of Tye. So much development it is possible to see between 1550 and 1625. It showed itself in the composition technique of the period and, as we should expect, Byrd who plumbed the emotional and spiritual depths was the most adventurous experimenter. There is a world of difference between the joy in musical technique of Fayrfax and the joy in expression of Byrd and Gibbons.

THE ENGLISH LANGUAGE AND MUSIC

Latin left the composer to find his own rhythms with the usual result that he ceased to be forced into rhythmic invention. His mind tended to run in set channels. But English with its elasticity, its frequent harshnesses, its tripping dactyls, its feminine endings, made him think afresh and trim his music to the rhythmic richness of the language. It gave him really less melodic rein but compensated with rhythmic stimulation. Thus was the unique and subtle rhythmic counterpoint of the period forced upon him. Squareness, the balance of four-plus-four would not work; instead, we find Byrd writing with an engaging lilt and a felicitous over-balance:

Ex. 13

Treble from Magnificat of Byrd's Short Service

As he pro - mised to our fa - ther A - bra-ham

---

[1] This is a strange comment by a writer who knew the greater warmth of Byrd's Latin music and the wonderful emotional range of Tallis' *Lamentations*, perhaps the finest work of its period.

which springs from the rhythm of the text. And if we turn from the rhythmic flow of the words to their sound, we notice that the beauty of English words is lavish but often harsh. Sibilants, palatals, clusters of consonants crunch from the lips and tongue and spoil the singable vowels; but they are the expression of the vision behind the words which caught the composer aflame. Palestrina set his sonorous, vowelly liturgies in a cool, placid style well fitted to the broad Latin phrases. A handful of stock progressions sufficed him to 'bring all heaven before our eyes', a rarefied, unearthly vision, the vision of a man looking upwards away from men. Even in the non-liturgical, emotional *Stabat Mater* the warmth is there but the even, harmonic flow of the music is never disturbed. The harsh, lovely English tongue turned the thought of our own composers inwards into their own hearts. They loved God but loved their neighbour more. It was the protestant view, the view of a man with his feet firmly planted in this world. Thus if Palestrina had one mood, Byrd and Gibbons had a hundred—all the human gamut. Their harmony reflected their outlook. No handful of chords would do for them; the voices clamoured against one another rhythmically, harmonically, and led them to music which, had he heard it, would have made Palestrina stop his ears. Each voice must sing as it felt and let the rest go hang. The Elizabethan choir was, in fact, a body of individualists; the resultant texture of their music shows all the roughness, all the rich treasures which individualism brings with it.

10

CHOIR MUSIC TO THE DEATH OF GIBBONS

2. TECHNIQUE

RHYTHM

The gist of the rhythmic technique can be studied in a familiar phrase of Merbecke:

Ex. 14
From the Booke of Common Praier Noted

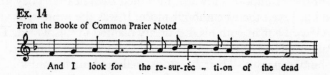

And I look for the re- sur-rec - ti-on of the dead

Accent in a musical phrase such as this is assured in three ways: a long note acquires accent if surrounded by shorter notes: a high note takes accent if placed in the midst of lower notes (and vice versa); and in the ending or cadence the last note tends to be accented because of the harmony, implied or heard. Thus we see accents on *look, for, -rec-, dead*. *Look* gets its accent from the preliminary run up the scale. It is followed immediately by another accent, this time the result of length, on the word *for*. Such pairs of contiguous accents are common in English; a good example is found in Psalm 48:

> The hill of Zion is a *fair place*, the joy of the *whole earth*: upon the *north side* lieth the city of the *great king*; God is *well known* in her palaces as a *sure re*fuge.

Merbecke's accent on *for* acts like a spring-board for the concatenation of short, quick syllables following it. Notice the second run, this time further up the scale, on *the re-sur-* to the accented *-rec-*, got by length and pitch. In speech *for* would not be stressed: sung, the phrase is better with an accent here, unless the singer dwelt for two beats on *look*. But sung thus not only would it lose much of its rhythmic point and charm but unanimity would be more difficult. Merbecke, at any rate, felt otherwise; he was a musician as well as an orator and realised the tame musical effect of a long series of unaccented syllables. The phrase is not, in fact, in what is today called speech-rhythm. It is a mixture of that and musical rightness and is characteristic of the technique of the period. Such rhythms will be found freely strewn on every page of the music of the time. Other examples will help to show the principle:

Ex. 15

Treble from Mundy's O Lord the maker (Transposed)

O ___ Lord the mak - er of all ___ thing

where the stress on *of* serves a similar purpose, and:

Ex. 16

Treble from the Magnificat of Gibbons' Service in F **(Transposed)**

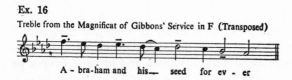

A - bra-ham and his ___ seed for ev - er

where the principle is clear at the word *and*.

For church purposes the music never moved with fixed regular accents. Time-signatures in the modern sense with their attendant bar-lines are therefore never found.[1] The single voice-part has a rhythm arising out of the music itself in combination with the words. As often in the printed part-books the words were not written in for whole stretches, much latitude was apparently left to the singer or his choirmaster—nowadays to the editor—to find the underlaying which best suited the passage.[2] His part thus proceeded like good prose, now in groups of two, now in three, much

---

[1] Time-signatures were prefixed but only to show the subdivision of the unit-notes, long, breve or semibreve. Except at rare changes of this subdivision they may thus be disregarded. Bar-lines as indicators of regular or irregular accents are also unknown in the part-books. The singer presumably accented his music by ear and according to the text he sang. The *Tudor Church Music* edition inserts them for help to the eye at irregular intervals—usually in four-two and six-two groups.

[2] Extant part-books occasionally show the underlaying inserted by hand, indicating how some careful precentors or choirmasters tackled the problem.

like plainsong except that for reasons of harmony and unanimity there must be a stricter unit-beat in his mind as he sang. In the following passage bar-lines and time-signatures are inserted in the modern manner to show the rhythmic scheme at the back of the singer's mind if he is to deliver the phrases well;[1] it is not necessarily the only scheme that would fit:

Ex. 17

Tenor from Gibbons' Hosanna

Thus to find the rhythmic structure of his part must be the singer's first duty; it was forced upon a sixteenth-century choirman as scores were apparently unknown and he sang from a part-book containing only his part.[2] Reading a new work must therefore have been difficult, but once the work was familiar the use of a single part-book must have added to the independent reading and freedom of the individual singer.

With such a scheme it can be imagined what endless possibilities there were in rhythmic counterpoint. Such counterpoint is indeed the salient feature of the music. To show the effect a typical example is given in which the rhythm of the parts is shown by bar-lines:

---

[1] This method of indicating the rhythms would of course be too worrying to the eye to be of practical use. The Fellowes editions use a stress-mark to show where the chief accents occur when these conflict with the inserted bar-lines or with one another. This seems the most satisfactory method.

[2] Part-books: usually five each for Decani and Cantoris, making ten in all for the whole choir plus duplicate treble books. Books Decani 1 and Cantoris 1 would contain all the top parts of anthems even if, for example, in a men's anthem this was the first alto. Thus books Decani 4 and Cantoris 4 would contain the lowest part of all four-part anthems but the next to lowest of five-part works. There would be no bass parts to four-part works in books 5.

6 Moſes, Aaron and Samuel,
    as prieſts on him did call: (well
When they did pray he heard them
and gave them anſwer all.
              (ſpake,
.7 Within the cloud to them he
   then did they labour ſtill,
To keep ſuch laws as he did make,
according to his will.

8 O Lord our God, thou didſt them
   and anſwerd'ſt them again: (hear,
But their inventions puniſhed,
   which fooliſh were and vain.
              (fore
9 O praiſe our God and Lord thereupon his holy hill:
For why? our God whom we adore,
   is the moſt holy ſtill.

Cantus & Baſſus.   PSALM C.   *Proper Tune.*

ALL people that on earth do dwell, ſing to the Ld with chearful voice:

Him ſerve with fear, his praiſe forth tel, come ye before him and rejoyce.

Medius.   Pſalm 100.   *A. 3. Voc.*

ALL people that on earth do dwell, ſing to the Ld with chearful voice:

Him ſerve with fear, his praiſe forth tel, come ye before him and rejoyce.

Baſſus.   Pſalm 100.   *A. 3. Voc.*

ALl people that on earth do dwell, ſing to the Ld with chearful voice:

Him ſerve with fear, his praiſe forth tel, come ye be fore him and rejoyce.

2 The Lord ye know is God indeed,
   without our aid he did us make:
We are his flock, he doth us feed,
   and for his ſheep he doth us take.

3 O enter then his gates with praiſe,
   approach with joy his Courts unto:
Praiſe, laud, and bleſs his Name al-
   for it is ſeemly ſo to do. (ways,

                                 4 For

A page from John Playford's 'Whole Book of Psalms'

Chamber organ by Snetsler

Ex. 18

Extract from Gibbons' O Lord increase my faith

The expressive power of these rhythmic waves on the word *charity* can be matched on any page of the period. Nothing could better suggest to the listener a dwelling, a meditation on 'charity' than these gentle eddies with their delightful overlappings.[1]

MELODY AND UNDERLAYING

To divorce melody from rhythm is impossible: the melody is the up and down movement hung on the rhythm. We may, however, here shortly consider the habits of the composers so far as the pitch-shape of the phrase goes.

Church music of the period rarely sounds as if the composers wrote a melody and then accompanied it in the part-song manner; such a method was used in the secular 'ballets' and is found in some settings[2] of hymn-like melodies by Dowland in the seventeenth century. In the church music there is at times some atavistic

[1] For contrast with the modern technique see the last few bars of *Though I speak*–Bairstow (publ. Banks) where a similar meditative effect springs from the counterpoint. The rhythm used is that of Gibbons.

[2] Some inner parts of these settings, recently discovered, are very ornate, the melody and bass remaining simple. Apart from the 'short' services the outstanding example of block harmony is Byrd's *Christe qui lux*, a beautiful setting in faux-bourdon of a plainsong melody which appears in each of the five parts in turn.

feeling that the main interest lies in the tenor, the other parts making a faux-bourdon; but on the whole the interest is shared by all the parts, except in the 'short' services where the treble and tenor sometimes have a more adventurous line than the other voices, none of whom, however, in the average short service[1] can be said to sing anything approaching a 'melody'.

Melodic habits are best understood by remembering Morley's dictum that the full close (that is, the perfect cadence) can come only at the full stop in the text.[2] The method is never to write a 'tuney' phrase of eight bars or so, but to divide the text into short clauses and set each either harmonically or contrapuntally. Thus in Gibbons' *O Lord, increase my faith* the text is cut up as follows, a short melody being given to each clause:

O Lord, increase my faith – – strengthen me – – and confirm me in thy true faith – – endue me with wisdom – – charity – – and patience – – in all my adversity – – sweet Jesus, say Amen – – sweet Jesus, say Amen – – sweet Jesus, say Amen.

In each little phrase there is always a studied lack of regular lilt to preserve the soberness which Cranmer suggested, and the melody moves, as in all the music of the time, English and foreign, stepwise with an admixture of short leaps. English music is, how-ever, often lax in this principle,[3] the bass sometimes moving a fourth and then another in the same direction, or a part ending one phrase on, say, F-sharp and beginning the next on the F-natural above. Gibbons's magnificat in F shows the following in the treble:

Ex. 19

serv – – ant

---

[1] Short service: a simple, block-harmony setting designed to get over the ground quickly.

[2] On page 178 of his *Plaine and Easie Introduction to Practicall Musicke*, 1597, where he makes the following astute remarks, 'Lastlie, you must not make a close (especiallie a full close) till the full sence of the words be perfect: so that keeping these rules you shall have a perfect agreement, and as it were a harmonicall concent betwixt the matter and the musicke, and likewise you shall be perfectly understoode of the auditor what you sing, which is one of the highest degrees of praise which a musicion in dittying'—that is, setting words to music—'can attaine unto or wish for.'

[3] See Ex. 15, the first four notes.

The small notes are in the part, and whether they are meant to be sung as written or as a portamento, the octave leap to an unstressed syllable is a bold, almost unwarrantable stroke needing much care in the performance. In contrapuntal passages a few simple melodic formulae are used again and again because of the ease with which they work in imitation. Cadence idioms such as:

Ex. 20

(a) Alto in Tallis' Salvator Mundi
Cadence in E-minor

te de— prec-a - mur, De - us

(b) 1st treble in Gibbons' Hosanna
Cadence in E-flat

in the name of the—— Lord

(c) 1st alto in Gibbons' Hosanna
Cadence in E-flat

that com-eth in the name of— the   Lord

are used as perfunctorily as Mozart and Handel used theirs. Both these sets of formulae were indeed the stock-in-trade. They are perhaps the first idioms to strike a modern listener and seem to give the music its peculiar flavour, but to a contemporary they were banal, and a too liberal use of them, though perhaps attractive to us, shows the composer with a lazy mind. That men like the incomparable Byrd could use them for expressive ends is shown by the final bars of his *Agnus Dei* from the three-part mass, a lovely message based entirely on a cadence formula.

UNDERLAYING

Worthy of notice too is the tendency to sing sheer melodic phrases on unimportant, unaccented syllables, an idea which seems for ever to have departed from our music. It lasted, indeed, to Purcell, who writes:

Ex. 21
Treble from Purcell's Rejoice in the Lord

a - gain I—— say,— re - joice

The most common use of the idiom is in the three-time dotted rhythm which is always underlaid thus:

Ex. 22

Is - ra - el

Not only does this underlaying give a tripping, forward-moving feeling to the phrase, but it is easier to sing than the modern plan of giving the first two notes to the first syllable of the word. The sixteenth-century method gives the singer a better chance of easily pronouncing his consonants and the two notes on -*ra*- throw the secondary accent—usually on the third beat of a three-beat metre —back a quaver, so producing a temporary syncopation which prevents the passage becoming 'waltzy'. Just as Shakespeare varies the dull jingle underlying blank verse so the Elizabethan composer fights shy of a too regular metre. For the same reason four quavers are always split into one plus three rather than two plus two, as

Ex. 23
Tenor from Weelkes' Hosanna

Ho — san — — na

CONTRAPUNTAL TEXTURE

In its counterpoint, both rhythmic and melodic, lies the glory of this music. Its attractive freedom is the product of two idioms, the lack of regular accent and the use of short melodic 'points' for imitation. If one voice can be singing an accented note while another is singing an unstressed syllable the contrapuntal possibilities become limitless; if in addition only short phrases, a breath long, are used for imitation the resulting fugato becomes freer to work and can easily be prolonged to any length desired. To show the freedom obtained on this system we need only contrast it with the counterpoint of the early nineteenth century where a regular accent makes the entries start always on the same beat of the bar-metre, where the four-plus-four-bars form of the composition forces the unwilling imitations into its unyielding chains, and where the prevailing tonic and dominant harmony dictate only certain possibilities of imitation and even more strongly restrict the sort of phrase which can be imitated. The difference is also seen by contrasting Tye's childlike imitation in:

Ex. 24

Extract from Tye's Laudate nomen (words added later)

where the composer is shackled by his regular metre, with the consummate freedom of Byrd's:

Ex. 25

Extract from Byrd's Three-part Mass

The points used in the imitations are simple, easily recognisable—an important point to the listener—and enter so naturally that the whole texture shows that apparent ease which is the hall-mark of a mastered technique. Between these extremes of lucid simplicity and thoughtful complication the Tudor composer expressed himself in counterpoint. In simple and complicated passages alike the point starting the fugato was always childishly obvious. On paper nothing could look simpler than:

Ex. 26
Extract from Byrd's Ave Verum

Its effect in the atmosphere of the church service is indescribably expressive. Yet the device of echoing a treble phrase of three notes by the under parts is little more than a stock idiom, turned by Byrd into 'something rich and strange'.

The normal procedure in a fugato is for all the voices to take part, the interval of entry being free but tending, because of voice compass, to be at the fourth or fifth. The old tetrachord rule which answered a leap of a fifth by a fourth is usually kept, so retaining the music in the mould of its own mode. A familiar example is the opening of Tallis' *Salvator mundi*:

Ex. 27
Opening of Tallis' Salvator Mundi

Here the point is not conjunct after the leap but uses an oscillatory phrase on *-vator mundi* which makes for a certain stiffness not found in the later work where conjunct motion was almost a rule and gives more ease to a fugato passage.

GIBBONS' COUNTERPOINT

Gibbons is guilty of an experimental mind and we find him occasionally trying other methods:

Ex. 28
From Gibbons' O Lord increase my faith
Sweet Je — sus, say   A — men

Sweet Je — sus, say A - men

This shows a point in two parts used not very convincingly. Verbally it is a repetition of a phrase already satisfactorily treated, while here it is left too undeveloped to have much musical *raison d'être*. The parts are rhythmically too similar and the drop of a sixth in the alto seldom comes off. A daring experiment which does come off, however, is found in the *Gloria* to *Nunc Dimittis* in the service in F. Here Gibbons writes a masterly and unobtrusive accompanied canon at the fourth below between treble and alto. This lengthy piece of canonic writing is a rare feat contrasting with the usual short-phrase technique. In both these cases one might imagine the two parts accompanied by a continuo in the manner of the seventeenth century.

HARMONY AND DESIGN

Consecutive fifths and octaves, later banned absolutely, were not considered so forbidding before 1600. A melody underlined at the perfect fifth or octave is more thoroughly underlined than at the third or sixth because the 'perfect' intervals remain unvaried whereas passages in thirds and sixths mix the major and minor types. (See Ex. 29(a).)

Consecutive perfect intervals are objectionable only where incongruous within a general style, and even in classical harmony they rarely offend the ear if one of the chords is a seventh, or some other chord of more than three essential notes; classical theorists allowed them, for instance, in the resolution of a German sixth. They are the primitives of harmony, the oldest chords used and, like the trunks and earliest branches of a tree, are the strongest. It is their stark strength that makes them too prominent, and therefore incongruous, where other chords all contain thirds and sixths and more 'delicate' intervals. In the sixteenth century the occurrence was disliked, yet the sound of 'consecutives' was often made. Ex. 29 (b) and (c) are from Palestrina:

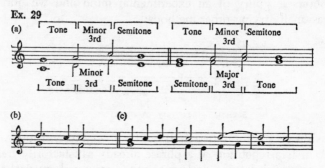

There is little need to consider the vertical, chordal aspect of this music. To say that it consists of triads and their inversions with prepared sevenths is to state nothing useful. The technique of dealing with suspensions was formal though various ornamental resolutions were cultivated which Palestrina did not use. They are easily recognisable.

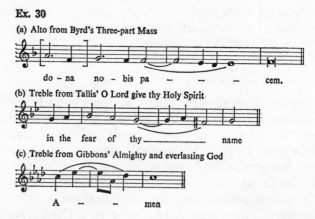

The chief harmonic interest is to be found by considering the way in which the music moves from cadence to cadence. A prevailing contrapuntal texture is relieved by formal cadences in more or less block harmony, each fugato leading to a cadence after which another fugato starts. A typical design is found in the familiar *O Lord, increase my faith* of Gibbons:

A: *O Lord, increase my faith*
    block harmony leading to a plagal cadence on E.

B: *strengthen me*
  echoing phrase founded on the G chord.
C: *and confirm me in thy true faith*
  block harmony leading to perfect cadence on A.
D: *endue me with wisdom*
  imitative counterpoint: two entries at the unison founded
  on the A scale, two entries at the octave founded on the E
  scale.
E: *charity and patience*
  imitative counterpoint at the fifth and sixth on *charity*,
  leading to a perfect cadence on E for *and patience*.
F: *in all my adversity*
  imitative counterpoint at the fifth, leading to a perfect
  cadence on D.
G: *sweet Jesus, say Amen*
  echoing phrase leading to perfect cadence on B; repeated
  leading to a perfect cadence on E.
H: *sweet Jesus, say Amen*
  two-part point repeated, leading to a final perfect cadence
  on A.

By 'modulations' the sixteenth-century composer did not mean
key changes, but cadences on different degrees of the mode or
scale. In that Gibbons piece, belonging to the early seventeenth century, we observe cadences, perfect or plagal, carefully arranged so that two similar ones are not used consecutively,
and nowhere before the final cadence does the music come to a
complete halt; it has no sections. The whole is, in fact, definitely
in the A mode: it revolves about A as round a pivot. When the
words *sweet Jesus, say Amen* first appear there is a sudden feeling
of softness, almost of 'modulation', one might say, as the music
moves for the only time to a new, rich cadence, that on B. The
feeling is at once cancelled by the next cadence on E, a cadence we
have heard three times before. Such is the usual ground-plan of the
Elizabethan anthem; in very long works the music sometimes
comes to a definite halt midway, but there is no attempt to write
successive sections in contrasted keys. Extended canticles like *Te
Deum* or the Nicene Creed are treated as the anthems: the variety
of cadences saves them from becoming dull. To say that Gibbons'
anthem here analysed is in mode A or the Aeolian mode is pure
convention. It begins with A as a centre, often comes back to its

pivot, and ends with A in the tenor; but it is no more entirely in the Aeolian than Beethoven's Fifth Symphony is all in C-minor. It is, however, clearly not in A-major, despite the C-sharp in its final cadence. The conventions of *musica ficta* had by 1625 caused the modes to group themselves into two kinds, those like our modern major scale and those like our minor. The transformation could hardly be called complete before 1660 but in 1625 it was well on the way. In *musica ficta* accidentals were added to the seventh and sometimes the sixth of the mode to provide a cadence in which the note a semitone below the final of the mode was used instead of the real seventh, which was a tone below. The results of thus sharpening the seventh and sixth may be tabulated as follows:

Ex. 31

Plain form of the mode   Form used in Musica Ficta

From the above it follows that the Dorian and Aeolian lost their distinctiveness, merging into a scale identical with our modern minor.[1] A piece written in the free form of the Dorian sounded exactly like a piece transposed from the free Aeolian. Ultimately the sameness of the two modes restricted the harmonic vocabulary which under the free modal system had been very rich. The 'minor key' of 1700 left the composer with a handful of possible cadences *in the key*—a harmonic famine compared to the plenty under the free modal system. The free form of the Mixolydian was identical with the Ionian, our modern major. Only the Phrygian stood aside from this dual grouping because of the second note of its scale, which, unlike the second of any other mode, was only a semitone above the final. The mode was occasionally used with D-sharp and F-sharp when it became identical with the Dorian and Aeolian, but never with D-sharp and F-natural in the same chord, unless as a freak experiment. The characteristic Phrygian cadences with the F-natural were too beautiful to be dropped and have continued to this day:

Ex. 32

ENGLISH CADENCE

The free modal system has left many such traces still to be found in our modern music. It gave rise to the so-called English cadence, to be seen on any page of sixteenth-century work; it was formed by using the descending form of the scale in one voice simultaneously with the ascending form in another. The three examples following show it in stages of increasing dissonance:

[1] Morley makes it clear that his contemporaries no longer imagined themselves to be using a mode but some part of the 'Gamut', i.e. the scale of all notes within the normal vocal compass, upwards from the G below middle C. They sang it to syllables which reminded them of the most common 'modulations'. Thus they sang not just G, A, B, etc., but G-Sol-Re-Ut, A-La-Mi-Re, etc.

Ex. 33

(a) From Byrd's Five-part Mass (2nd tenor in small notes)

(b) From Byrd's Christe qui lux (plainsong in 1st bass in small notes)

(c) Essential Parts only from Tallis' Salvator Mundi (2nd tenor in small notes)

Of these examples we may note that the first was used by Purcell (died 1695) as a conscious antique—as in *Rejoice in the Lord* at the words *let your requests be made known unto God*—and the others died out with the passing of the sixteenth century.

SOME CHORAL POINTS: (*a*) DESIGN BY CONTRAST

Design in music is attained by contrast and repetition. In Elizabethan church music repetition was sparingly used but contrast was secured by the successive use of block harmony and counterpoint, by the variety of cadences, and by other contrasts which delight the ear by first satiating it with sonority and then bringing it relief by the employment of a thinner texture. At this last method the composers of the sixteenth century were no less adept than the composers of other periods. We find a deft use of pitch contrasts, especially in the more ambitious works like Weelkes' *Hosanna to the son of David* where the higher voices batter the ear with loud, close harmony alternating with deeper, rich effects obtained from the six voices engaged. In five- and six-part work, indeed, the increased number of voices is used rather with such an end in view than to add to the complexity of the counterpoint. Relief is given to the ear by a careful use of differing combinations. In four-part works there is always a liberal use of two- and three-part passages, often following on the summing-up effect of some cadence. Only in the short services do we find all the parts singing all the time in the manner of a hymn-tune; these are the 'bread-and-butter' work of the period and the best that can be said of them is that they get over the ground quickly and sometimes beautifully. The only contrasts used are the alternating passages for decani, cantoris and full.

SOME CHORAL POINTS: (*b*) CHORDING

As one would expect in contrapuntal work the layout of the chords often breaks acoustical laws; the shape of the melodies will, of course, always account for the oddity. Even in five-part work chords occur without the third, the only apparent reason being that the composer liked them. Gibbons ends his *Nunc Dimittis* in F with:

Ex. 34

It looks a poor enough final chord on paper but seems to sound well in a building the size of a church. Except where a large number of parts are singing, the score is usually playable by the two hands, which shows that large gaps between the notes of a chord were studiously avoided; spacing is even, the inevitable consequence of keeping the compass of each voice within, as a rule, a ninth or a tenth. The singer is seldom, if ever, called upon for the extreme notes of his compass and that keeps the music sober in spirit. Melodically the parts are always easy and the short-phrase technique ensured that the singer had time to breathe—points often forgotten in more recent works. A glance at any page will reveal a score littered with rests, the breathing spaces so essential not only to the singer but to the attention of the listener. And if after a rest the part enters on a point, before the rest the composer is invariably careful to end his phrase musically with a note of some length on which the singer can dwell with satisfaction. There is no 'snatch a breath and on again' feeling left in the singer's mind.[1] In compass, alto parts alone give some anxiety to the modern choirmaster; the extremes used in all voices are somewhat as follows (in actual sounds):

Ex. 35

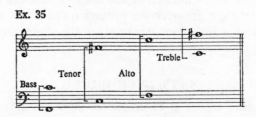

From this it is clear that the alto was expected to have an effective range of the same compass as that of other voices. The counter-tenor, a light head voice of tenor quality, was capable of delivering good notes in all parts of this range; our modern alto is a poor voice beside this, being often inaudible below D (above middle C) and incapable of anything higher than the C above. At times, therefore, editors have had to do some arranging in order to ensure an audible delivery of some of the low notes; it is still often the modern choir-master's duty to allow a tenor to lend a helping hand at difficult places.

PITCH

Most works of the period are now transposed up often as much as a minor third. It is presumed that ecclesiastical pitch in the

---

[1] The long phrases fashionable in modern works suit a large choir where any one singer can break the phrase without being noticed; the normal cathedral choir with perhaps only two men to each under part is essentially a 'chamber' combination and can seldom 'bring off' the sustained intensity required in these long phrases.

sixteenth century was higher than that now used. Ouseley in his edition of Gibbons' works quotes the following note from Tomkins' *Musica Deo Sacra*, published in 1668. It is found only in the Tenbury copy.

Ex. 36

Sit tonus fistulae apertae longitudine duorum pedum et semissis: sive 30 digitorum Geometricorum. (Let this be the pitch of an open pipe two and a half feet, or 30 inches, long.)[1]

A pipe thirty inches long produces a note which we should call a slightly sharp G; this would seem to make our modern transposition up a minor third a trifle on the sharp side. At any rate, this transposition brings all the voice parts within a singable compass, though it sometimes makes the tessitura of the tenor lie a little high.

NOTATION

The whiteness of the printed page should not restrict the choirmaster in his choice of a vigorous pace where it is effective. The minim should be looked upon as in a hymn-tune—merely a convenient symbol for the unit-beat; it is well, often, to imagine the score printed in notes half the length.

ACCOMPANIMENT

The works are seldom sung today with accompaniment. What the contemporary practice was no one knows. The 'sketch' scores extant give only the leads, when these are conductor's scores or meant to be played from. They were used as 'reminder' scores by players already familiar with the work. We do not know for certain whether choral music was often sung entirely unaccompanied in the late sixteenth century. Works by Tallis, Byrd and others were accompanied during the 1620's and under the Laudian regime, for organ books exist.

---

[1] Tomkins also says that the beat of the human pulse gives the normal duration of a minim. This suggests that we still tend to sing music of the period too slowly, especially when we see 'white' notes.

11

CHOIR MUSIC TO THE
DEATH OF GIBBONS

3. THE REPERTORY

SERVICES: MODERN USE

For the ordinary parish choir the Tudors and Jacobeans do not provide much. An increasing number of choirs can tackle the idiom, but the music itself, being originally written for the cathedral service, does not readily fit into a modern parish church service. The Great Services are apt to be lengthy, complicated and difficult besides requiring well-trained singers in the individual parts, while the Short Services, being mere formal settings designed to get over the ground quickly, are not very elevating to listen to for present-day unmusical congregations, many of whom rightly claim a share in the singing of the canticles. For churches where the congregation do not claim this right and for cathedrals there is some simple work of much charm.

THE MASS

Of the settings of the mass one hears the three by Byrd in three, four and five parts. The three-part is perhaps the most tenderly moving piece of liturgical music in the whole repertory and provides one of the few instances of its composer working on a small canvas.[1] Nothing so lovely as the *Agnus Dei* has ever appeared from any pen. The four- and five-part settings show Byrd playing with long contrapuntal lines which need time for their development: the result is a trifle too lengthy but broad and majestic to those who have the patience to allow it to run its full course. As settings to be used on festive occasions they are ideal but their atmosphere demands a mass done with the full comple-

---

[1] Another is his St. John Passion. Like the Byrd masses and motets this was probably sung by a very small choir in the Duke of Norfolk's chapel. Probably only one voice was allocated to each part.

ment of servers and liturgical exercises, and they both need a choir of efficient cathedral standard.

THE GREAT SERVICES

One may say the same of the Great Services which, even if they were tackled by the choir of the ordinary parish church, would hardly fit the scheme of parish church services. But the Great Services of Byrd and Weelkes[1] are noble if complicated settings and show their composers at their highest.

THE SHORT SERVICES

The Short Services used are chiefly those of Byrd—five-part—and Gibbons, in F—four-part. Gibbons is less baldly chordal and indeed solves a problem Byrd never attempted, that of using contrapuntal means without becoming lengthy. The Gibbons setting in F is indeed little short of a marvel of reticent and quickly moving beauty. The chordal settings of Byrd perhaps look dull on paper; one must remember, however, that they are the forerunners of many such settings by seventeenth-century composers. They set out to be little more than written-out chant settings where the chant varies. To this simple idea Byrd brings a wealth of rhythmic invention and cadence variation which make the settings as lovely in their way as the old method of singing the canticles to a plainsong chant. They perhaps keep too obviously and humbly to the dictum of 'to every syllable a note', but they fit well into the service despite their dull appearance on the printed page and the type is traceable through the simple settings of Byrd's successors, Bevin, whose short service in the Dorian mode is often sung, Child, Rogers (settings in D, F and A-minor), Blow, Boyce and even Goss. Other excellent and useful Short Services are supplied by Richard Farrant[2] (evening setting in A-minor, sometimes wrongly

---

[1] Weelkes, Thomas (born between 1570 and 1580—died 1623). In 1600 he was organist of the 'Colledge at Winchester'. 1602, Mus.B. Oxford (New College) and soon after organist of Chichester. An outstanding writer of madrigals, ten services, all very incomplete but showing an interesting experimental mind, and about forty anthems, many in MS.

[2] Richard Farrant (date of birth unknown—died 1580). Before 1564, when he became Master of the Choristers at St. George's Chapel, Windsor, he had been a Gentleman of the Chapel under Edward VI. Reappointed in 1569 to the Chapel Royal without relinquishing the Windsor appointment.

described and printed – first by Boyce – in G-minor), John Farrant[1] (evening setting in D-minor) and Nathaniel Pattrick[2] (service in G).

ACCOMPANIED SERVICES

Byrd's 'Second Service' is accompanied and roughly follows the old plainsong and faux-bourdon method: in place of the plainsong he gives a 'verse' to one of the voices following it by a verse set for chorus. The method is followed later in such services as Wise, in E-flat, Purcell, in G-minor, and the much later Walmisley, in D-minor; this type of strophic setting of the canticles has, indeed, nearly always produced interesting work.

ANTHEMS: FOUR-PART

It is fortunate for the normal four-voiced choirs of today that the Elizabethans have left a handful of pearls of great price which even choirs of slender resources can tackle. Any choir which does not use them all is not doing its duty by the Tudor inheritance, unless it be a choir where altos and tenors are hard to come by; being in four parts instead of the normal five or six, they can be performed by any reasonable choir which is not afraid to sing unaccompanied. Tye's *O come ye servants* (*Laudate nomen*) is little more than a hymn-tune with a 'point' set in the middle, and the contemporary *Lord, for thy tender mercy's sake* of Hilton (in the edition by Fellowes or that of the Church Music Society) is similar; but both make a good beginning for attacks on the Tudor repertory. Tallis offers two little gems, *If ye love me* – one of the few anthems of Tallis composed to English words – and *O Lord, give thy Holy Spirit*, and Byrd a deeply felt *Ave verum corpus*,[3] while Weelkes provides in *Let thy merciful ears* a tender miniature of no great difficulty. The rest, if somewhat harder, are all beautifully wrought: Gibbons' *Almighty and everlasting God* and *O Lord*,

---

[1] John Farrant (was living in 1600). Organist of Salisbury 1598–1602. John Farrants appear as organists of Christ Church, Newgate, Ely (1567–1572) and Hereford (1592–3) though they – or he – are probably not the same man as the Salisbury Farrant.

[2] Nathaniel Pattrick (date of birth unknown – died 1594–95). About 1590 he was Master of the Choristers at Worcester. Tomkins, his successor at Worcester, married his widow.

[3] Not, of course, written as an anglican anthem.

increase my faith need certainty in the leads, a feeling for the beauty of the text and the power to deliver the word-rhythms. Lesser-known composers are represented by Redford[1] (*Rejoice in the Lord*, a fine work of some breadth and thus unique among the smaller works, for all the others exhale a more subdued atmosphere; Redford's work is buoyant and vigorous with its cross-rhythms and strong accents, and ends with a fine cadence on *Amen*); Farrant's *Call to remembrance* and Hooper's[2] *Teach me thy way* strike a more thoughtful note while Mundy's[3] *O Lord, the maker of all thing* (*Rerum creator*) matches its moving text so well in spirit that one is inclined to think it one of the most successful of all these four-part works.

ANTHEMS: LARGER WORKS

The really representative work of the period is to be found in the larger anthems which may be placed beside the madrigals as the finest products of a remarkable generation. A glance at the corpus of this music as found in the volumes of *Tudor Church Music* will show not only that it is impossible to consider all the works but that only a percentage of it can be tapped by our choirs. At its best it can be as grand in its effect as a movement of a Beethoven symphony, and sung in its proper place and in the setting of the English service it is even more stirring; at its least effective it is always consummate in technique and never in bad taste—which can be said of the worst work of no other period. Little purpose would be served by giving short reviews of a mere handful of works; we may perhaps get the best idea of the general corpus of Tudor work by studying the characteristics of the work of three of the great names of the period.[4]

[1] John Redford (approximate dates, 1485–1545). Chorister, vicar-choral and organist of St. Paul's. The authenticity of *Rejoice in the Lord* has never been questioned; it is a remarkable production for its date.
[2] Edmund Hooper (1553–1621). 1588, Master of the Children at Westminster, 1603–4, Gentleman of the Chapel. 1606, organist of Westminster. There are a handful of services and anthems. He contributed to Este's *Whole Book of Psalms*, 1592, and to Ravenscroft's *Psalter*, 1621.
[3] William Mundy (date of birth unknown—died about 1591). Vicar-choral of St. Paul's and 1563–4, Gentleman of the Chapel.
[4] A list of works recommended for study will be found at the end of this section of the book.

12

THREE COMPOSERS

TALLIS

Tallis,[1] the earliest in date of the three great names, produced work which is always technically fine and serve as a model to be copied and improved upon by his pupil Byrd. The direct, classical quality of his style was more the product of his own genius than the result of modelling himself on the technical complexities of his precursors. Tallis at the time of the publication of the Book of Common Prayer was already a man of forty-five or so and the bulk of his work was written to Latin words; for that reason it smacks of the continental Palestrina style which relies more than later English work on purely musical methods to attain its effect. If Tallis had composed more to vernacular texts it is possible that his genius would have been moved to new paths of expression; but thus to carp is merely to say that his music was of its time. His genius made his work monumental, a perfect model for the youthful Byrd who called him 'a father in musicke'. The five-part *Salvator mundi* which has become part of the modern repertory attempts something more and achieves an unforgettable fusion of the grand style and a moving pathos which reflects the emotion of the text. The clashing English sevenths on the word *redemisti*, the effective repeat at the beginning—a device more common in the

---

[1] Thomas Tallis (*c.* 1505–85). In 1540. on the dissolution of Waltham Abbey he received forty shillings wages and bounty, which suggests that he had been organist or Master of the Choristers there. About 1540 he became a Gentleman of the Chapel. In 1557 Mary granted him part lease for twenty-one years of Minster (Sheppey), and in 1574–5 Tallis and Byrd who were then joint organists of the Chapel Royal were granted a monopoly by Elizabeth to print music and music-ruled paper. Under this licence most of the music of the period was printed. Tallis died at Greenwich and was buried in the parish church. A commemorative plate will be found in the present church. Publications in his lifetime are: *Cantiones Sacrae*, 1575 (with Byrd) and five English anthems in Day's *Certaine Notes*, 1560–5. There are a few Latin services and about fifty motets. Besides about thirty English anthems, of which ten or so are adaptations (some possibly by Tallis himself), there are two English services, the Dorian *Te Deum*, and settings of the preces, responses and litany.

madrigals than in the motets, here consummately used to drive home the urgency of the cry *Salvator mundi, salva nos*—the repeated note figure on *auxiliare*, like the earnest utterance of a crowd, and the long downward movement in pitch, dynamics and intensity of feeling of the last two pages are all used with the unconscious greatness of genius without once halting the onward march of the music.

BYRD

Byrd[1] caught the nobility of style of his master and fused into it a new, more human pathos; the resulting music is wonderfully rich, like Shakespeare at his finest, where oratory and feeling combine to make great art. Byrd, despite his rather over-developed sense of justice and his consequent love of lawsuits, was a serious-minded man as well as the most accomplished master of music technique in his day: he could handle his eight parts with ease as well as cling stubbornly to his Roman faith in days when that sometimes meant the threat of execution. But he had other qualities: he believed in his heart as well as in his mind the dogmas of his faith (a rarity even in serious-minded men) and could in addition carry over into his music his strong emotional conviction. The result is a giant in music who even in experimental work like his keyboard pieces could surpass all his contemporaries. His mind attuned to great things loved to toil at a large canvas with a serious subject; the lighter side of madrigal writing was not in his

[1] William Byrd (1543–1623). Organist of Lincoln, 1562, where in 1568 he married Julian Birley. In 1569 he was sworn in as a Gentleman of the Chapel, taking up the appointment (after the custom of his day) in 1572, when he worked in association with Tallis who was also possibly his tutor. The monopoly granted to Tallis and Byrd passed solely to Byrd on the death of Tallis and later to Morley and then to Este. From 1572 to 1592 he lived at Harlington, Middlesex, where his wife and family—and sometimes himself—were often the object of persecution against the Roman Catholics. In 1593 he moved to Stondon Place in Essex, buying the lease for £300 from the crown who had previously taken it from a Roman Catholic named Shelley. Byrd was possibly buried at Stondon. His work includes: three masses, *Cantiones Sacrae*, 1575 (with Tallis), a series of Latin motets and further similar books by himself alone in 1589 and 1591. In 1605 and 1607 followed two books of Latin Gradualia. There are also fifty or so Latin works in manuscript. English services include the Short, Second, Third and Great together with the litany and a setting of the preces and responses. Of the English anthems, of which there are fifty or so, some were published in *Psalms, Songs and Sonnets*, 1588 and 1611, and in *Songs of Sundrie Natures*. There are in addition 15 verse-anthems.

make-up, but he could at times produce miniatures as fascinating as *Christe qui lux*, with its simple chordal setting of a plainsong compline hymn, and the moving *Ave verum corpus*. With space in which to work, however, he is more at home and is certain to produce majestic and highly vitalised music suited to the inspiring texts he chose.

GIBBONS

The third great name, Gibbons,[1] brings us to music of a different sort. Gibbons was more 'English' than the others and a protestant; he wrote only to English texts and like all protestants had his feet firmly set on the earth. He is moved more by the drama of human things than by the dogmas of the theologians. If he could thrill to the dramatic Palm Sunday story in *Hosanna to the Son of David*, he loves rather to linger over words like 'look upon our infirmities', 'in all our dangers and necessities', or 'O Lord, increase my faith', the eternal cry of the Christian struggling in a world at odds with his ideals. He shows to advantage in the two saint's day anthems, one for John the Baptist–*This is the record of John*–and the other for Peter–*Almighty God, who by thy Son*. The human touch in both is new and unmistakable; in the former the conversation gives a vivid character sketch of the baptist's blunt vigour; *and he answered, No* is set to a short, almost unmannerly cadence, while the earnest heart beating beneath the camel's hair shirt is felt in the impassioned utterance *and he said, I am the voice of him that crieth in the wilderness*. No one can forget the simple, telling effect of the word *earnestly* in the Peter anthem. Gibbons, in fact, shows almost a romantic tendency, a judgment corroborated by the study of his madrigals which are often tinged with a sorry cynicism, the sure sign of a romantic. Gibbons' faith is not the easy faith and adoration of Tallis and Byrd in an incense-breathing milieu but shows the heart-searchings and questionings of a thoughtful protestant.

[1] Orlando Gibbons (1583–1625). 1596, chorister at King's College, Cambridge; 1604, organist of the Chapel. In 1619 he was made one of the king's 'musicians for the virginalls', and in 1623 organist of Westminster, where he conducted the music at the funeral of James I. He died at Canterbury while attending the new king who had gone to meet his bride from France, and was buried in the Cathedral, where there is now a commemorative plaque and bust. Little of his music was printed in his lifetime. There are two services (F and D-minor) and about forty anthems of which more than half are verse-anthems. There are no Latin works.

GIBBONS, THE MUSICIAN

As a musician Gibbons must be considered the last of a great tradition writing in a reactionary style when all the bright young men around him were experimenting with new means. With the counterpoint of the old school he paints more the world as it is than as it might be. He is not very adventurous with his melodies but can weave a pattern of intertwining lines with an adroit hand; this he does without allowing himself to run to the heavenly lengths of Byrd, a concession, perhaps, to the conditions of his generation when choirs were being reduced in numbers and when the first rapture of the reformers was possibly cooling off. The most he concedes to a changing world is to write a few anthems with string accompaniment; the two saint's day anthems mentioned above are thus provided and enable Gibbons to set the model of a new idea, that of a verse or solo anthem with accompaniment. But the vocal line of the solos is written in the old idiom with perhaps a slight enlargement of the compass compared to his chorus parts—it might well be another string part—and there is no attempt at a 'tune' with a bass such as others like Dowland and Campion were already writing, or of chords held as the accompaniment to a vocal recitative, a device already gaining favour. Gibbons is, of course, great enough for the charge of reactionary not to matter; as much might be said of Bach or Elgar.

GIBBONS' AND WEELKES' 'HOSANNA'

It may be interesting and instructive to contrast his glorious, full-blooded setting of *Hosanna to the Son of David* with that of his contemporary Weelkes. At a glance Gibbons is more consistently contrapuntal; only at the phrase *peace in heaven* are there some low three-part chords: at no place is there a rest for all the voices simultaneously. He works in seven parts for richness of sound, all the parts being *divisi* except the bass. There is a fine sense of form and climax; note, for example, the upward-rising scale in the opening phrase followed by the downward-moving four notes on *blessed is he*, or the last trombone-like entry of the bass after a lengthy silence. The whole is sonorous and gives the effect of the glory of God sung by a choir of worshipping cherubim and seraphim in some distant heaven. Weelkes' setting paints a different picture, one of silver trumpets uplifted for the pageant of a king's reception. Here we find block harmony, the effective use of simultaneous rests—for the singers, that is, not rests of sound in an echoing cathedral—and the two trebles are exploited in their highest register to give brilliance. The form is made clear by alternate block chords and a contrapuntal texture. Note the crescendo of the three central hosannas obtained simply and effectively by adding parts to the original three, the whole being a kind of return to the opening hosannas. The general result is one of vigour and brilliance and aptly contrasts with the gorgeous solidity of Gibbons' setting.

13

ORGANS AND ORGAN
ACCOMPANIMENT TO 1600

SOME EARLY INSTRUMENTS

Mention of organs in Christian churches before the eighth century is scanty, though it is certain that instruments of the organ type with pipes and bellows together with sliders to admit the wind were known to the Jews and Greeks in pre-Christian times and were in use in the services of the early church. Contemporary writers would obviously mention or describe only the most famous organs, and bearing in mind that such organs were not perhaps always typical of their time, we may briefly mention some of them. An organ is stated to have been used in the nun's church at Grado in Spain before 580; it contained thirty treble pipes, two to each note, and such a compass of four octaves was probably rare at the time. A similar instrument, possibly, was that set up a hundred years later by Pope Vitalian in a church in Rome. It is a certain Aldhelm who shows us, by referring to the Anglo-Saxons' custom of painting the front pipes of their organs, that organs were to be heard in England as early as the year 700. Fifty years later Pepin (714–768) set up in a church in Compiègne an organ sent by the Byzantine Emperor Constantine Copronymus VI, while in 811 or 812 Charlemagne his son had two organs in Aachen, one a copy of his father's and the other a gift of Haroun Alraschid, the work of a builder named Giafer. These stories seem to suggest that the Arabs and the people of Constantinople were as well advanced in the art of organ-building as they were in most musical matters and influenced the west in their organs no less than in their mathematics, alchemy, hymns and monastic ideals. It is interesting to find that England was always a good market for organs and during the tenth century Dunstan (925–988) set up famous organs with metal pipes in the abbey churches of Malmesbury and Abingdon. At the same period Winchester had the largest organ then known, a monster having 400 pipes, which suggests reduplication of notes in profusion so that, as customary at the time, the octave and fifth of the note played was sounded; its date coincides with the first experiments in organum where the earliest counterpoints moved in octaves, fourths and fifths with the canto fermo.

MECHANISM AND USE

The instruments described above were all simple in type and incapable of being 'played' in any manner approaching present-day conceptions. Under each pipe was a sliding lath which was pushed in to admit the wind and drawn out to silence the pipe. Most organs had two or more pipes sounding over each lath with no arrangement for shutting off any one rank of pipes. On the laths were marked the names of the notes, a device followed on the later keyboards, and few organs apparently contained more than seven or eight notes. These details are given in a treatise, *De Diversis Artis*, liber iii, written during the eleventh century by a monk who calls himself Theophilus and who also gives directions for cutting the mouth of the pipe to produce loud and soft tone; the principles governing the shape of flute-toned and diapason-toned pipes were apparently universally known. Such organs could be played possibly at the speed of the plainsong though one would imagine that their use as accompanying instruments would not help towards rhythmic elasticity in the singing.[1]

IMPROVEMENTS: LEVERS AND SPRINGS

At the end of the eleventh century two important innovations were applied to the instrument: the sliding laths were replaced by laths acting as levers which had to be pressed downwards to open the valve to the pipe—a much simpler operation for the player—while springs, probably made of horn, were provided to bring the valves and levers back to the closed position. The levers were attached to the valves by ropes and were ordinarily three to five inches wide and a yard or more in length, while they had often to be depressed as much as a foot; the player, now called appropriately *pulsator*, would certainly need to thump or at least to give the lever a strong jerk as at the present-day carillon console. Much quicker playing was naturally possible with this lever and spring

[1] We have no proof that they accompanied singing. Chaucer mentions 'the merry organ that on masse-days gon', as if organ playing, like bell ringing, marked festivals.

action. During the years after 1100 organs were provided with more and more pipes sounding at various concordant intervals from the note marked on the lever, and thus the organ continued for three hundred years.

THE NOTES OF 'MUSICA FICTA' ADDED

It was not until the fourteenth century that the new notes of musica ficta were added to the range of pipes; the Winchester organ of the tenth century had already contained pipes to emit the B-flat (the 'lyric semitone', as it was called) and now the F-sharp was added to help in Mixolydian cadences, then C-sharp for the Dorian mode, E-flat to provide another lyric semitone for the Lydian mode and last of all G-sharp to give Aeolian cadences. The octave now contained twelve notes,[1] the levers for these new pipes being placed a few inches above those for the diatonic notes so that the performer could knock down the diatonic levers with his wrist, his fingers operating the new notes of *Musica ficta*. Towards the end of the century another experiment made it possible to enlarge the compass of the organ without having a console of unwieldy dimensions: this was the roller which allowed the levers to be placed in any desired position and not as hitherto directly under their own pipes. By this means the pipes could be posted on the soundboard in any convenient arrangement and more widely spaced—which is better acoustically—and from now on we find the familiar V arrangement of the pipes; the organ no longer had all its weightier pipes at one end.

ACCOMPANIMENT BEFORE 1400

It is clear that such organs as these could hardly have been used to play music in more than two parts (the wrist and fingers were used rather as the heel and toe ends of the shoe in modern pedalling), but they were doubtless employed to accompany the early attempts at harmonised singing and may even have given would-be composers an opportunity of finding new effects to be tried later with voices. Their clumsy levers must, however, have made

[1] It should be noted that with organs all tuned to an untempered scale the notes of *musica ficta*—C-sharp, E-flat, F-sharp, G-sharp and B-flat—were not equivalent to D-flat, D-sharp, G-flat, A-flat and A-sharp, which latter set of notes never entered into the minds of composers until the wild and daring experiments of such men as Dr. John Bull in the seventeenth century.

even simple improvisation difficult and it is perhaps significant that noticeable advance in the technique of composition was made after the keyboard had become more manageable in the following century. The tone of the organs before 1400 must have been a little wearying as no one had yet invented any device for shutting off any one rank of pipes.

BIRTH OF THE MODERN ORGAN

During the years between 1400 and 1500 the modern organ was born. By 1500 the console of levers had become a keyboard with the sharps on the same 'manual' as the naturals (though still a little above them), the keys—thanks to the roller—becoming small enough to be operated with the fingers of the performer and being covered with black and white material in the reverse order of present-day keyboards. As the keys approximated more and more to the modern width so the compass of the keyboard was enlarged from one octave to four up from F at the foot of the bass stave. Often below this F, a pipe for C was added played from the E key next below, a device later extended to include all the diatonic notes below F and known as the 'short octave'. Nor was appreciation lacking for the effective use of the low notes of the organ; pipes of sixteen- and even thirty-two-foot pitch were made on the continent while as early as 1418 an organ was built having an octave of pedals with its own sixteen-foot pipes. But in most organs having a pedalboard the pedals were merely attached by ropes to the manual action and thus worked as if on a modern organ one drew 'Great to Pedals' and had no pedal stops drawn.[1] In passing, it is extraordinary to note that pedals did not appear in English organs until 1790, three hundred years later. The invention and application of the spring-box made it possible to shut off any rank of pipes and thus indirectly caused experiments to be made in altering the shapes of the various components of the pipes to produce new timbres: by lessening the scale or diameter of the diapason pipes string-tone was produced, and the stopped (stoppered) diapason gave another new timbre; tapering the pipes gave the Gemshorn type of tone and reeds like the trumpet and vox humana appeared. By 1500 the organ begins to assume a modern look with its black and white keyboards, its pedalboard,

---

[1] Village organs can still be found in England which do the same, though the coupling is not made with rope.

its stop levers, symbolic of a rich variety of tone-colour, and its pipes stacked on the soundboard in V shape.

THE SIXTEENTH-CENTURY ORGAN

This, then, is the type of organ which served for the accompaniment of the services during the Reformation period. Such organs were built by itinerant builders—a necessity at the time in such a profession—and on similar instruments, but without pedals (though not without sixteen-foot tone), Byrd and his contemporaries performed. Many of the cathedrals had two organs, 'the great orgones' and 'the small orgones', which may possibly have differed in pitch for accompanying voices of either tenor or bass compass, the former being naturally the larger and more important instrument of the two. There is, however, very scanty information about English organs during the Reformation period and it is not even certain whether the settings of services and anthems were accompanied or not. What look like organ scores exist; the use made of them is doubtful but no doubt any accompaniments there may have been merely reduplicated the voice parts. In the verse-anthems which appeared before 1625 the accompaniment is in most cases intended for strings; it is not clear what conclusions may be drawn from the fact. What is certain is that the post of accompanist or organist was often shared among as many as three or four persons in the cathedrals and Royal Peculiars, which suggests that it was not considered a very important element in the musical establishment. The only reliable early English specification extant is that of the organ set up in the 'P'isshe of Alhalowe, Barkyng, next y\ᵉ Tower' which was only a small instrument consisting of three stops, a diapason and 'dowble principalls throweout', and built by one Anthony Duddyngton in 1519. Tonally it seems unenterprising when compared with continental organs of the same date in churches of equal importance, but it is unwise to make further comparisons with such a lack of evidence. A hundred years later in 1606 the organ built by Dallam for King's College Chapel, Cambridge, contained two manuals and a 'shaking stoppe'; this again was not a large organ for the time, since by 1560 the two-manual organ with pedals at St. Mary, Lübeck, had a third manual added and by the end of the seventeenth century had on the Great thirteen stops, on the Swell fourteen, on the Choir fifteen and on the Pedal fifteen. The English organs were probably conservative in tone, relying mainly on diapasons with some contrasted softer stops, and not carrying much mutation work. Reeds were familiar enough in the continental organs and in the regals—small portable instruments—but seem to have been little used before 1600. Perhaps here, too, the hand of the more zealous and Calvinistic reformers showed itself. If accompaniments are used today—as in verse-anthems—it will therefore be in keeping to confine them to flue-work for the most part with a sparing use of sixteen-foot tone.

The article *Organ Mass* in Grove's *Dictionary* gives a summary account of the increasing incursions of organ music into the liturgy from the fourteenth to the sixteenth century. Note that this influenced the design of vocal music and that, by the 'alternation' method, whole sections of *Kyrie, Gloria,* etc., were not sung at all, but imagined during the organ verset. For a fuller account of this see Reese's *Music in the Middle Ages* and his *Music in the Renaissance.*

BOOKS AND MUSIC RECOMMENDED FOR FURTHER STUDY

The Prayer Book and Englishing of the Services

A New History of the Book of Common Prayer, Procter and Frere
(*Macmillan*, 1901–1932)
The Background of the Prayer Book, C. S. Phillips (*S.P.C.K.*)
*Cranmer's First Litany, 1544, and Merbecke's Book of Common
Prayer Noted, 1550*, J. Eric Hunt (*S.P.C.K.*, 1939)
An attractive book of facsimiles with a summary of recent
research in these subjects.

Music and Composers

English Cathedral Music, E. H. Fellowes (*Methuen*, 1941), which
in chapters 1–9 sums up all that is known about the period.
The English Madrigal, E. H. Fellowes (*O.U.P.*, 1925), which
though outside the subject gives the background of secular
and cathedral music-making under the Tudors with plenty of
illustrations of contemporary documents, etc.
Voice and Verse, H. C. Colles (*O.U.P.*, 1928) deals with the questions involved in setting words to music.
William Byrd, E. H. Fellowes (*O.U.P.*, 1936)
Orlando Gibbons, E. H. Fellowes (*O.U.P.*, 1925)
Tudor Church Music, Denis Stevens (*Faber*, 2nd ed. 1966), which
includes an E.P. disc.
The prefaces to the volumes of *Tudor Church Music* (*O.U.P.*)
are full of useful matter. For the study of the technique of com-
position of the period, the following should be consulted:
Contrapuntal Technique of the Sixteenth Century, R. O. Morris
(*O.U.P.*, 1922)
Music and the Reformation in England, 1549–1660, Peter le Huray
(*Jenkins*)

MUSIC

SERVICES

Byrd: Masses in three, four and five parts.
          2nd, accompanied Service.
          3rd, Short Service in five parts.
Gibbons: Short Service, in F.
Tallis: Dorian *Te Deum*.
          Lamentations.

ANTHEMS

Byrd: Ave verum corpus. Miserere mei. Christe qui lux.
          Justorum animae. Sing joyfully. O praise the Lord, ye
          saints above. Haec Dies. Laudibus in sanctis.
Gibbons: O Lord, increase my faith. Almighty and everlasting
          God. This is the record of John (accompanied). Al-
          mighty God, who by thy Son (accompanied). Hosanna
          to the Son of David. O clap your hands together
          (eight-part).
Morley: Nolo mortem peccatoris.
Mundy: O Lord, the maker of all thing.
Philips: Ascendit Deus. Cantantibus organis.
Redford: Rejoice in the Lord.
Tallis: If ye love me. O Lord, give thy Holy Spirit. Salvator
          mundi.
Weelkes: Let thy merciful ears. Hosanna to the Son of David.

It should be noted that the following composers not mentioned
in this book are worthy of study: Dering, Morley, Philips, Tomkins, Whyte. Other composers not mentioned have supplied useful works for the modern repertory; the above list is one of music
recommended for study on the lines laid down in this book.
Gramophone recordings are not given as new recordings are
frequently made and old recordings as frequently go out of
pressing. For recent recordings consult the gramophone com-
panies' catalogues.

PART III

THE SEVENTEENTH CENTURY

14

CHURCHMANSHIP AND THE
PRAYER BOOK FROM 1559 TO 1662

ELIZABETH

With protestant interference during the reign of Edward and the Catholic persecutions of Bloody Mary to warn her, Elizabeth determined to tread warily, but her careful attitude could not stop the rift created by the first Act of Uniformity.[1] The advanced faction, all of whom had fled to Frankfurt and Geneva during Mary's reign, returned to England when they saw the bloodless methods of the new queen. In their hearts nothing short of the abolition of the Prayer Book—any prayer book—would satisfy them, and the history of the next eighty years is the story of their continual nagging at ceremonies and vestments until the Book of Common Prayer was ousted in 1645. The 1559 Book, founded as it was on the protestant Book of 1552, could not succeed in pleasing the 'Roman' Catholics any more than it did the captious 'Puritans' as they may now be called. In 1570 Pope Pius V, more downright than his predecessor who had not strongly objected to the 1559 Book, published a Bull of Excommunication against the English Church which made further conciliation impossible between England and Rome. Those opposed to the Book for protestant reasons included many who unwillingly conformed, others who felt they could not sincerely conform and the Puritan party who must henceforward be considered as anti-church, though they themselves thought they were the true Church and had, while in Geneva, brought out a rival book of Forms of Service. No sooner had James I ascended the throne in March 1603 than a puritan Millenary Petition, purporting to have a thousand signatures, was presented to the king. James called a conference in the following January at Hampton Court and in February issued a few minor alterations; but in reality the Elizabethan Book remained as well as the dissensions.

[1] See page 67.

SCOTLAND

A Prayer Book was foisted on the nonconforming Scots in 1637 after negotiations between Laud and Maxwell which had lasted for eight years, but it failed to please and never came into general use. Its importance lies in its influence on later revisions: in the 1662 Book it suggested the rubrics concerning the offertory and the manual acts in the consecration; its form of consecration prayer was later incorporated into the Scottish Liturgy, formally adopted in 1731 by the Church of Scotland which had been disestablished in 1688. Through this Liturgy it later influenced the American Liturgy of 1789.

THE DIRECTORY

The failure of the Scottish Book may be said to have precipitated the events in England of the next few years. By the summer of 1640 the Puritan party had gained enough power to force the ejection from parliament of the bishops. The episcopacy was abolished, the bishops themselves imprisoned, and the Church became presbyterian. But it was only an interim measure; in 1643 a so-called Westminster Assembly, consisting partly of lay members, ousted Convocation and overthrew the Church of England. Two years later the Book of Common Prayer was replaced by the 'Directory for Public Worship of God in Three Kingdoms'. It was forbidden to use the Prayer Book in public or private worship and fines and other penalties were to be inflicted on any minister who did not use, or even spoke against, the Directory.

THE PURITANS IN TRIUMPH

Puritanism had triumphed. Its services and Prayer Book made illegal, the Church of England as an organisation no longer existed, though its buildings were freely used. The Directory, true to its title, prescribed no forms of service but merely issued instructions on how 'meetings' should be conducted. All vestments were to be put away, the communion-table was to be moved into the body of the church (the minister as in the primitive church facing the congregation), while west-end fonts, wedding rings and burial services were all scrapped. Directions were given for the 'Singing of Psalms'—that is, psalm-tunes—which implied that no choir was necessary. Music, in fact, apart from psalm-tunes, was strictly banned; organs were silenced, removed, or in some places despoiled by zealots, while many choir libraries were destroyed in fits of iconoclasm. The purifying of public worship was complete. A model was given for all future nonconformist services. The puritan mind, indeed, started its reasoning from the axiom that in public worship all expression is immoral, the inner feeling needing no material manifestation. Carried to its logical end it becomes Quakerism; but most of the Puritans of the Rebellion would not go so far. They allowed kneeling, they allowed psalm-tunes, though they shuddered at surplices and choir music. As a result the history of nonconformist music is from now on a melancholy tale of hymn-tunes in eight-eight and eight-six. In Germany it culminated in the Bach Passions; in England it reaches its climax in revivalist hymn-tunes and the music of the Salvation Army. Art, say the Puritans, must at any price be banished from the religious gathering; hymn-tunes serve a useful purpose, and they alone may remain.

THE RESTORATION

While Charles II was waiting at The Hague, presbyterian divines were sent to entreat him not to use the forms and ceremonies of the Book of Common Prayer in his private chapel. If he did, they asserted, he would scandalise all religious men. He replied that he intended to consult parliament about the matter and meanwhile would have surplices worn in his chapel as he had always done. He later promised a revision of the Prayer Book and on March 25th, 1661, the nine surviving bishops and other divines met at the Savoy Hospital intending to make a stand about ceremonies and vestments. The Puritans in their usual manner claimed to be representative of the Church of England and submitted long lists of carping criticisms. The churchmen, feeling their position stronger as the conference went on, answered their captiousness with curt refutations. On December 20th the Book of Common Prayer was adopted by both Houses, and on May 19th, 1662, it was given the royal assent.

THE 1662 BOOK

The Book was provided with a new Preface, Cranmer's preface being retitled 'Concerning the Service of the Church'. Scriptural passages were altered to conform to the 1611 Bible and minor alterations to the number of six hundred were made throughout. The psalter was designedly left untouched, the old version being thought more singable. The musicians, in fact, were considered not only in this; in the famous rubric, 'In quires and places where they sing, here followeth the anthem', they were given authority for an already old custom. Choirs and their organists settled down to the business of rebuilding themselves, their organs and their repertories.

TOLERATION

From now on the Presbyterians, Independents and other non-conforming groups form a sect outside and separate from the legally established church. Within the church there is also peace for a hundred and fifty years, as the 1662 Book broke little new ground and no doubt churchmen had grown tired of continuous squabbling. The settlement was a decidedly protestant one, showing the influence of the puritan mind. Toleration of some sort had been established and the church could now go ahead with its services unmolested by the puritan element. If toleration degenerated into lethargy the fault could be laid at the door of secular influences during the next century, of which more later.

15

CONGREGATIONAL MUSIC FROM 1549 TO 1662

1. RESPONSES AND PSALMS

THE MUSIC OF THE CONGREGATION

Life for a choirmaster during the eventful years after 1549 must have been varied, interesting and sometimes dangerous. The Englishing of the service caused little trouble in anthems and other such musical settings, but every present-day choirmaster will know that the congregation's part in the service and the psalms would present interesting problems; for upon the active participation of the people in the service the Book of Common Prayer had laid much stress. Even at the service without music this ideal was not easy to attain, at least in the parish churches, for it may be presumed that few of the people could read: hence, perhaps, the bidding before the general confession at matins and evensong, *saying after me*.[1] At the musical service the congregation, who before the publication of the first Prayer Book had been accustomed to join in very little of the service, would find itself still unable to sing in for example the psalms and canticles, or the creed and *Gloria* at the mass. It seems, indeed, possible that no one really did tackle this problem, either to provide a 'people's music' or to teach them to sing it; the congregation were indeed excluded from those very parts of the service which the Prayer Book meant them to undertake. It is only in recent years that their claim to sing their own liturgical parts of the services has been reasserted and music provided for them to sing, after their being denied their rights for three hundred and fifty years. During that period the problem was solved by providing them with something else, the true 'people's music' of the period—the metrical psalm and the hymn.

[1] Which means, presumably, 'saying as I say'.

THE SOURCES OF INFORMATION

What little they could sing is to be found in a handful of books
which by their fewness in number prove beyond doubt how little
was done to tackle the question. Of these Merbecke's *Boke of
Common Praier Noted*, 1550, is the only real attempt to provide a
solution. It was never re-edited to conform to later Prayer Books
and is therefore negligible for the history of the period. There is
nothing to show that the book was widely used or even influential,
though we may surmise that its methods were those generally
followed, at least in the priest's parts and the responses. In 1560,
following the 1559 Book, Day's *Certaine Notes* gives simple four-
part settings to parts of the mass and canticles and notes the
psalms in the vague way Merbecke had done, but to a different
tone. There was probably little change in the priest's parts and the
responses before the Commonwealth, and this is corroborated by
some interesting publications which appeared after the reinstate-
ment of the church service in 1660 designed to remind and instruct
those who were re-establishing the services. The first of these was
Edward Lowe's[1] *A Short Direction for the performance of Cathedrall
Service*, published at Oxford in 1661, which gives the preces,
responses and litany as sung in pre-Commonwealth times and
adds a version of Tallis' responses and litany as 'Extraordinary
Responses upon Festivalls'. In 1662 two compilations of anthem
words were published, one by Stephen Bulkley in York, the other
being a collection of the words of fifty-one anthems as sung in
Dublin Cathedral. These and the famous collection of the Rev.
James Clifford[2] entitled *The Divine Services and Anthems usually
sung in the Cathedrals and Collegiate Choirs of the Church of
England*, published in 1663, are valuable because they give the
choir repertories during the first half of the century together with
the earliest Restoration additions. They prove that it was not
until 1660 that the sixteenth-century works dropped out of the
cathedral lists, and as Clifford's collection contains the words of
nearly four hundred anthems it may be taken as a careful and
representative catalogue made no doubt by Clifford during his

[1] Edward Lowe (1610–1682), chorister under John Holmes at Salisbury.
About 1630, organist of Christ Church, Oxford. 1660, one of the three
organists of the Chapel Royal. 1662, Professor of Music at Oxford.

[2] James Clifford (1622–1698). 1632, chorister of Magdalen College,
Oxford. 1661, minor canon of St. Paul's. He lived to be present at the
opening of the new St. Paul's in December 1697.

years of enforced idleness. In 1664 Clifford republished his work
with additions containing 'Brief Directions for the understanding
of that part of the service performed with the organ in St. Paul's
Cathedral on Sundays and Holydayes'; in a second edition the
chants for the psalms, *Venite* and *Quicunque vult* are given. By
means of these books it is possible to piece together the history of
the singing of the psalms, responses and other service music
between Merbecke's book and 1650.

THE TRADITIONAL RESPONSES

The setting of the responses given by Merbecke was a transcription and translation of the old method, to be sung in unison.[1] The
reformed choirs, however, seem early to have shown a desire to be
always singing in four parts—a disease still rife—and precentors
and choirmasters probably made their own arrangements. Tallis is
often quoted as the author of the usual harmonised version as sung
today,[2] though it is very bald and might have been made by anyone. It is possibly this version or something very like it which was
sung on all ferial days in cathedrals throughout the two hundred
years following 1600. More ornate settings by sixteenth-century
composers are extant,[3] some using the plainsong version as a canto
fermo, others adventuring into the realms of fantasy. That they
were ever widely used is very unlikely, except for the Tallis set;
they are choir pieces and though of little use in a parish church
today can yet find their place in the cathedral service. Tallis' set
with the plainsong in the tenor—often called the Festal Responses
—has always been freely used in the English service on festive
occasions, as we see in Lowe, and is perhaps best now retained for
marking off certain seasons of the church's year. Sung as faux-
bourdons by the choir with the people singing the plainsong *canto
fermo*—after adequate rehearsal—they can no doubt sound effective;
but elaboration of these parts of the service in the ordinary parish
church is, truly speaking, hardly worth while. The method of
singing responses has varied from a deliberate 'chanting', the
usual plan up to the end of the last century, to a talking speed as

[1] His preces differ from those used today, which date from 1662.

[2] As published by the Church Music Society and the School of English
Church Music.

[3] *Six Settings of the Preces and Responses by Tudor Composers*, ed. Ivor
Atkins and E. H. Fellowes. Obtainable at S.P.C.K. or O.U.P.

commonly used today. In the old cathedral tradition the Tallis set was accompanied with a fairly full organ, but modern usage tends towards the disuse of the organ, so that the word-rhythms can have free play.

THE PSALMS

Until the Commonwealth there were apparently three distinct methods of singing the psalms, in which we include the strophic canticles: they were sung to the plainsong tones, the less ornate tones and endings being usually chosen, as in Merbecke and Day, because they were better suited to an English text; they were presumably sung (as they had often been before 1549) to plainsong with alternate verses in faux-bourdon usually but not always founded on the tone as a *canto fermo*; finally, certain psalms, as, for example, Psalm 51, were given special verse by verse, chant-like settings. Byrd and others have left such settings; the composer usually scores the first few verses only, perhaps leaving to precentors and choirmasters the arranging of the remainder. The history of the three methods is far from complete owing to the destruction of choir-books during the Commonwealth, but the existence of three different ways side by side shows that the problem was at any rate tackled from all angles. The crucial difficulty at the time was not the actual fitting of English to music intended for a Latin text; it was a rhythmic difficulty brought about solely by the insistence of the choirs on singing in harmony. Harmony, especially at the cadence, creates accent and those who arranged the psalms for singing found, as we still find, that it is not always easy to get the word- and syllable-stress to coincide with the musical accent. In the plainsong tones the stress could be moved from one note to another or 'hanger' notes could be inserted where the words required it. In the harmonised versions of the tones there could be no such adaptations and a rhythmic scheme to fit all—or nearly all—contingencies had to be devised. The evidence (found in extant manuscript choir-books) shows that many schemes were tried; as, at the Restoration, two chants were singled out by Lowe and Clifford as being best known, we may assume that their rhythmic scheme had been found the most satisfactory. The chants are these:

Ex. 37

(a) Christ Church Tune

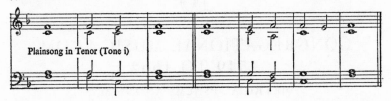

Plainsong in Tenor (Tone i)

(b) Imperial Tune

Plainsong in Tenor (Tone viii)

The first follows the rhythmic scheme (shown by the addition of bar-lines in the modern manner) of Tallis' setting of Psalm 2; its authorship is uncertain, Tallis and Batten both being suggested. The Imperial Tune is by Child. Both have the plainsong in the tenor and in both the first note of the plainsong—the reciting-note—is repeated in the following chord, a subtle device which enabled the singer to get in a subsidiary accent before the final accent at the cadence. However vague the history of harmonised chanting is between 1549 and 1645 it is at any rate certain that at the Restoration the general livening up of the service caused the complete rejection of all plainsong tones, the discontinuance of the faux-bourdon method and the joyful, carefree adoption of the rhythmic scheme of the Christ Church and Imperial Tunes. A spate of Anglican chants followed (some called 'Double Tunes' disregarding the structure of the psalms) and English chanting set out jauntily on its tortuous path. Not until S. S. Wesley, a premature pioneer, and after him the present generation, did anyone think of studying afresh the rhythmic principles involved.[1]

[1] See page 218. In Robert Bridges' *Collected Essays, XXI-XXVI*, the whole question is skilfully dealt with both historically and theoretically in more detail than is possible here.

16

CONGREGATIONAL MUSIC FROM 1549 TO 1662

2. METRICAL PSALMS AND HYMNS

PROTESTANT INFLUENCES

If the nonconformists found ritual an abomination they found in music—of a certain type—an indispensable aid. The modern street-corner service, the negro revivalist meeting use music today to get at the hearts of those they seek to influence, and Luther (and Huss before him) appreciated the value of hymns. A hymn with its catchy melody, its easily remembered rhythmical text, could sum up succinctly some point of the Christian doctrine; teaching and pleasurable emotion were combined to lay siege to the hard heart of man. Unlike the office hymn of the medieval church, the hymn-tune soon became the folk-music of protestant congregations; it has remained the folk-song of most church-going people to this day. Indeed, for many nonconformists the psalm-tune and hymn might be considered as a substitute for the church priest—the legitimate avenue of approach for a man to his God. In a hymn the plain man can praise his God in simple words set to a simple tune. Luther, with psychological insight, took well-known, well-liked secular tunes (much as the Salvation Army does today) and set Christian texts to them. Why should the devil have all the good tunes? The result was an expressive medium which needed no trained choir for its performance; left with little or nothing to sing in the service according to the Book of Common Prayer, church-people in England, like their nonconformist brothers, took to hymn-singing as their own part of the service.

PSALM-TUNES: BOURGEOIS

If the root and branch reforms in Germany allowed these new-fangled chorales to flourish, churchmen elsewhere were more conservative. Instead of making new texts for their hymns based on the Bible, those responsible in England, France and Geneva were content merely with translating the psalms into metrical verse, a fashion which had spread from Clément Marot's courtly French translations first published in 1542. Forced to flee from France, Marot worked on in Geneva and after his death Théodore Béza completed the translation of the whole psalter in 1562. Also working in Geneva with Calvin and Béza was Louis Bourgeois[1] whose fine melodies were unknown until recently because they were set to words in uncommon metres. Robert Bridges in the *Yattendon Hymnal* has provided them with equally fine texts and in this form Bourgeois has made his début to modern congregations. Bourgeois had a contemporary worker in Claude Goudimel, hardly less famous, but in Bourgeois' work we find a rhythmic resource and a melodic and harmonic grace which make him the Palestrina of the psalm-tune.

STERNHOLD AND HOPKINS

The fashion for psalm-singing in this new way now well established, we see it in England spreading within the church, where the dividing line between churchmen and non-conformists was not yet well defined. The legality of singing these extra-liturgical products was questioned and finally admitted in 1559; the older office hymn (itself once the subject of legal controversy) was no longer sung. Thomas Sternhold had published in 1549 nineteen psalms which, after his death, were added to by the pen of John Hopkins and published at Geneva in 1556 in an edition with tunes. The book, following the custom of the time, had a Form of Prayer prefixed and was considered by its exiled devotees as a rival to the 1552 Prayer Book, already repealed under Mary. It was not, however, until many revisions had taken place that a Standard Edition was published in 1562 containing the 'Whole Book of Psalms Collected into English Metre' together with a large appendix consisting of prayers of all kinds, thus making the book a

[1] Louis Bourgeois (born about 1510). A native of Paris, he was in charge of the music at the Huguenot church in Geneva under Calvin from 1541. Imprisoned by his employers in 1551 for using harmonies and dismissed in 1557, he left Geneva leaving behind him a psalter containing eighty-five tunes, many of which were his own, written to translations by Marot and Béza. Harmonies being forbidden in Geneva, Bourgeois published the harmonised versions in Lyons. Their excellence may be sampled in *Calvin's First Psalter*, edited by R. R. Terry, and *English and Scottish Psalm Tunes* by Maurice Frost (*S.P.C.K.* and *O.U.P.*).

complete vade-mecum for the running of the services. Musically the book was poor, as the ballad metre, 8.6.8.6, occurred frequently enough for one tune to do duty for many psalms; indeed, only one-third of the psalms had 'proper' tunes.

THE 'STANDARD EDITION'

From now on the Standard Edition was republished, added to, its tunes harmonised—first by Day in 1563—and other tune-books provided by 'Damon', Cosyn, Este, Barley and Ravenscroft. The last's *Psalter* of 1621 became very popular and continued the incomprehensible oddity, first introduced by Este, of naming its tunes after towns and villages of the British Isles. Hitherto tunes were merely named after the psalm they were set to: the 'Old Hundredth' thus means the tune to psalm 100 in the Standard Edition, later called the 'Old Edition' to distinguish it from the 'New' Standard Edition of 150 years later. The Standard Edition did not exhaust the ambitions of psalm versifiers and many other collections were published, as those of Archbishop Parker[1]—a private translation of the whole psalter containing Tallis' celebrated 'canon' tune—and Sandys' 'Paraphrase' of 1636–8 with tunes by Henry Lawes. Such collections would be used only in private chapels or at family prayers; they are of interest to us as source-books for good hymns.

TATE AND BRADY

After the Interregnum it was slowly felt that the old Standard Edition was played out. Playford's *Psalms and Hymns*, 1671, tried hard to reform the dull musical settings, but his *Whole Book of Psalms*, issued in 1677, merely proved that his first book had made no headway by pandering to the unskilled, for it set the tunes in three parts instead of four.[2] The time was ripe for a New Version, which was produced in 1696 by Nahum Tate, the Poet Laureate, and Dr. Nicholas Brady, authorised by William III as an alternative book to the Standard Edition and renamed the *New Version* to distinguish it from the *Old Version*, as the old Standard Edition was now called. Henceforward the two books were used side by side. In both the tunes were undistinguished, though some solid melodies, like the 'Old Hundredth', have survived. There is in

[1] See page 37.   [2] See page 130.

English hymnody of the time very little to compare with the inspired products of Luther and Bourgeois; England had not yet
entered into its own, and the day of the hymn proper had not yet
dawned.

HYMNS OF THE PRIMERS

The medieval office hymn was hardly a hymn in the modern
sense; even if its tune were 'catchy' it was never intended to be
heartily sung by a congregation, but was an artistic product. The
modern hymn shows no verbal subtleties and its music, at its best,
shows a mixture of the styles of a folk-song and a national 'anthem'.
Words and music, if they are to suit a large and unskilled crowd of
singers, need to be obvious, in the best sense, and unsubtle. The
origins are to be found less perhaps in the Latin office hymns than
in the carols and other non-liturgical effusions used at pilgrimages,
theatrical performances and other semi-religious gatherings. When
the office hymns were cleared away by the zeal of the reformers
the metrical psalms took their place. But by 1600 signs were
already noticeable that a new form of spiritual song was coming to
birth. Tucked away in the appendices of primers—manuals of
private devotions—and compilations of psalms, hymns sporadically appeared, by which is meant devotional metric songs of a
personal and generally non-scriptural type. If they had not the
congregational feeling of the true hymn they were at any rate
pointers at a time when the émigrés of Geneva discouraged any
text not based on the Bible. Their verse was seldom content with
the limping doggerel to be found in the average collection of
metrical psalms emanating from Geneva or London, and has some
little affinity with the fine work of its period—the age of Spenser,
Shakespeare and Donne.[1]

[1] Here are two specimens of doggerel to be met in Este's *Psalter* of 1592:

> O come and let us now rejoice
> And sing unto the Lord,
> And to our only Saviour
> Also with one accord.
> (*Ps.* 95)

> What man soever he be that
> Salvation will obtain,
> The Catholic belief he must
> Before all things retain.
> (*Quicunque vult*)

PRIVATE COLLECTIONS

The first collection of such hymns was George Wither's *Hymns and Songs of the Church*, 1623, famous because not only might it be called the first hymn-book but its verses were given melodies and basses by Orlando Gibbons whose fine tunes have recently found a place in our modern books and make a splash of colour amid the drab psalm-tunes of the Standard Edition. The hymns of Wither were the forerunners of greater work by George Herbert, the saint of Bemerton, Henry Vaughan, self-styled the Silurist, and the incomparable Robert Herrick, some of whose work was set in 1701 in Henry Playford's *David's Harp New Tun'd* by Blow, Clarke, Turner and Croft; the tunes are used today though the verses are too intimate and fanciful to be sung by large bodies of voices. Pointing more obviously in the direction of the real hymn are the famous morning and evening hymns of Thomas Ken, Bishop of Bath and Wells; though neither of these can be considered great poetry they show a solid worth which makes them suitable to be sung by a large congregation. We must also add the famous hymns contributed by Addison to the *Spectator*. It must be remembered, however, that none of this work was published with a view to congregational singing; its avowed aim was to help private devotion. It was left to Watts and the Wesleys not only to write hymns but to popularise them in the British Isles.

It should be remembered that Luther issued only some eighty chorales, most of which were German versions of *Kyrie, Gloria, Credo*, etc., canticles for Vespers or *Detemporelieder*, i.e. office hymns proper for feasts and fasts of the kalendar; others were for use during the Administration of Communion. Luther and 'orthodox' Lutherans maintained a ceremonious high celebration as the main Sunday and feast-day service until after Bach's lifetime. Bach was among those who upheld the elaborate choral-orchestral music as well as 'Dr. Luther's chorales' against the desires of the ultimately victorious Pietists, who wanted a congregational service similar to that of Calvinists but with 'human hymns'.

THE MODERN HYMN

The modern hymn was, in fact, destined to be born outside the church: its cradle was Congregationalism. Of the nonconformist sects, the Presbyterians adopted in 1564 the Scottish Psalter, a book steeped in the Genevan dye and founded on the Standard Edition of two years before, and the Baptists discouraged hymn-singing in favour of the more scriptural psalms; the Independents, later to be called Congregationalists, published in 1694 their *Collection of Divine Hymns,* and it was this book which pointed the way to the work of Watts who began his ministerial career four years later and was destined with the Wesleys to create English hymnody.

17

CONGREGATIONAL MUSIC FROM 1549 TO 1662

3. THE PERFORMANCE OF PSALM-TUNES AND HYMNS

THE SIXTEENTH CENTURY

We may imagine that the zealous followers of Luther and Calvin at first often sang their psalms in unison and private with any available accompaniment, or none. But as their congregations grew those who were musical as well as devout wished for something better. The story of Louis Bourgeois is typical: after serving a term of imprisonment for attempted innovations he was opposed by the dour Calvin for wishing to arrange the singing of the Huguenot Church at Geneva in four parts, and finally dismissed.

THE SEVENTEENTH CENTURY

By the middle of the seventeenth century four-part singing was, where possible, looked upon as normal: Este's *Book of Psalms* of 1592, like Playford's first book, 1671, is arranged for a four-part choir. This, of course, did not imply that congregations sang in four parts, but that there was an accompaniment and probably some body of singers more skilled than the rest. In 1677 Playford published his book with settings in three parts: in this book, as in subsequent compilations, the melody and bass are set out in one stave system, the third part, or 'medius'. being given separately. The accompanist, where such existed, would play from the upper staves, filling in the harmonies in the manner of the time. Members of the congregation interested enough to buy the book would perhaps put in a little bass or 'medius' as it suited their voices; but there was undoubtedly a decline among cultured people in musical skill which worsened during the following hundred years, if we are to judge by the increasing number of pages given over at the beginning of every tune-book to an explanation of the rudiments of music.[1] Playford, in his preface to the 1677 book, says: 'In our

[1] Possibly, of course, the musical prefaces were meant to instruct the less

late Forefathers' days (upon the Restauration of our Church to its Primitive Purity and Discipline) it was, That some holy and godly Men brought the present use and manner of singing Psalms into the Publick Service of our Church, following herein the Examples of the *Reformed Churches* in *France* and *Germany*: But Time and long Use hath much abated the wonted Reverence and Estimation it had for about 100 Years after this Establishment.' Playford, in fact, even had misgivings about some of his three-part settings, and thinking they might be hard to learn says: 'Likewise all such Psalms and Hymns whose Tunes are long, and may seem difficult to some, have Directions over them to be sung to other short Common Tunes.'

GALLERY CHOIRS

Rude gallery choirs were being formed in the country churches and we may suppose their musical knowledge went little further than Playford's short introduction; some, however, may have taken to heart his quaint injunction: 'These are yᵉ most usefull Instructions I think necessary for a Young Beginer (being confin'd to so little room) but for a farther knowledge in this excellent Science I referr you to Mʳ PLAYFORDs Introduction', i.e. his famous *Introduction to the Skill of Music*. One may suppose that few of the congregation, then as now, took the trouble to acquaint themselves with the paraphernalia of the rudiments.

ACCOMPANYING INSTRUMENTS

Until after the Restoration England had been backward in supplying organs to its churches; it was not, indeed, until the middle of the ninetenth century that harmoniums began, as in Hardy's novel, *Under the Greenwood Tree*, to oust the gallery orchestras. It is only in our own time that organs are to be found in almost every village church. During the eighteenth century the accompaniment was often left to a solitary bassoon playing the bass, the gallery choir, we hope and presume, singing in four parts. Playford is more optimistic when he explains: 'The *Church-Tune* is placed in the *Treble* Part, (which is the *Cantus*) with the *Bass* under it, as most proper to joyn Voice and Instrument together, according to Holy *David's*

cultured members of congregations who had presumably never been able to read music.

prescription, *Psal.* 144.9. And since so many of our Churches are
lately furnished with Organs, it will also be useful for the Organist
and likewise for such Students in the Universities as shall practise
Song, to sing to a Lute or Viol.' By 1761, Arnold in his *Compleat
Psalmodist* gives a long list, with prices and manufacturers, of
instruments which may be used, though whether he is quoting
instruments actually used in church is not quite clear. Possibly his
guitar was meant for private devotions only, but he is certainly
enthusiastic about 'Church Organs of the Machinery Kind', which
though useful could hardly be said to enhance the artistic side of
worship. They are, he tells us, 'so contrived as to play (having
Barrels fitted to them for that Purpose) a set of Voluntaries, also
most of our ancient Psalm-Tunes, with their Givings-out and
Interludes, Ec. which are very commodious for Churches in
remote Country Places, where an Organist is not easily to be had
or maintained, and may also be played by a Person (unskill'd in
Music) who is only to turn a Winch round, which causes the
Barrels to play the Tunes they are set to; which Organs also
generally have, or should have, a Set of Keys to them, that a
Person might play on them at Pleasure, notwithstanding the Barrels, Ec.' He mentions 'Box-Organs' 'of a very small Structure',
which 'may be had of the Organ Builders, also at most Music-
Shops in London, from ten to fourteen Guineas Price . . . ; of this
Kind, as well as of the large Organs, you may have Tunes of your
own chusing set upon the Barrels, and as many Barrels with
different Sets of Tunes (made to put in and take out alternately) as
you please'. He then mentions the harpsichord, 'double-keyed' or
'common' (i.e. with two manuals or one), and 'the Spinnets', with
the 'Guittar, a very pretty and gentle Instrument, and now very
much in Vogue' and goes on: 'The Bassoon being now in great
Request in many Country Churches, I presume therefore, it will
not be improper for me here to acquaint my Reader, that it makes
an exceeding good Addition to the Harmony of a Choir of Singers,
where there is no Organ, as most of the Bass Notes may be played
on it, in the Octave below the Bass Voices: The Bassoon requires
a pretty strong Breath to blow it, but it is not at all difficult to
learn to play upon, all the Instructions, belonging to it, being only
a Scale of its Notes.'

INTERLUDES

The Interludes which the barrel-organ was competent to play
were to be heard performed between the lines of hymns, entirely
ruining both the melodic structure and the text of the hymn. In
Stopford's edition of Chetham, 1811, one of these interludes is
written out thus:

Ex. 38

The Trumpet appears after every line and a note is added: 'The
Air of this Hymn is generally sung over first as a Solo, and
repeated in full Chorus.' Arnold remarks that 'the Reading
Psalms being ended a short Voluntary is performed on the Organ',
a practice now completely discontinued.

THE PARISH CLERK

Before the advent of Sunday Schools towards the end of the
eighteenth century many country congregations were doubtless
unable to read and the text of the hymn to be sung was often read
out by the parish clerk whose duties included those of precentor.[1]
Despite his usually humble origin, he chose the tunes, announced
the hymns and was the object of hopeful admonitions in charges
delivered by the bishops to their clergy.

AMATEUR COMPOSITION

The picture is indeed not very elevating. Nor was the music sung
any better. Flighty three-in-a-bar tunes abounded and every tune-
book is careful to mark in the 'trillos' much beloved of the singers
of the time as a mark of musical breeding and acquaintance with
the opera. Such music was not easily eradicated; then as now your
hymn-singer was pious but stubborn. Amateurs in composition
thought, as they still do, that their piety absolved them from
keeping the inexorable rules of harmony. Arnold roundly casti-
gates them: 'I could have wished, for their own Sakes, they had
kept their Compositions to themselves, and that they never had

[1] At worst the hymn or metrical psalm was 'lined out' by the clerk, i.e.
with the tune broken so that one or two lines could be read at a time.

exposed their Ignorance by exhibiting their Compositions to the Public View; that they had followed the Art of teaching the Compositions of their Superiors, instead of composing such whimsical flighty Psalm-Tunes (as several Authors late have) since most of their Compositions cannot be reckoned any other than an unconnected Jumble of Notes confusedly put together, being founded on no musical Rules. . . .'

18

CHOIR MUSIC

1. THE NEW TECHNIQUE

EMERGENCE OF THE SOLO

The story of the protestant outlook between the Prayer Books of
1559 and 1662 might be summed up as the establishment of man's
opinion as the final arbiter in religious matters. With a queer
disregard for the personal, unreliable emotional complexes which
fashion a man's opinion, the protestant substituted for the authority of the church that of himself. The humanism of Erasmus had
resulted in an outbreak of individualism; personal opinion was
raised to the rank of a philosophy and science believed in the
authority of nothing but the five senses. In music, which includes
church music, a breakdown of the community spirit of counterpoint gave place to the emergence of the solo; already in Dowland,
the sweet singer, we see the beginnings of a new form, the solo art
song with accompaniment, and the finest composer at the end of
the century, Purcell, was also an accomplished singer.

THE TRANSITIONAL CAROLINE COMPOSERS

In church music the composers working between 1625 and 1650
were unknowingly bridging the gap between the experimental
verse-anthems of Gibbons and those of Purcell.[1] These transi-
tional Caroline composers whose actual works matter more to the
historian than to the choirmaster are rather interesting than vital
or usable. Christopher,[2] the son of Orlando Gibbons, never
secures release from the tentacle clutch of his father's style and
vacillates between the old and new idioms. Child,[3] who can write

[1] Verse-anthems: Gibbons, page 103; Purcell, page 139.

[2] Christopher Gibbons (1615–1676), born at Westminster, became a
chorister at the Chapel Royal. 1638, organist of Winchester. 1660, organist
of Chapel Royal and Westminster Abbey, and private organist to Charles.
Buried in the cloisters at the Abbey. Very little church music.

[3] William Child (1606–1697), taught by Bevin, organist of Bristol. 1632,
organist of St. George's, Windsor and Chapel Royal. 1643, retired to a farm

moving Latin motets of the old type, tries by perpetrating rather
foolish experiments in harmony to keep up with the times; he lives
in fact to a ripe old age, old enough to mimic the gay demeanours
of the restored court, but none of his more ambitious work is
anything but an exercise in the declamatory style rounded off with
a few quasi-joyous hallelujahs.[1] Henry Lawes[2] is so keen on the
just accenting of his words, over-praised by Milton in a famous but
rather undiscriminating sonnet,[3] that he forgets to write music; in
justice to him, however, for he was a competent musician living
in an unfortunate age, one should add that he sometimes forgets
his accent and dissolves into real music. Matthew Locke,[4] more
famous in operatic efforts, can be effective and show good command of feeling, but he lacks the urge of genius which is needed to
solve the problems by a few masterpieces. Benjamin Rogers[5]

near Windsor and composed church music. 1660, chanter of Chapel Royal
and private musician to Charles. Buried at St. George's. Publications: 1639,
First Set of psalms, later renamed 'Choise Musick' and often called Choice
Psalms, consisting of twenty anthems. Undated: *Divine Anthems*. Many
services and anthems in MS. He gave £20 towards the new town hall at
Windsor and paved the choir of St. George's.

[1] For his services see page 145.

[2] Henry Lawes (1595–1662), gentleman of the Chapel Royal and Clerk
of the Cheque. Wrote a few anthems including *Zadok the priest* for the
coronation of Charles II. His church music, except the fine hymn-tunes to
Sandys' version of the psalms, is not so important as that written for masques,
especially that for 'Comus'. Publications: 1637, *A Paraphrase upon the
Psalms*, the Sandys tunes. 1648, *Choice Psalms*, William and Henry Lawes'
joint work.

[3] Beginning: Harry, whose tuneful and well measur'd song
            First taught our English music how to span
            Words with just accent . . .
—an unsuspecting slight on Byrd and Gibbons, one presumes.

[4] Matthew Locke (1630–1677), chorister of Exeter. 1661, Composer in
Ordinary to the king. A convert, possibly, to Rome, he was appointed
organist to the queen. Wrote anthems for the Chapel Royal, of which *Lord,
let me know mine end* was given in Boyce and so presumably remained in the
repertory. Publications: 1666, *Modern Church Music*, a kyrie and creed
composed for the Chapel but 'Obstructed in its Performance before His
Majesty, April 1, 1666' and in this publication 'Vindicated by the Author'.
Other anthems and some Latin hymns appeared in published collections of
the time, while some were given in Tudway's MS. collection.

[5] Benjamin Rogers (1614–1698), chorister of St. George's, Windsor.
1639, Christ Church, Dublin; 1641, lay-clerk at Windsor. During the
Interregnum taught in Windsor, being re-appointed as lay-clerk in 1662.
1664–1685, organist of Magdalen College, Oxford. Many services and

manages a successful but unremarkable fusion of the old and the new.

THE BAR-LINE AND WORD-ACCENT

The problem was new in the history of music, and history waited in vain for a genius big enough to resolve it. And so the matter had to run its course, a course lasting a hundred years from 1600. A new tyranny had arisen—the bar-line. Just as churchmen had rejected the unmanageable prose versions of the psalms, replacing them by metrical translations, so now they insisted on a regularly recurring accent in their music. In the previous century the lighter effusions like ballets and folk-songs had shown a regular beat, but in serious music (madrigals, motets, anthems, plainsong) such a practice was eschewed. After 1600 the regular accentual system spread like a plague and for three hundred years music went on hammering out its tom-tom beat.

FORM AND KEY

If the introduction of the bar-line had been the only innovation, however, progress in the new music would have been rapid and easy; but other new elements confused the issue. The rejection of contrapuntal methods—perhaps because they were played out, perhaps because choirs were depleted, perhaps because of the growing worship of 'personalities' and achievement—created an accompanying difficulty, that of form. Knit as it was with the contrapuntal texture, the form of the sixteenth-century motet was clear enough. Now new ways of giving shape to the music had to be invented and two other elements made that the more difficult: they were the chosen text which had a form of its own and key which, when the music consisted mostly of a solo and accompaniment, became too easy to handle (the possibilities of modulation became theoretically limitless when the accompaniment could be relied on to help the singer through a difficult passage). To us the system where a key with its attendant relative keys helps to define the form by giving point to contrasting sections and restatements seems a simple notion; we are used to whole sections of a symphony in C-minor being in any key but C-minor. In a seventeenth-century composer the old modal idea of a centre of gravity to

anthems, some printed in collections, including Boyce. His *Hymnus Eucharisticus* is sung each year on May 1st from the top of Magdalen tower.

which one was always returning after certain permitted cadences— not, be it noted, *sections* in a related *mode*—was too strong to be overcome quickly. He therefore tends to vacillate between too much modulation, as in some of the secular works, and no modulation at all, as often in the verse-anthems. One has to remember that the contemporary composer seldom knows even what he is trying to discover: in music as in scientific work the story of Röntgen finding X-ray phenomena during the process of looking for something else is often repeated.

LENGTH

If form and key both gave trouble, length added to it. The anthem was gaining in importance as the appeal of the liturgical part of the service diminished. If today evensong seems but a dull ante-room vigil for a sermon, it became in seventeenth-century musical establishments but the prelude to the anthem. Pepys' attitude to the anthem was typical of the end of the century: he regarded it as the tastiest morsel of a social banquet. Anthems grew in length as they grew in importance; few Tudor motets take more than five minutes to perform but the composer after 1630 was increasingly faced with filling out effectively his quarter of an hour.

THE SOLUTION

Small wonder is it, then, that little lasting music was produced between the death of Gibbons, 1625, and the birth of Purcell, 1659, or that still less is sung in our churches. This triple problem of form, key and length was solved at the keyboard and in the orchestra where there were no words to embroil the already complicated issue; for the question of word-accent in conjunction with regular bar-lines was no small problem in itself. At the keyboard it was solved only when composers ceased trying to imitate vocal counterpoint and frankly fashioned their pieces on the dance with its clear-cut sections. Byrd had written music of both types for the virginals, but one could hardly expect instrumental composers to see at once which type to use as their model, so that the fifty years after 1625 are really a melting-pot period. By taking up the story again in 1680 or so we can examine what has been evolved.

THE VERSE-ANTHEM

In a typical Purcell verse-anthem like *Rejoice in the Lord alway*, which we take because it is familiar, we find the work preceded by a short instrumental prelude for strings (here on the composer's favourite ground-bass device which gives the work its nickname of *The bell anthem*) and thereafter divided into sections by further instrumental ritornellos; in the usual editions these are either not given or shortened down to a few bars, though Purcell certainly meant them to be there. The work is thus a kind of suite of movements all in the same key or in keys with nearly related tonics. Usually the alternations are between major and minor—sharp and flat keys as Purcell would have called them—rather than between tonic and dominant, which is used only in see-saw fashion as yet during fugal entries. Here the alternations are C-major and A-minor; the more usual alternation, between C-major and C-minor, is seen in *Thy word is a lantern*. Contrast is obtained by changes of time-signature, entry of the chorus in two places, both similarly containing the verse interjections *and again*, and by the string interludes. A plain restatement of the first verse section is placed before the final entry of the chorus, and by repeating the same section *piano* at the start of the work the composer drives it home to the listener so that it is easily recognised on its return. It must not be supposed from this instance, however, that such restatements are normal; perhaps in this slight but pleasing work Purcell was frankly out to please 'the town', and hoped the town would go away humming his tune—as it still does. No attempt is made at spiritual subtleties and the general effect is secular and 'jolly', and therefore typical of the more cheerful Restoration anthems.

HARMONY AND MELODY

Coming to the details, we may note that the counterpoint runs smoothly in a preconceived harmonic mould where the harmonies are very much in our familiar C-major and the cadences are frequent and already stereotyped. Asperities in the counterpoint remind us, always politely, of the Elizabethans, as at the words *let your requests be made known unto God*. The words are deftly placed over a metric basis, except at the word *alway* where the music has its own swing rather than the word.

RECITATIVE IN TEMPO

But we need to search a more serious type of anthem, or a work containing recitative to see how careful Purcell is over this matter of syllable-accent; one needs to remember that he was a trained singer as well as a composer. In recitative, as seen in the anthems produced after 1660, we find a fully developed technique which is entirely new compared with Elizabethan methods and just as effective; it is indeed at times capable of a deep human pathos. Unlike recitative on the continent English recitative is meant to be sung in strict time. Purcell's

Ex. 39
Bass.Verse from Purcell's Behold I bring you glad tidings

tid-ings of great _____ joy, ____ which shall be to all__

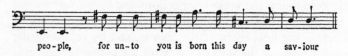

peo - ple,   for un-to   you is born this day   a   sav-iour

is the forerunner of Wesley's

Ex. 40
Men's Recitative from Wesley's Blessed be the God

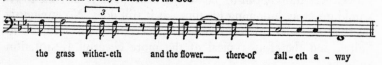

the grass wither-eth   and the flower____ there-of   fall - eth a - way

both the true metrical descendants of Merbecke's semi-metrical

Ex. 41
From Merbecke's Creed

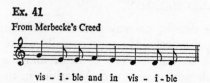

vis - i - ble and in vis - i - ble

though modern choirmasters sometimes allow their singers to take too much liberty with note-lengths. Purcell learnt his word-setting from Locke via Humfrey and from his own experience as a singer; he improved on his models by making his work not only a good and careful setting of the words but also vital as music.

THE RESTORATION STYLE

The music of the Restoration composers had thus settled into two main types, the verse-anthem and the full anthem which was the child of the Tudor motet. The verse-anthem was essentially a suite of movements for varying ensembles of solo voices with or without instrumental interludes, interspersed often with choruses for the full choir or entire sections for one solo voice. In the light of later developments it seems to us as a form to lack any real organic growth, being held together more by the connecting ideas in the text than by any musical magnetic force. But that was a defect of all the music of the time, including for example the Bach cantatas of twenty years later, and must be looked at with a blind eye. Within that flimsy framework a new method of expressive solo song has been evolved, recitative in tempo. Purcell at least has succeeded in writing good tunes which do not mangle the words and musicians in general have submitted to the tyranny of the bar-line. Of the old tradition little seems left; the noble impersonality of Byrd has been for the most part replaced by a more homely expressiveness which, though always effective in its pathos, is yet the expression of an individual. The old English roughnesses in the counterpoint and a few echoes of the modal system give evidence of the continuity of the tradition. But a more deep-rooted change is noticeable in the texture: the invention of the methods of figured-bass show that the lazy composer thought of his chords first and his melody second, at least in the solos. Metrically considered the music began to move in balanced phrases instead of in the easy alternation of two- and three-rhythms of the previous century. The church had been fighting against regular metre ever since the days of Augustine; it succumbed because all music had succumbed. A major influence upon church music was that of the theatre—not necessarily frivolous. The lyrical sections of Restoration and later English church works are more often like airs in Lully's tragedies than like elaborate Italian arias with much vocal display to a single syllable. Lully's careful setting of French set an example.

19

CHOIR MUSIC

2. CHOIRS

CHOIRS UNDER THE STUARTS

Under the Stuarts the choir at St. Paul's which had contained thirty 'gentlemen' was whittled down to contain only six vicars-choral, and Bumpus[1] quotes an anonymous manuscript in the British Museum showing that choirs were depleted so that the existing singers could obtain a living wage by compounding the salaries or in some cases to line the canon's pockets. Possibly a rise in the cost of living cut into the resources of endowed bodies who always suffer first under economic stress. Be that as it may, choirs were certainly becoming smaller during the years before 1645. The suppression of the church service saw the complete disappearance of choirs; as a hundred years before at the dissolution of the monasteries, the singers were turned loose on the world and there followed during the Cromwellian period a reawakening of secular music-making.

THE PURITANS AND MUSIC

The Puritans were opposed to music only in church; Cromwell himself was keen enough on music to take down the organ in Magdalen College Chapel, Oxford, and have it re-erected for his own amusement at Hampton Court Palace, while rumour has it that he was fond of Dering's Latin motets. But cathedral libraries were ransacked and destroyed—not too thoroughly, it seems, for later research workers have found a fair amount of Elizabethan work—and the organs forbidden to be used—the puritan burghers of Norwich destroyed their cathedral instrument with furious zeal —so that after eleven years of silence a good deal of reconstruction was necessary. Small organs were bought cheaply by taverns, especially (as Pepys tells us) the Thames-side taverns in or near London. Many clergy and organists must have retired to brood

[1] Bumpus, *A History of English Cathedral Music*, vol. 1, page 92.

over lost traditions or to make notes on the old services with the aid of an illegally hidden Book of Common Prayer. Dr. Child optimistically busied himself with writing anthems against the expected return of the monarchy.

RESTORATION CHOIRS

At the Restoration men like Child, Lawes and Christopher Gibbons returned to their posts at the Chapel Royal only to find that they themselves belonged to a past age. As Tudway reports: 'His Majesty, who was a brisk and airy Prince, coming to ye Crown in ye flow'r and vigour of his Age, was soon, if I may so say, tyred wth ye grave and solemn way, and ordered ye Composers of his Chappell to add Symphonys, &c., with Instruments to their Anthems, and thereupon established a select number of his Private Musick [i.e. band] to play ye Symphonys and Ritornelles which he had appointed. . . . The old Masters, Dr. Child, Dr. C. Gibbons and Mr. Lowe, organists to his Majesty, hardly knew how to comport themselves with these new-fangled ways. . . .' In the choirs themselves problems not only of personnel but of the forgotten service came to the fore. Some of the newly appointed lay-clerks would be re-established old members of the choirs, some of the younger ones may have been choirboys in the old days, and others would undoubtedly be newcomers.[1] The chief trouble was of course the absence of any tradition among the boys, for a good choir cannot be made out of raw boys in under three years. At first the verse-anthem, already evolved as an art form before the Commonwealth, became a necessity and a fashion for it was re-created. As late as 1664 a cornet[2] (not the modern brass instrument but a treble-compass wooden instrument with a cup mouthpiece) was used in Westminster Abbey to supply missing or inadequate parts. In the Chapel Royal Captain Henry Cooke[3]

---

[1] In the newly formed Chapel Royal choir only five men remembered—or thought they remembered, perhaps—the old methods of singing the service.

[2] The cornet (or cornett), judging from cathedral account books, had often been used, as it was later in the Bach cantatas, to *double* the melody. As a contemporary, Randle Holme, says: 'It is a delicate, pleasant wind musicke, if well played and humered.' Its compass was two octaves up from D at the foot of the treble stave.

[3] Henry Cooke (born about 1616, died 1672), probably the son of a bass who had come from Lichfield to the Chapel Royal choir. Cooke possibly served as a boy in the Chapel Royal choir; he entered the army on the

was appointed Master of the Children. His dynamic energy soon bent itself to the task of re-establishing the choir on the lines of military discipline. By reviving an old privilege he managed to stock his choir with the best boys in the country–they were taken to London willy-nilly for 'the service of the King'–whom he made into the most distinguished choir of boys ever got together. As well as having a fine voice Cooke was a knowledgeable musician and an excellent teacher, and knew it–Pepys calls him a 'vain coxcomb'–so that in a short time his boys were writing creditable anthems before their voices broke. The subsequent history of his boys–Pelham Humfrey, the king's favourite who succeeded Cooke, John Blow, William Turner, Michael Wise[1]–is the history of church music for the next fifty years. Books, surplices, instruments to eke out the treble line quickly appeared; the gentlemen were told to be decently robed in a surplice–perhaps some 'puritans' had objected–and to be punctual, while no deputy system was to be allowed. For the boys a good musical education plus writing and Latin was provided and with the king's permission and, no doubt, encouragement the band of instrumentalists was organised.[2] The whole establishment was in perfect working order within three years of starting from nothing–no mean feat.

Royalist side, was in the retreat from Newcastle to Yorkshire and was promoted to a captaincy. During the Commonwealth he probably studied singing in Italy, and he taught in London. 1660, a bass and Master of the Children at the Chapel Royal. He was a fine singer and composed, though sometimes ungrammatically. At his death the Crown owed him £500 for wages.

[1] For biographies see for Humfrey, page 149, for Blow, page 146, for Wise, page 146. Purcell was admitted later probably through the recommendation of his uncle.

[2] It was worked on the shift system. See also note 3, page 147.

20

CHOIR MUSIC

3. THE REPERTORY

SERVICES BEFORE 1650

As attention was centred away from the liturgical service until 1660, when a few more enterprising settings began to appear, there is little work of the first half of the century on which to report. Bevin[1] and Batten,[2] whose work figures in modern cathedral lists, came at the parting of the ways and though talented produced little more than competent workaday settings. Child and Rogers wrote settings of the short-service type which have been retained; their work has a charm which matches well with the quiet of the cathedral service on ferial days. It is easy to call such work dull. Actually it is wrought with care in the word-setting and part-writing, and in the short-service idiom it comes off remarkably well. The short service is in fact only one step removed from the chant and psalm-tune and its ideals are simple; it seeks to provide daily fare for the cathedral service by being short, straightforward, unpretentious and not too elaborate. To judge it as dull by comparing it with more elaborate settings where the music has time to develop is as unreasonable as to find a hymn-tune dull because it cannot compare in musical interest with a full-dress anthem. Settings of the time seldom include the communion service which was no longer given enough prominence as a service to warrant the presence of the choir; where settings were

[1] Elway Bevin (born probably between 1550 and 1560; 1634 he was described by Laud as a very old man), pupil of Tallis, vicar-choral at Wells 1575–1584 and probably organist of Bristol from 1589 onwards. Possibly a Roman Catholic. He taught Child and was a capable theoretician, being the author of a *Brief and Short Introduction to the Art of Musicke* which contains some clever and diverting canons. The D-minor service appears in Boyce. Three or four services and a few anthems exist in MS.

[2] Adrian Batten (born before 1600, died in 1637). 1614, vicar-choral and organist at St. Paul's. There are many services and anthems some of which appear in Boyce. His famous *Organ Book* is a short-score copy in Batten's autograph of works by sixteenth-century composers.

made they consisted only of the *Kyrie*—sometimes the responses
to the commandments—and creed, the choir and most of the congregation being apparently accustomed to leave before the canon.
This is true of all complete services until the middle of the nineteenth century.

SERVICES BY COOKE'S BOYS

The rest of the settings of the canticles still sung today were
written by Cooke's boys. Blow's[1] straightforward setting in the
Dorian has admirably caught the sober feeling of the Tudor short
service and makes a useful unaccompanied setting for ferial days
despite its conscious archaisms. His service in F with its fluttering
quaver thirds on *rejoiced* in *Magnificat* shows its composer at
his best and is an outstanding product for its time, showing vitality
and dignity with a love of the words of the liturgy seldom met
with in its day: neither work is at all tarred with the brush of
Restoration hilarity or Restoration pathos. Wise and Purcell are
less frankly archaic. Wise[2] in a delightful little service in E-flat
uses the new style with laudable effect. He manages to get over the
ground quickly but without hurry, exhibiting a reticent joy uncommon in his day; from his other work we can infer that Wise, like
Blow, had a deep sense of the dignity and beauty of the service.

PURCELL

The G-minor Purcell[3] setting is also a successful effort in the

---

[1] John Blow (1648–9–1708). As one of the first children of Cooke's choir
Blow wrote some youthful anthems and with Humfrey and Turner wrote his
share of *I will always give thanks*, usually known as the Club Anthem.
1673, Gentleman of the Chapel Royal and Master of the Children. 1677,
Mus.D., the first musical degree granted by Lambeth. Organist of Westminster except from 1679 to 1695 when Purcell held the post. 1685, Composer
in Ordinary to the king. 1687–1693, Almoner and Master of the Choristers at
St. Paul's. 1695, joint tuner with Father Smith of the king's instruments.
1699, Composer to the Chapel Royal. Wrote many services and anthems of
which only a small proportion was published by the composer. Most of his
work still remains in MS.

[2] Michael Wise (1648–1687), one of the original choristers in Cooke's
choir. 1663, lay-clerk at St. George's, Windsor. 1668, organist and Master of
the Choristers at Salisbury. 1675–6, Gentleman of the Chapel Royal.
1686–7, Almoner and Master of the Choristers, St. Paul's. The E-flat
evening service and some of his anthems appeared in Rimbault.

[3] Henry Purcell (1659–1695), chorister in the Chapel Royal choir, first

new style. Like the Wise setting it is composed verse by verse on the principle of the full anthem with verses—Walmisley's famous service in D-minor of over a century later is another fine instance of the same method—a plan which admirably suits the musical setting of the strophic canticles. Purcell's *Gloria*s are particularly noteworthy in this excellent service. The B-flat service sounds like the sort of thing the previous generation had been aiming at and never attained. In both these services Purcell obviously took his work in hand seriously and with a love and appreciation for the text. He wrote them in full court dress, as it were, displaying all the learning and ingenuity of which he was capable. Despite his canons four in one and four in two in the G-minor service, carefully pointed out by Boyce with admiring italics, he succeeds in writing a worthy successor to Gibbons in F, recapturing its classic spirit and giving us a short service with more than the usual contrapuntal interest which nevertheless never dawdles. Like Gibbons, Purcell solves the problem of writing a musically interesting short service with the finger of genius.

ANTHEMS BEFORE 1650

Because of its experimental nature little of the work of the transition period is used today, but in some cathedrals a handful of works has been kept in the repertory or rescued from oblivion.

under Cooke and later under Humfrey, where he had lessons in writing, Latin, lute, viol and organ. When his voice broke in 1673 he developed a bass and counter-tenor voice and was an accomplished singer. 1673, apprenticed to Hingston, supervisor of the king's instruments; he tuned the organ at Westminster Abbey from 1674 to 1678. At Locke's death in 1677 he was appointed composer to the king's 'violins' (string band) which played in shifts of 5 or 6 monthly in the Chapel Royal services when the king was present. 1679, organist of Westminster where the music staff consisted of 4 singing minor canons, 12 lay-clerks—one of whom was Master of the Choristers—and 10 boys. 1682, bass singer and joint organist of the Chapel Royal with Edward Lowe (see page 120); here there were 32 singing men, including 8 clergy, 3 organists, a Master of the Choristers and the Clerk of the Cheque, all of whom worked on the shift system. 1683, Purcell became keeper of the king's wind instruments at a salary of £60 per annum, and in 1685 was appointed harpsichordist (conductor) in the king's private music (band). After 1688 James II had a private Roman Catholic chapel at Whitehall and the Chapel Royal was rather neglected. In 1690 Purcell began his collaborations with Dryden which took him into the fashionable world and induced a spate of secular music. There is little church music after about 1685.

On the whole the work of Child and Rogers has charm without much striking inspiration, though Locke can at times manage to be himself rather than a mere precursor of Purcell. The few full anthems, because they are tied to the old style and do not seek out new methods, are usually more effective than the experimental verse-anthems. There is hardly need to mention particular works, but we may notice Batten's *Sing we merrily*, Child's *O Lord, grant the king* and Locke's *Sing unto the Lord* and *Lord, let me know mine end* as typical and still usable work of the period. As Locke was one of Purcell's models it will be of interest to give a few bars of the last:

Ex. 42

From a Verse in Locke's Lord, let me know mine end

RESTORATION WORK

The verse-anthems of the Restoration vary much in effectiveness but seldom in one particular; unless of a pathetic type they must contain at least one 'Allelujah' chorus. They all need good professional soloists in the alto, counter-tenor, tenor and bass, and with a good performance can be fine and moving. The boys' parts are usually easy and short.[1] Humfrey,[2] despite his reputation for worldliness and frivolity, can touch stirring depths as in, for example, *Hear, O heavens*; Wise, whose verse-anthems are perhaps the best of the period and are certainly the most sung, has a fine command of expressive recitative and that characteristic solo-voice counterpoint to be found in all this work. His most representative work is contained perhaps in the quartet *The ways of Zion do mourn*, *Prepare ye the way*, *Awake up, my glory* and *Awake, awake, put on thy strength*. Purcell's verse-anthems present quite a vocal problem, his counter-tenor parts—possibly sometimes sung by himself—requiring an accomplished singer with an extended range, and his bass parts—written for the Rev. John Gostling, a bass with a 'Russian' compass—descend with alarming frequency to low E's and D's. Apart from the cheerful *Rejoice in the Lord*, *Thy word is a lantern* is a thoughtful work well worth performing, while the famous *O sing unto the Lord* with its string accompaniments and its vocal roulades needs well-trained singers to bring off its vigorous declamatory phrases. Blow who is really at his best in his full anthems writes in *I was in the spirit on the Lord's day* an anthem which, while perhaps missing the full import of the words, contains some music of real urge with its glorious leaps of a tenth, though it is overlarded with Hallelujahs. His Latin 'motet' *Salvator mundi*, one of a series, shows him in a different vein: it has a spaciousness achieved by a recitative-like counterpoint alternating with massive chords which are not only harmonically arresting but exploit to the full the glories of a large building. This fine work can rank equal with that of Tallis on the same text as a stirring setting of a moving theme. His other full anthems, some of which are now republished,[3] show always a fine sense of the choral import of his texts.

[1] It may be noted that anthems with string accompaniment are usually those written for the Chapel Royal where the strings were employed normally on Sundays when the king was present.

[2] Humfrey, Pelham (1647–1674). Also spelt Humfry, Humphrys, etc. Chorister at Chapel Royal 1660 under Cpt. Cooke, where he composed some anthems including his own section of the Club Anthem. 1664, sent abroad by Charles II with funds from the Secret Service; studied with Lully. 1666–7, Gentleman of the Chapel, and 1672, Master of the Children and Composer in Ordinary. Some secular music, several excellent anthems and an evening service in E-minor.

[3] *Fourteen Anthems by Blow*, ed. C. Hylton Stewart (*O.U.P.*). Obtainable separately.

PURCELL'S FULL ANTHEMS

Purcell's full anthems show him at his best as a church composer. The verse-anthems are often beautiful and show an unusual facility with irregular bar-rhythms, often moving in groups of three and five, besides a wide range of expressiveness; but they do not always exhibit real church decorum and reticence. In his full anthems, on the other hand, he can command the massive and sober dignity of Blow with the pathos of Wise as we find in the eight-part *O Lord God of hosts*, where the solos are infused with real feeling, or the five-part Latin work *Jehova, quam multi sunt* which moves along with expressive majesty and contains some well-wrought counterpoint. The lovely *Remember not, Lord, our offences*, in five parts, gets its solemn and moving effect by simple means, exceeded only by the four-part *Thou knowest, Lord*. This little work of genius was written in March 1695 for the funeral of Queen Mary and by November the composer himself was dead.[1] The numerous rests, the absence of any counterpoint, the recitative-like setting of the feminine endings *holy*, *mighty* all combine to create a moving contakion. *Soul of the world* from one of his two odes for St. Cecilia's Day is often sung. Its text has little to do with the Christian religion, but the celebration of the patroness of organists is made the excuse for performing in church this excellent, exhilarating piece of writing. Its knowledge of choral effect, the alternating rich harmony and cunning counterpoint, the runs on the words *scattered atoms* give not only a thrill but the clue to Handel's effective writing.

NEGLECT OF PURCELL

Until the rediscovery of the Tudors Purcell was often called the greatest English musical genius. It is well to remember that by the general public Purcell has not yet been discovered. Like the Tudors' his idiom is not a modern one and to be savoured to the full it needs continuous hearing; the public which loves its Handel would as certainly respond to Purcell his forerunner, just as one can like Beethoven and Haydn or Byrd and Tallis. But composers do not become popular merely because they typify a certain phase of history: Purcell would be liked for himself, the personality of the man. That however can only become possible when he is given a

---

[1] Purcell had set the words twelve years before, but re-set them in 1695.

hearing. There are practical problems in performing his verse-anthems which were written for a specialised milieu of singers with a professional technique and a small string combination of five or six players. It is surely possible to re-create that milieu, if not during the service, at least on special occasions. The solos for counter-tenor are a difficulty but surely not an insuperable one. The revival of the Bach church cantatas has shown what might be done.

PURCELL AS CHURCH COMPOSER

To assess Purcell's value as a church composer is rather difficult. Not only did he die at an age when he was still developing but he wrote practically no church music during the last ten years of his life: it was just during that period that his command over technique was progressing further than that of any of his contemporaries. The sure hand in *Thou knowest, Lord*, one of the few church works written during the period, shows what might have been expected of the composer if he had lived to return to writing for the church. In some works Blow equals him as a church composer. Humfrey and Wise can be as moving in solemn recitative; and if Purcell shows a rhythmic invention to be sought in vain elsewhere among contemporary verse-anthems, he had not, by 1685 or so, succeeded in unifying the form, a problem he might well have solved if he had lived. He cannot be specially blamed for his optimistic secularity, a characteristic of the time, when the anthem was, at bottom, a piece of entertainment rather than an act of praise; his moving passages are an expression of the subjective spirit of the age. In *Thou knowest, Lord, Remember not, Lord, our offences* and perhaps in the two services he achieves the objectivism of Blow, a sort of impersonal beauty inspired more by the angels than the audience, but he never once attempts the sublimity of Blow's *Salvator mundi*, almost a freak for its period. Remembering Purcell's music for the theatre, his string fantasias and his sonatas, we may well regard him as a genius who wrote for the church rather than as a wholly dedicated church composer.

21

RESTORATION ORGANS AND ACCOMPANIMENT

PRE-COMMONWEALTH ORGANS

There seems little doubt that English organs before the Commonwealth were conservative in their tonal scheme compared with continental organs of similar importance. Dallam's organ at York Minster, begun in 1632, had two manuals, the Great consisting of a 'recorder' stop as the sole contrast to the usual ranks of diapasons and the Choir merely of one flute and one recorder; there were no pedals, no reeds, no mixtures, the only mutation stops being a twelfth and a twenty-second. The organ at Magdalen filched by Cromwell for Hampton Court was very small; built by the first generation of Harrises in 1637 it was a two-manual instrument, the Great having two open diapasons, two principals, two fifteenths and two twenty-seconds while the Choir had one stopped diapason, one fifteenth and a recorder. Tonally, a continental stimulus was needed and it was the Commonwealth which indirectly provided it.

CONTINENTAL INFLUENCES: THE RESTORATION ORGAN

In August 1643 parliament passed an order abolishing 'superstitious monuments' and in the following May it went further and passed an act for the demolishing of 'monuments of idolatry and superstition' among which were counted church organs. Only a few instruments—as, for example, those at St. Paul's, York, Durham and Lincoln—survived the Commonwealth; the others were demolished like the Norwich organ or removed and sold to private enthusiasts. Builders and organists alike had to find other pursuits and by 1660 the only competent builders were the Dallam firm, Thamar of Peterborough, Preston of York and Henry Loosemore of Exeter. Thomas Harris, a member of an old pre-Commonwealth firm, had gone to France to earn his living in a country where organs were not classed as superstitious monuments; full of continental ideas he re-established himself in England at the Restoration with his son René (Renatus) who carried on the business after his father's death in 1672. A German builder, Bernhard Schmidt, better known as 'Father Smith', was appointed 'organ-maker in ordinary' to Charles II and given a workshop in the palace of Whitehall. In the organs of Harris and Schmidt we first see the influence of continental tonal schemes though they contained no Pedal organs. Extant instruments of these two men which still retain some of the original pipe-work show that both Harris and Schmidt were masters of the art of pipe-making and -voicing, though in a famous competition held in the Temple Church where both erected an organ in 1664 that of Schmidt was judged the better. It was Schmidt who erected the instrument in the new St. Paul's, a three-decker of twelve, nine and six stops; its erection caused friction with Sir Christopher Wren who, when asked to allow the organ to be enlarged beyond the original scheme, called it a 'confounded box of whistles'. Here it would seem that the architect was in the right in his refusal to enlarge the organ chamber in defiance of the original plans; it is seldom, however, that church architects can be made to see that the organ chamber must be an essential and well-thought-out part of their plans.

THE RESTORATION TONAL SCHEME

The organ accompaniments of the period could not be said to lack variety, but the instruments were wanting in the deeper-toned pipes played from a separate Pedal organ which give the characteristic effect of a held pedal note with shifting harmonies above. Sixteen-foot tone was, however, to be found on the Great and Choir and it was the common practice to play the bass on a sixteen-foot manual stop and the upper imitative or filling-in parts as found in many anthems of the period on the other manual, usually the 'chayre' organ. It is thus not an anachronism to use the pedals when performing works of the time and no doubt plenty of sparkling reeds were to be heard in the strongly rhythmic anthems of Purcell's day. The favourite stops of the period were the 'cornet' and 'trumpet' which were usually arranged so that the notes below middle C could be cut off allowing the player to accompany a trumpet melody with a softer stop on the same manual.

ORGAN PITCH

A word may be said about the pitch of organs at this time. It was not kept constant even by the same builder, Schmidt, for example, calling a note produced by a pipe a foot long A in Durham and C in Trinity College, Cambridge. Since 1495, the date of the famous organ at Halberstadt (A=505.8), the pitch had been steadily sinking until in 1690 the Hampton Court instrument had A= 441.7 and in 1713 the organ at Strasbourg had A=393.2. The mean pitch used from Purcell till the early nineteenth century made A=about 420, which is little different from the modern French 'diapason normal' of A=435 at 59° Fahrenheit, equal to C=522 as used by the B.B.C. today. To get a true idea, therefore, of the pitch of Restoration music as the composer heard it we should transpose down not more than a semitone. We have seen that music of the sixteenth century must usually be transposed up a tone or more as the ecclesiastical pitch between 1570 and 1625 was high; but there is no real need to transpose Restoration music as the compass of the voices—apart from the difficult counter-tenor parts—gives no trouble to the present-day singer.

ACCOMPANIMENTS

Accompaniments during the seventeenth century were not treated in the careful modern manner; even in 1760 Boyce, when the full choir is singing, is content to give only a figured bass leaving its decoration to the ingenuity of the performer. Most of the published accompaniments are the work of modern editors; those edited before 1900 need careful scrutiny for chords are sometimes inserted which were never intended by the composer. Many old piano scores of Handel's *Messiah*, for example, always give the dominant seventh in the perfect cadence whether it appears in the voice and orchestral parts or not; in the typical Handelian and Purcellian inverted cadence the penultimate chord of the sixth is often made into a dominant seventh inversion thus:

Ex. 43

The tenor G of the first chord should of course be F. The same editions of Restoration and eighteenth-century anthems are perhaps too conservative in their slavish following of the voice parts, for there is no doubt that men like Purcell and Blow played a much freer accompaniment during the full sections of their anthems much as a modern imaginative organist accompanies a hymn or psalm when a good choir is singing. The final chord which is frequently left without a third in the voice parts might perhaps be filled in on the organ, especially when it is the final chord of the whole composition. In the verse and recitative portions of anthems it behoves the accompanist to keep his part as simple as possible, though occasional imitation of the solo voice parts is quite in keeping. The typical arrangement of two imitative parts (written out by the composer) over a figured bass sounds fuller if provided with quiet accompanying chords though this would not have been possible with Restoration organs which had no pedalboard. Finally, to retain the spirit of this music contrast rather than shading should be the rule: few places will be found where the *crescendo* or *diminuendo* is of the essence of the passage. The swell-pedal had not yet been thought of.

BOOKS AND MUSIC RECOMMENDED
FOR FURTHER STUDY

PRAYER BOOK

A New History of the Book of Common Prayer, Procter and Frere (*Macmillan*, 1932)

PSALM-TUNES

Hymnody Past and Present, C. S. Phillips (*S.P.C.K.*, 1937)
English and Scottish Psalm Tunes, Maurice Frost (*S.P.C.K.* and *O.U.P.*)

MUSIC AND COMPOSERS

English Cathedral Music, E. H. Fellowes (*Methuen*, 1941)
Voice and Verse, H. C. Colles (*O.U.P.*, 1928)
  Studies the technique of suiting words to music.
Henry Purcell, Denis Arundel (*O.U.P.*)
Purcell, J. A. Westrup (*Dent*, 1937)
Music in the Baroque Era, Manfred Bukofzer (*Dent*)

MUSIC

The best way to study the style of the period is to 'browse' in Boyce's *Cathedral Music*. Most of the following are published separately, and are recommended as being representative of their composers:

UP TO 1650

Batten: Sing we merrily. Deliver us, O Lord our God.
Bevin: Short Service in the Dorian.
Child: O Lord, grant the king. O pray for the peace.
        Sing we merrily (seven-part)

Locke: In the beginning. Lord, let me know mine end.
Rogers: Services in D and A-minor (for the Short *a cappella*
          type of service).

COOKE'S BOYS

Blow: Services in the Dorian and F.
          I was in the spirit. I beheld and lo! My God, look upon
          me. Bow down thine ear. Let thy hand be strengthened.
          Salvator mundi.
Humfrey: Hear, O heavens. Rejoice in the Lord.
Purcell: Services in G-minor and B-flat. *Te Deum* in D.
          Thy word is a lantern. Thou knowest, Lord. Remember
          not, Lord. Jehova, quam multi sunt.
Wise: The ways of Zion. Prepare ye the way. Awake up, my
          glory. Awake, awake, put on thy strength.

PART IV

FROM CROFT TO WESLEY

22

THE CHURCH

TOLERANCE

The Book of Common Prayer of 1662 set out on its uneventful path with no flourish of trumpets; though it was a protestant book, its compilers made it clear that the nonconformists were not going to be included as part of the established church. Once that was clear the word toleration began to be whispered in ecclesiastical politics and the religious troubles of over a hundred and fifty years can be presumed to have ended. The nonconformists, realising that from now on they must fend for themselves, put their house—houses might be more accurate—in order and to the tune of Watts' hymns sang their way through a century of enthusiasm. Within the church, however, toleration degenerated to tolerance; going to church became, as for Addison's Sir Roger de Coverley, a pleasant social duty. The church as a Christian body, losing touch with the momentous events in the outside world of thought and politics, went slowly to sleep, especially in the cathedrals where the services were droned out day by day with diminishing thoughtfulness. The musical establishments followed suit: poor as indeed some of the organists and composers of the period were, it is yet surprising that they did their daily job for the most part with sincerity and conscientiousness.

OUTSIDE INFLUENCES

The minds of thinking men which for so many years had been concentrated on religion shifted their interest. Using the new experimental methods suggested by Descartes, men like Boyle, Newton, Faraday probed the phenomena of physics and chemistry, explained away the spacious firmament and seemed to drive the mysteries from life. Writers like the mordant Voltaire extolled the Newtonian physics and derided the shams and social unawareness of current Christianity; the French Encyclopedists proved that no God was needed to sustain a determinist universe. Social unfairness of all kinds was uncovered and with the advent of machine-run industry the evils of society and the franchise became the topic of the hour. In France the growing discontent was precipitated by Beaumarchais' *Figaro* (set later to sparkling music by Mozart) into the Revolution which soon belied its watchword of freedom and resulted in a dictatorship. England passed unhappily through the troubles leading to the Reform Bill. Thinking men were too occupied with these vital things to bother about drearily recited church services out of touch with the world. Even the fanatical preaching of the Wesleys, both churchmen, failed to rouse the church from its torpor; their followers split off from a church with whose members they had political as well as dogmatic differences. The state of the world, ecclesiastical and political, is vividly pictured in three dissimilar but contemporaneous events. In 1831 Gaisford was installed as Dean of Christ Church, Oxford, and is reputed to have ended one of his Christmas sermons with these remarkable words—more remarkable when one remembers the sort of audience out of term time who heard them: 'Nor can I do better, in conclusion, than impress upon you the study of Greek literature, which not only elevates above the vulgar herd, but leads, not unfrequently, to positions of considerable emolument.' Unconscious cynicism could hardly go further. In 1832 the Reform Bill made the first attempt to distribute the franchise more fairly, and in the following year John Keble preached his famous sermon on National Apostasy, thus initiating the awakening of the church known soon as the Oxford Movement.

THE OXFORD MOVEMENT

The ministry had become the resort of those seeking an easy and respectable profession, but by Keble's sermon and the ensuing tract warfare the standard of better things was already being raised. The Tractarians rediscovered the church as a God-made institution with the communion as its Christ-given service. Slowly the church was to begin to take itself seriously, to use its missionary powers not only abroad but at home. Parish churches everywhere formed surpliced choirs, cluttered their chancels with choir-stalls and organs and set about aping the cathedral service. Enthusiasts ordered copies of French missals to discover how the communion service should be performed. Church-going became once more the fashion, even for unbelievers. The cathedrals, safely ensconced in their endowments, lagged far behind especially in the matter of their choirs where the education of the boys was often as disgraceful as the housing of the choir-school. Miss Maria Hackett wrote impassioned letters to every dean in the country, making herself a veritable Florence Nightingale in the cause of cathedral choristers. Sir John Stainer improved the choir conditions at St. Paul's and Sir Frederick Ouseley founded a college where cathedral singing could flourish and be studied. If the Victorian churchgoer of the middle of the century was smug he was at least busily smug. Convocation was revived in 1852 and a committee was formed to inquire into questions of ritual which by then, thanks to the Tractarians, had become a burning brand of controversy; though no common decision was reached in 1871, they issued a revised lectionary—a great improvement on the old—and a year later the Act of Uniformity Amendment Act gave official sanction to shortened services and other unimportant customary departures from the Book of Common Prayer. A further attempt in 1879 to deal with the problems of vestments and the octaves of certain saints' days proved abortive: it is possibly well that it was so, for accurate knowledge of liturgical history was not yet available and a revision then might have made the whole question more difficult later.

23

CONGREGATIONAL MUSIC
THE ESTABLISHMENT OF THE
ENGLISH HYMN

1. THE EIGHTEENTH CENTURY

WATTS

The Genevan motto, 'back to the Bible', and the resultant swing of the people's part in worship from the pre-Reformation liturgical chants to metrical psalms placed an emphasis on the psalter which gives the reformed service–church and nonconformist–an old testament atmosphere. There is something more Mosaic than Christian about Calvin, the Roundheads or the services of the Restoration which makes such poets as Bunyan, Crossman and Herbert stand out as Christian lights who lighten the prevailing Mosaic gloom. It was the vision of an ardent youth of twenty, Isaac Watts,[1] which first laid the axe to the metrical psalms. Most of his hymns which were to become popular and influential twenty or thirty years later were written by 1700 when Watts entered the Independent ministry, and we find him among the first to waken the nonconformists, and after them the churchmen, from their old testament torpor. Watts' hymns are steeped in the grace, dignity and zeal of the gospels. Even when at times he degenerates into eighteenth-century bombast the new testament imagery is there; at his best he has the charm and simplicity of Luke. Watts, indeed, never wanders far from the Bible and most of his hymns are para-

[1] Isaac Watts (1674–1748), born at Southampton. His father had been twice imprisoned for his religious convictions. Though offered a university career by generous Southampton friends, Watts in 1690 entered the Non-conformist Academy at Stoke Newington. From 1694 he spent two years at home, where he wrote most of the hymns to be published later. 1696–1702, tutor to the son of a prominent Puritan, after which he was ordained pastor of the Mark Lane Independents. Owing to continuous ill health he retired in 1712 to become the guest of Sir Thomas Anthony until his death. D.D. Honoris Causa, Edinburgh, 1728. Publications: 1707–9, *Hymns and Spiritual Songs.* 1706–9, *Horae Lyricae.* 1719, *Psalms and Hymns.*

phrases rather than direct inventions. He writes in the metres of the metrical psalms but his verses are as a breath of fresh air driving out their stale doggerel. His hymns became quickly popular and had no small influence in their time, an influence which has never diminished; they are the first consistent corpus of English hymns, setting this truly national product on the road it was to travel.

THE WESLEYS

Following the work of Watts came the gargantuan labour in preaching and hymn-writing of the Wesleys, John[1] and Charles.[2] Both highly emotional men, John was impressed by the hymn-singing of some fervent Moravian brethren whom he met on board ship when travelling to his missionary work in America. He soon took to translating and adapting German hymns. Later, during their itineraries round England on horseback, the two brothers, who both saw the emotional power of hymns to soften hard hearts already pounded in their sermons, wrote their hymns *ad hoc* for each meeting. The six-thousand-odd hymns of Charles thus hurriedly penned contain a score or so of masterpieces, countless excellent hymns marred here and there by passages too purple for use today, and, as one can expect from such an output, much sheer dross. He would allow no polishing of his verses, though modern compilers perforce pay scant attention to his wishes. John, the life and soul of the fraternal combination, was responsible more for the ideas behind the actual publications, but he too contributed a number of fine hymns and translations. In every modern hymn-book the Wesleys are drawn upon almost more than any other single source and among the 'hundred best'

[1] John Wesley (1703–1791). 1714, Charterhouse, and 1720 to Christ Church, Oxford. Ordained in 1725, he went back to Oxford as a Fellow in 1729, joining his brother's group of 'Methodists'. In 1735 on his way out to Georgia he was influenced by a party of Moravian monks, took, like them, to vegetarianism and set to work to learn German. In 1728 he suffered a 'conversion' and split with the Moravians two years later, disagreeing with their quietism. He gave up active work in 1761, owing to ill health, preaching his last open-air sermon at Winchelsea in October 1790.

[2] Charles Wesley (1707–1788). Educated at Westminster, whence he went to Christ Church, Oxford, in 1726, and formed his group of seventeen 'Methodists'. Thereafter he worked with his brother. The itinerant preaching of the two began in 1741 with the formation of the United Services of Methodists. The 'New Chapel', City Road, became in 1778 the headquarters of the movement. Charles unlike his brother John enjoyed a happy marriage.

hymns, if one were constrained to attempt such a compilation, a round score would be by one or other of the brothers.

THE TUNES OF THE EIGHTEENTH CENTURY

The few excellent hymn melodies by Jeremiah Clarke and Croft which appeared round about 1700 were, like those of Gibbons eighty years before, allied to texts unsuitable for the rough and tumble handling of a congregation; instead of starting a steady stream of good, 'English', workmanlike melodies they were quickly forgotten. Neither Watts nor the Wesleys had the good fortune to have a Clarke in their entourage, but they had all the means of popularising the melodies to which their works were sung. A poor florid style abounding in six-four cadences, appoggiaturas, parallel thirds and sixths *ad nauseam* and a preponderance of three-in-a-bar became the 'vogue'. To write an acceptable melody in this style needed not invention but practice to acquire the trick of decorating a dull harmonic structure; the amateur composer came into his own. A hymn-tune is so short, so obvious in form, that it must, argued the amateur, be easy to produce melodies—and basses, with a little experiment—in hundreds. Produced they were. A German bassoon player called Lampe may be noted as a type: he was attached to the Wesley circle and, wanting to use his talents to the full and *ad majorem Dei gloriam*, took to composition. His tunes ran always along the same track with always the same decoration scheme; no atom of striving to match the words or to suggest godward movement of the soul mars their suave banality, but there is usually a good bassoon part for a bass, and a graceful vocal line in the melody which in a convert of 1770 must have occasioned as much pleasurable emotion as the sugared harmonies of a century later did to the contentedly righteous Victorians. Among the inevitable hits and misses accompanying such a salvo of melodies we may note *Richmond* as a hit. It has a salt sea-air feeling, a bracing of the muscles to meet 'the surge's angry shock' to which it is often sung, and it convinces one of rock-like strength in spite of a too obvious third line. Its characteristic drop of a seventh in line four, so beloved of the eighteenth-century aria-singer, is a bold but successful experiment for congregational melody. The Wesleys themselves had apparently some qualms about the worst of the florid tunes to which their hymns were sung and in 1781 published *Sacred Harmony* where there is a larger proportion of simpler tunes. The florid tunes which to us seem vulgar deeply moved the singers of the time and one can imagine the emotional fervour conjured up by the tunes after a fiery sermon of John in some English meadow, when many of his listeners had fallen down in fits, foaming at the mouth, or had had an attack of conscience accompanied by an equally disturbing fit of the 'jerks'. Whether such storms always led their willing victims on to other more desirable states is a question which sometimes troubled even the Wesley brothers—as it should trouble our present-day missioners.

24

CONGREGATIONAL MUSIC
THE ESTABLISHMENT OF THE ENGLISH HYMN

2. THE NINETEENTH CENTURY

ACCEPTANCE OF THE HYMN

Just as John and Charles Wesley, though remaining churchmen, preached their sermons not only in churches but in the open air or in the converted iron 'Foundery' at Moorfields (1739), so the establishment which they effected of the true English hymn took place as it were outside the church. Once again, as by the reformers' metrical psalms, the church was challenged by some new evolution. The fiery new testament concoctions of Watts and the Wesleys went to the head after the old testament doggerel of Sternhold and Hopkins or Tate and Brady, and even churchmen began to drink of their draughts with relish. The famous 'Olney Hymns', 1779, of the poet Cowper and his converted naval friend Newton helped to settle the new standard. As often before, the question of legality arose, coming to a head in 1820 when a Sheffield parson, Thomas Cotterill, foisted his own hymn-book on an unwilling congregation. In a lawsuit with a characteristic English ending, Cotterill had to withdraw his book, but the Archbishop paid for a new edition out of his own pocket on condition that he supervised the publication. 1820 may thus be taken as the date at which the church accepted the hymn as a definite part of its worship. The Old and New Versions slowly became extinct; no longer were they considered the Mosaic Decalogue of extra-liturgical singing in church.

SEASONAL HYMNS AND PSALMS

In the preface to his *Psalms of David for the Use of Parish Churches*, 1791–the tunes were arranged by Dr. Arnold and J. W. Callcott, organist of St. Paul's, Covent Garden–we find the

Rev. Sir Adam Gordon writing, significantly enough in these days of the rising tide of hymns, a long apologia for the use of psalms in public Christian worship. The book is also significant for other reasons. We read in the preface: 'My chief wish and aim, have been to apply such subjects to their respective seasons, as either in an obvious, or prophetick sense, relate to the history of man's redemption. . . . And as, in all works of a serious nature, the value of authorities cannot be too much consulted, I have profited, in the choice of *some* subjects, by the ancient custom of singing the *introits*, which were psalms appointed for each Sunday or holiday, and on some account rendered proper for the day, by their containing something *prophetical* of the *evangelical history*. Being driven to some strait, to accommodate a psalm for every Sunday after Trinity, without being subjected to much *repetition*, I had recourse to the above precedent for assistance. . .' The psalms in the book are, in fact, arranged by Sundays—an idea suggested by Bishop Gibson as early as 1724 in one of his charges but presumably not carried into effect—and a few seasonal hymns are included: for example, *Jesus Christ is risen today*[1] makes an appearance and a hymn for sacramental use is found based on the melody of the minuet in the overture to Handel's *Berenice*, and set, by adding a preliminary note, to the words *My God and is thy table spread*.

TRANSLATIONS

This book, in no way different from many others of the last decade of the eighteenth century, shows a reawakening of the liturgical sense which was perhaps part of a more fundamental idea soon to find expression in the Oxford Movement—that of the authority of the church. It was perhaps also suggested by the new enthusiasm for the study of history by means of contemporary documents, the fashion for which had been set by Voltaire. In 1827 Bishop Heber published his book of hymns and John Keble his *Christian Year*, both unpractical as hymn-books but combining the seasonal, liturgical sense with hymns instead of with psalms as private meditations. After 1833, the year of Keble's famous sermon, the appeal to the authority of the church rather than to that of the Bible forced the high-church party, hitherto rallied against the hymn, to reconsider its position. The hymn had been an integral part of the medieval service, and provided it now

[1] First appeared in the *Lyra Davidica* of 1768.

showed liturgical fitness and expressed the voice rather of the church than of individuals it was accepted. Feverish translation from the Latin began, led by the work of Isaac Williams, John Chandler, Mant, Newman, Oakeley and Copeland who used corrupt French breviaries of the seventeenth and eighteenth centuries as their sources.

NEALE

The greatest translator of them all, John Mason Neale,[1] was the first to go back to the medieval originals, copying their metres and producing careful and imaginative versions. His medieval cast of mind demanded too the plainsong melodies and the help of Thomas Helmore, a musical parson, was enlisted. The tunes must have sounded strange to the ears of 1860, but the interest in plainsong was slowly growing in England and throughout Europe; it was to issue ultimately in the palaeographic work of Solesmes. Neale's untiring pen produced collection after collection of translations of Latin and Greek Orthodox hymns, all of which have been tapped by subsequent compilers of hymnals, and if his versions are often naïvely humorous and have had to submit to much editing, his work must nevertheless be considered monumental.

GERMAN HYMNS ENGLISHED

The repertory of translations was further widened by versions of the Lutheran chorales. John Wesley had already awakened the interest, and the enthusiasm of Mendelssohn and S. S. Wesley for the works of the little-known J. S. Bach together with the stimulus of a royal household which still conversed in German made the appearance of the famous *Sacred Hymns from the German*, 1841, of Frances Cox and the *Chorale Book for England*, 1863, of

---

[1] John Mason Neale (1818–1866). Educated at Sherborne, he was a scholar of Trinity College, Cambridge, in 1836. He was ordained in 1842, becoming at once incumbent of Crawley, Sussex. In 1843 he travelled to Madeira and on his return three years later became Warden of Sackville College, East Grinstead, an old almshouse, at a salary of £28 p.a. Eleven times he gained the prize for the Seatonian Prize Poem, and, a great traveller abroad, he is reputed to have spoken twenty languages. In 1854 he founded the Sisterhood of St. Margaret, and was much persecuted by bishops and the mob—he was mobbed in Liverpool—for his advanced ritualistic tendencies. He contributed much to the understanding of the Eastern Church.

Catherine Winkworth inevitable. The pietistic and symbolic trend of the texts, however, and the lengthy solidity of the German tunes do not easily strike a sympathetic note in the hearts of most English churchgoers, though there are signs today that the ever-growing popularity of the Bach Passions and Cantatas is making the chorales, at least in their Bachian settings, better known and loved.

'HYMNS A. & M.'

Thus, when in 1861 *Hymns Ancient and Modern* was first published, its 273 hymns could justify its title, drawn as they were from all sources—Watts, the Wesleys, and newly made translations from Latin, Greek and German originals. The evangelical party, who had first welcomed the Watts-Wesley hymn and whose enthusiasm remained unabated, were also responsible for a number of new hymns of the *Abide with me* type. With its numerous translations of medieval hymns, however, the new hymn-book seemed to its contemporaries to be definitely a high-church book, but it lived to see itself championed by moderate then low churchmen against a high-church newcomer; such are the queer fashions of hymn-singing churchgoers. Despite its alleged high churchmanship in 1861, however, it became immediately popular and went through many editions. In each edition new hymns were added, chiefly by contemporary authors, so that by the turn of the century it might have been retitled *Hymns Modern and Ancient*.

VICTORIAN TUNES

The music of the first edition was drawn from old sources for the most part, but Monk, the musical editor, Dykes and Ouseley, both parson-musicians, contributed original tunes. The proportion of contemporary tunes in later editions was considerably higher and caused the book to soar to an astronomical circulation. Between 1906, the date of publication of the *English Hymnal*, and 1930 or so it was just these Victorian tunes which were most criticised. Dykes especially came in for castigation and now that the controversy is less heated it is fitting to form a judgment of his output, the type *par excellence* of the Victorian hymn-tune. The tunes are very vocal, rhythmically unadventurous and approximate in type to the Victorian part-song. Their harmonisation dates them more than anything else. At its worst, as in *Hark! my soul, it is the Lord*, it matches the bland pietism of the text by insistence on the dominant seventh, a chord of fateful fascination to the Victorian. The melodies of Dykes' hymns are, however, often good and with some simple harmonic changes might be accepted by any musician. These nineteenth-century hymns have as definite an atmosphere as a Bourgeois psalm or an eighteenth-century hymn, and these rather personal, sometimes smug, emotional words and tunes can, if we are not just prejudiced, produce an effect of happy confidence. The worst of them are no worse than the dross of any other period; the best of them, especially after careful re-editing of some of the more emotional moments, are quite worthy of a place in the repertory of English hymnody. Dykes, like the rest of his fellow-contributors to *Hymns A. & M.*, moved in a limited emotional ambit and in that he had a sure touch. No possible objection can, for example, be raised to his excellent tune for *The king of love my shepherd is*, except for the weak, easy harmonisation of its last line. As with Neale's humourless medievalism, a little judicious editing is all that is needed. In *O come and mourn* and *Still throned in heaven* Dykes' music is so reminiscent of Gibbons' as to belie its period and composer. It is probably finest where its provenance is obvious but the faults of its period not so—as in *Holy, Holy, Holy* and *The king of love*.

N.B. Phillip's opinions on 'judicious editing' have been reprinted, though they are questionable.

25

CHOIR MUSIC

1. GENERAL

OUTLINE OF THE PERIOD

After Purcell the traditional stream of English church music begins to dwindle and widen. The masterpieces which crowd between 1570 and 1625 thin out considerably during the next eighty years or so; from 1715 onwards the works of genius are more spaced still and not usually of such a high order, while the tradition itself becomes weaker as the years creep towards 1900. Not that there are fewer composers; there are more. But the leaven is less. Two hundred years saw extraordinarily little change of style and it would be arbitrary to imagine 1800 as a dividing date. The number of major works is quite small and the term genius can seldom be applied to the composers of the period. On the other hand, shoals of competent, useful and dull work appeared during the whole period, many outside influences were at work and some collections of the music of the cathedral repertory were made.

COLLECTIONS OF CATHEDRAL MUSIC

Three collections of the existing repertory had been made during the preceding century. The first was that of the Rev. John Barnard, Minor Canon of St. Paul's, published in 1641; the collection was published not in score but in the Elizabethan manner in part-books. No complete set survived the Commonwealth according to Boyce, but a complete score has been compiled since from existing parts and is invaluable to modern editors. Barnard's work is useful as a source book for Tudor scores and is instructive in providing evidence of the repertory of cathedral choirs between 1625 and the date of its publication. Barnard also left a large manuscript collection of contemporary work with which he intended to form a second part to his work; the collection has survived. Tudway's large and valuable manuscript collection was made for Lord Harley. The other famous seventeenth-century collection, that of

Clifford, 1663, unfortunately contains words only; as the composers are mentioned it has often proved useful in tracing lost
anthems. Clifford also gave some very necessary 'brief directions'
for the conduct and understanding of the service and a small
collection of chants for the psalms, thus covering the ground of
Edward Lowe's *Short Direction for the Performance of the Cathedral
Service* already mentioned.

BOYCE'S 'CATHEDRAL MUSIC'

The famous three volumes of Boyce, his *Cathedral Music*, have
an interesting history. In 1752, Dr. John Alcock, in turn vicar-
choral, organist and master of the choristers at Lichfield, wrote on
a leaflet inserted into a book of chants he was publishing: 'As the
late Dr. *Croft* justly observes, among many other curious Particulars, (in the *Preface* to his *Anthems*) *That at this day it is very
difficult to find in the Cathedrals, any one ancient valuable Piece of
Musick that does not abound with Faults and Imperfections*; ... In
order to remedy which, my Intention is, to publish several of the
choicest ancient and modern *Services* compleatly in *Score*, (and
figur'd for the *Organ*) one every Quarter of a Year, as I have now
by me an exceeding valuable Collection of them. ... But as I
imagine many Persons will be glad to see in what Manner these
Services are to be done, I intend, by Way of Specimen, to print one
of mine, as it is perform'd at *New-College*, and *Magdalen-College*,
in *Oxford*: In the mean Time, I shall esteem it as a Favour, if those
Gentlemen who approve of this Scheme, will send their Names and
Places of Abode, to me. ...' Maurice Greene was apparently also
engaged on a similar collection, and Alcock on hearing of it handed
over all his manuscripts; Greene retired to the country to complete his work, but his untimely death prevented his finishing it.
Fortunately he commended his plan to his pupil Boyce who began
to publish his monumental work in 1760, the other two volumes
appearing in 1768 and 1778. Ten years after the date of publication of the third volume another edition was printed from the
same plates. To complete the story: Novello in 1841 reprinted the
work in separate parts with an additional organ-playing edition,
and again in 1848. Joseph Warren also edited the work in 1849
making several additions which brought the work up to date. The
original Boyce edition set out the music in score with C-clefs and
a figured bass for the organ; Novello and Warren both substituted

G-clefs and wrote out the organ part, usually a short score of the vocal parts. Arnold's Collection which when it appeared in 1790 sold only 120 copies was a supplement to Boyce containing a mixture of old and new services and anthems; its three volumes were re-edited by Rimbault in 1847.

SCHOLARSHIP

In the eighteenth century the exact work of modern palaeography was unknown. The historical sense of even Burney and Hawkins, the first two compilers of musical history, is necessarily extremely woolly when they deal with the remoter past. It is thus hardly to be wondered at that Boyce and Arnold could make neither head nor tail of the bar-free Tudors with their contrapuntal licence and rhythmic complications; they therefore 'corrected' them unblushingly in accordance with the rules of music as they understood them. A simple error, seemingly, due to an unavoidable lack of historical perspective, but it not only showed that the Elizabethans were no longer understood; it also proved that the bar-line had blunted men's rhythmic imagination so that the whole corpus of music before 1600, including plainsong, was a closed book to them. There is no real reason why Boyce should not have kept his bar-lines in his own compositions but still have been able to seize himself and teach to his choir the barless rhythms of the Tudors; but the Restoration period and the hundred years after it were an arrogant age which hung on the latest fashion and thought no music correct or even possible but its own. The sad consequence about Boyce's corrections is this: for a century and a half the music of Tallis, Byrd, Gibbons, even Purcell, and the rest was misunderstood, found dull and ungrammatical, and, worst of all, exerted no inspiring influence on composers; for most of the old music was obtainable only in the eighteenth-century editions. The story of the greatness of the Elizabethan giants was passed as a silly rumour from mouth to mouth but the music was found unconscionably boring. Church composers of the eighteenth and nineteenth centuries lacked not only the musical influence which the Tudors might have exerted on them but also the sense of pride in their heritage which might have made even a moderately talented man like Boyce a thousand times more vital and turned a man like Wesley into a second Byrd.[1] But it must be said in fair-

[1] Few can share this opinion of Wesley's potential.

ness that all honour is due to those who, like Boyce, strove in their unfortunate ignorance of the glorious past to keep their own work clean and competent.

FOREIGN INFLUENCE: HANDEL

It must not be supposed that the absence of the influence of the past was the only cause of the thinning out of inspiration. Into this body of church musicians working away in their cold and empty cathedrals came Handel, a brilliant young genius and a first-class imitator. With an enthusiasm lacking in his brother English musicians and with the insight of genius, he set to work to imitate and improve upon Purcell's inspired methods of handling words and large choral masses. Some years later the Handel oratorio with its noisy concert technique swept the board of fashion till it became 'the vogue' to go to the theatre for one's religious thrills rather than to the church with its reticent little 'chamber' choir. The too apologetic church musician gave way before this whirlwind from Hanover. Is it, indeed, fantastic to find a symbolism in Dr. Maurice Greene, with his coat off, blowing the organ at St. Paul's while his friend Mr. Handel extemporised for hours on end?

FOREIGN INFLUENCE: MENDELSSOHN AND GOUNOD

After Waterloo another tornado in the disguise of a zephyr descended, this time from Berlin. Mendelssohn, the young, beautiful and gentle lion of society, set a new fashion, not that of the sparkling orchestral works or the serious-minded organ sonatas, but that of the more sugar-sweet *Songs Without Words* or of *If with all your hearts*. His easy harmonies were made for imitation and composers of the weaker sort turned out their charming pieces. Later still Gounod, paying frequent visits to All Saints', Margaret Street, and showing undiluted admiration for the musical products of the English church, set the town afire with his dramatic, opera-like music and its exciting Spohr-like chords, its thundering marches, its bewitching orchestration. As well as works like *The Redemption* and *Nazareth* he wrote some anthems and services to show his imitators the way; they needed no such stimulus, however, and were already at work on their crashing *et resurrexit*s, diminished sevenths and thirty-two-foot pedal notes, while on Sundays they provided their psalms with wonderful illustrative accompaniments. The church had succumbed to the opera. A halt was at last called with the publication by the young Stanford of a service in B-flat; really this brought yet another influence to bear, this time more beneficial. It was that of Beethoven and the song-writing Schubert. The form and organ-parts of church music became more interesting, and though they could hardly be said to be in the English church tradition, now almost lost but for Wesley, they brought with them a really wholesome influence. Stanford himself had yet to learn better ways, the way of *The Lord is my shepherd* and *How beauteous*; other influences, too, were to help in the recovery, that of plainsong and the rediscovered Tudors.

26

CHOIR MUSIC

2. COMPOSERS OF THE TRADITION

BEFORE 1800

Despite outside influences there is running through the whole period a steady but narrow stream of work showing something of the old feeling. Curiously enough, during the eighteenth century the long list of second-raters went on mostly uninfluenced by Handel and producing libraries of useful but uninspired works in a watered-down version of the old style. Of their work, indeed, we may use Maurice Greene's quip about King: 'Mr. King is a very serviceable man.' And a serviceable pile of anthems and services came competently from the pens of King,[1] Kent,[2] Kelway,[3] Travers,[4] Nares,[5] Arnold,[6] Cooke,[7] Jackson[8] and William[9] and

[1] Charles King (1687–1748). Chorister at St. Paul's under Blow and Clarke. 1730, vicar-choral at St. Paul's. Chiefly sung are the services in F and C.

[2] James Kent (1700–1776). Chorister at the Chapel under Croft. 1731, organist at Trinity College, Cambridge. 1737, organist at Winchester. Publications: during his lifetime a volume of twelve anthems. Posthumously a service and eight anthems were edited by Corfe. Is said to have helped in the compilation of Boyce's *Cathedral Music*.

[3] Thomas Kelway (died 1749). 1726, organist at Chichester. Seven services and nine anthems extant, of which a few services have been published.

[4] John Travers (1703–1758). Chorister at St. George's, Windsor. 1737, organist at the Chapel. Service in F, Te Deum in D and some anthems, including the fine *Ascribe unto the Lord*. Some effective organ music.

[5] James Nares (1715–1783). Chorister at the Chapel under Croft and Pepusch. 1734, organist at York. 1757, Master of the Children of the Chapel. His harpsichord music is more original than his church music. Publications: 1778, *Six Organ Fugues*, *Twenty Anthems*. 1788, Morning and Evening Service and six anthems.

[6] Samuel Arnold (1740–1814). Educated at the Chapel under Nares. 1783, organist and Composer to the Chapel. 1793, organist at Westminster. 1786, Collection of Handel's works. 1790, *Cathedral Music*. Several services and anthems.

[7] Benjamin Cooke (1734–1793). 1757, Master of the Choristers at Westminster and the following year lay-vicar. 1762, organist at Westminster. Two services and about 20 anthems. The service in G was specially written for

Philip[1] Hayes and the rest, and continued, not quite so dully but as competently from Attwood, Goss, Smart, Walmisley, Ouseley, Barnby, Stainer and Sullivan. But of the eighteenth-century group there is nothing to say: their work is like the interminably similar psalm-tunes of the Old Version and while no one could conceivably work up any enthusiasm about it any cathedral organist would testify to the usefulness of much of this work in a musical establishment where two services and anthems have to be provided every day in the year regardless of the state of the choir, which even in the best-regulated establishments can fluctuate in health, personnel and numbers. The work of King and Kent and the rest was, indeed, the cathedral organist's standby until modern services began to appear in such numbers; if it is seldom inspired—though even the dullest services sometimes provide sixteen bars or so of pure lyricism—it never lacks charm or thoughtful part-writing and always fits admirably into the scheme of the average daily ferial service.

ATTWOOD

Attwood,[2] if he had had a less easygoing personality, might have brought to our church music the influence of his teacher Mozart, but he contented himself with writing a few charming trifles like *Come, Holy Ghost, Turn thy face from my sins*, or the sweetly pretty treble duet *Songs of praise the angels sang*, in all of which the

the newly added pedal organ at Westminster. Much organ and secular music.

Robert Cooke (1768–1814). 1802, organist and Master of the Choristers at Westminster. Evening service in C.

[8] William Jackson (1730–1803). 1777, organist and Master of the Choristers at Exeter. Service in F.

[9] William Hayes (1707–1777). Chorister at Gloucester. 1731, organist at Worcester. 1734, organist and Master of the Choristers at Magdalen College, Oxford. 1742, Professor of Music at Oxford. Services and anthems.

[1] Philip Hayes (1738–1792). Second son of the preceding and reputed to be the 'largest' man in England. 1767, Gentleman of the Chapel. 1776, organist of New College, Oxford, and the following year of Magdalen College. Anthems.

[2] Thomas Attwood (1765–1838). Chorister at the Chapel under Nares. Sent under royal patronage to Naples and Vienna at which latter place he took lessons with Mozart. 1796, organist at St. Paul's and Composer to the Chapel. 1836, organist at the Chapel. He did much to spread enthusiasm for the young Mendelssohn during his visits to England and so influenced English music indirectly. There are five services and about a dozen anthems, besides much organ and secular music.

pleasing melody has not the remotest connection with the sense of the words.

GOSS, WALMISLEY

Goss[1] and Walmisley[2] were capable of better things and each had something within him of the old spirit. Goss in *If we believe that Jesus died*, which has real power, or *The wilderness*, which is a cleanly written verse-anthem of some vitality, shows that in a better environment he might have created great things. Walmisley, who in such work as *From all that dwell below the skies* sedately adorns his text, was fired to real inspiration in the fine B-flat service and the D-minor evening canticles. This last is one of those extraordinary and unaccountable products which sometimes appear in art. It has a strong beauty, tenderness where it is needed –without sentimentality–a most praiseworthy accompaniment and a harmonic scheme nothing short of remarkable for its day. Here was something rich and strangely beautiful such as had seldom been achieved; even Walmisley himself could not understand it. It might be called his Kubla Khan: the story goes that he at first intended to put it into the fire. Sung at a rather majestic pace, as Walmisley intended it to be sung,[3] it can stand beside any of the great services of the English tradition. How this work of genius came to be written by the author of most of the anthems of Walmisley is a mystery perhaps solvable by the devotees of reincarnation; a more pedestrian solution may be found in the fact that Walmisley had a knowledge and sense of the work of the past rare in his day and was a keen literary man. If he had lived thirty years longer–he died at 42–there is no doubt that he might have developed much in advance of his contemporaries in the composition of church and secular music.

[1] John Goss (1800–1880). Child of the Chapel. 1838, organist of St. Paul's. 1856, Composer to the Chapel. Twenty-seven anthems of which the best known are *If we believe* (first performed at the funeral of the Duke of Wellington), *Praise the Lord*, *The wilderness*, *O Saviour of the world*. Two successful 'short' type services in A and E.

[2] Thomas Attwood Walmisley (1814–1856). 1833, organist of Trinity College, Cambridge, and St. John's. Later organist also of King's College Chapel and St. Mary's. 1836, Professor of Music at Cambridge. A cultivated musician–he had literary and mathematical gifts–he was an early champion of Bach and the serious study of the history of music in the university.

[3] According to the late Dr. Alan Gray who had it from a fellow organist of Walmisley.

SMART, OUSELEY, BENNETT, SULLIVAN

Henry Smart,[1] a little flamboyant sometimes, writes clean music which has often recognisable affinities with the traditional manner. Ouseley,[2] Bennett[3] and Sullivan,[4] each for his own reason, never managed to produce anything worth while. Ouseley was a competent and knowledgeable musician but the gods gave him little or no inspiration; exceptions must be made of a charmingly felt miniature *How goodly are thy tents* which breathes a spirit of real Christian joy and the tender eight-part *O saviour of the world*. Of Bennett and Sullivan, both excellent secular musicians, we need only say that the former writes a tolerable oratorio in *The Woman of Samaria* from which the innocuous *God is a Spirit* is often extracted for use in church—it is a miserable commentary on its fine texts—while Sullivan shows a singular lack of all the qualities which make his brilliant settings of Gilbert's verses so full of the sparkle of genius at play. In his hymn-tunes Sullivan is seldom anything but commonplace and can on occasion be vulgar.

BARNBY AND STAINER

Barnby,[5] a fine and rigorous conductor and an 'advanced' musician of the day, who introduced *Parsifal* to English audiences

[1] Henry Smart (1813–1879). Held various posts and was a fine accompanist and extemporiser. Hymn-tunes, services and anthems. Sir George Smart (1776–1867), a conductor of note, was in 1838 made Composer to the Chapel and produced some anthems.

[2] Frederick Ouseley (1825–1889). 1849, ordained deacon. 1854, founded St. Michael's College, Tenbury. 1855, Professor of Music at Oxford and Precentor of Hereford. Eleven services and about seventy anthems. Some secular music and excellent treatises on composition. Ouseley's first organist at Tenbury was the young Stainer, recommended by Goss.

[3] William Sterndale Bennett (1816–1875). Chorister at King's College, Cambridge. 1834–1835, organist at St. Anne's Chapel, Wandsworth. *Woman of Samaria*, op. 44, and anthems.

[4] Arthur Sullivan (1842–1900). Chorister at the Chapel when he composed and published his first work, an anthem. Many hymn-tunes and anthems.

[5] Joseph Barnby (1838–1896). Chorister at York, 1845. 1863, organist at St. Andrew's, Wells Street, and 1871, at St. Anne's, Soho, where he did inestimably good work by producing the Bach Passions. 1875, Precentor of Eton. Noted as a conductor and especially as an introducer of new works. His influence as a 'precision' choirmaster was wholesome. Many hymn-tunes, services and anthems, which hover, sometimes sentimentally, between dullness and flamboyancy.

and popularised the Bach Passions, translated his secular musical experiences and his fanatical love of the gaudier pages of Gounod into church music and occasionally produced horrible wonders which had no trace of the 'chamber' quality of church music about them. Stainer[1] may be compared to Ouseley: it seems that he always protested that he composed only because he was asked to provide simple music for the newly formed parish church choirs. His music, especially the services for the most part, is even in good taste until he attempts the dramatic; it is incredible that this pious and serious-minded young organist (who was only 48 when he retired from St. Paul's owing to failing sight) could pen the mock blood-curdling moments of his famous cantata. His tiny Sevenfold Amen no one could be ashamed to sign and church music owes both Stainer and Ouseley a debt of gratitude. Both men of deep conviction, Stainer, himself a brilliant accompanist, improved the music and the education of the choristers at St. Paul's, while Ouseley gave cathedral music a lasting gift in the college at Tenbury, whose foundation stone was laid in 1854. Besides establishing a world-famous musical library at Tenbury, Ouseley intended that there at least the cathedral tradition, which seemed to him near extinction, should flourish and be fostered. It was a fertile idea and the college has been the cradle of many church musicians.

[1] John Stainer (1840–1901). Chorister at St. Paul's. 1856, organist at St. Michael's, Tenbury. 1859, organist at Magdalen College, Oxford, and 1872, at St. Paul's. An outstanding accompanist and improvisor. 1887, *The Crucifixion*. A very active musician, especially on the educational side. Some useful and excellent reform work with the musical establishment at St. Paul's. Hymn-tunes, services, anthems.

27

CHOIR MUSIC

3. THE MUSIC

INSENSITIVENESS TO TEXTS

It is apt to be disheartening to contemplate this jumble of music which like Browning's fugue subject contains 'nothing . . ., that I see, Fit in itself for much blame or much praise'. Especially is it so when we consider that in, say, 1900 the music libraries of most choirs contained little else but this sort of work. The common fault of it all is not that it is generally unmusical or in bad taste; indeed, the taste of such men as Nares, for instance, is never in doubt, while few composers of today can surpass the Victorians in providing a good vocal line. With all of it the fundamental trouble is that its inspiration, where it has any, springs from the text only seldom. In music written for the church service the notes must catch fire from the words, themselves aflame with the deep meanings behind them. The composer must be moved by the words into music; when this verbal inspiration flags he is always tempted to fall back on purely musical devices. That was a real temptation to men like Tallis when setting liturgical Latin; Byrd and the rest in the following generation set a fashion of sensitiveness to words which has never been surpassed. After 1625 and before Purcell, composers like Lawes were so preoccupied with the words that they too often wrote dull music, but with Purcell himself the rival claims of words and music adjusted themselves once more. During the eighteenth and nineteenth centuries one sees spreading through secular and church music alike an increasing insensitiveness to words. A hundred reasons for it might be suggested, like the rise of purely instrumental music which evolved its own logic of construction, or (in England) the influence of Handel who never learnt to speak the king's English—the king himself could not speak it—or the meteoric rise in popular estimation of opera and the prima donna. Whatever the reasons, in theatre and cathedral alike the interest in the outward forms overbalanced the interest in content among the less notable composers: the result, as always in such a case, was unadventurous harmony and stereotyped rhythms.

THE RHYTHM OF EVEN NUMBERS

The matter worsens after 1800. Smart and Goss are usually careful but trip up at times as in Smart's

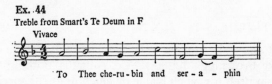

Ex. 44
Treble from Smart's Te Deum in F
Vivace

To Thee che-ru-bin and ser-a-phin

not a serious fault here if the music is sung flowingly with only one accent to a bar; but that sort of thing began to grow. The lovely unbalance of Byrd's answering phrases was slowly replaced by a dull, continuous see-saw of four-plus-four, so that in the least inspired effusions of 1860 or so words are mangled together to fit the Procrustean bed of four bars or repeated to fill out the phrases. In Boyce's

Ex. 45
Treble from Boyce's Te Deum in A

We praise Thee, O God; we acknow-ledge Thee to be the Lord

where the bar-lines might well be omitted, a phrase of four accents follows one of two. (In Boyce's time the bar-line had not yet achieved the tyranny it exerted later; that is evident, for instance, in the typical Handelian cadence where the accent cuts across the bar structure.) Smart's four-bar version of the same words:

Ex. 46
Treble from Smart's Te Deum in F
Vivace

We praise Thee, O God; we acknowledge Thee to be the Lord

balances perfectly and dully by giving a fast mouthful of syllables in the middle of the second phrase, the tenor having a specially difficult time with a leap to a top F at this point. Instances of

filling out the musical phrase by word repetition when it is under-
stocked with words are plentiful enough: Stainer who indulges
more than most sometimes creates laughable results. 'Whoso
believeth in him' is changed to the questionable axiom, 'Whoso
believeth, believeth in him', while a fugue subject has to carry the
remarkable understatement, 'as it was, it was in the beginning'.
Stanford succumbs badly at times, a flagrant example being found
in the B-flat *Te Deum* at the words, 'and we worship, we worship
thy name': here the words, 'and we worship thy name', have two
accents and the musical phrase three, hence the need for repeating,
for Stanford is intent on the restatement of his theme and sacrifices
the words to his musical needs. In the B-flat evening service the
four-accent musical phrase which has to carry the words, 'and his
mercy is on them that fear him' (three accents), and later 'as he
promised to our forefathers' (two accents), has, for the same reason,
its words spun out in the ugliest and most unsingable manner. In
the same work Stanford makes no attempt to match the difficult
dactyls of *lowliness, Abraham,* or that bugbear word *handmaiden,*
set so beautifully in the service in C.[1] This fetish of the even
number, seen no less on the Victorian mantelpiece than in the
Victorian music, has a devitalising effect; it is too easy to grasp and
in consequence makes an immediate appeal to the uninitiated
whose verdict on Tudor music is that it has 'no tune'. They
merely mean it is rhythmically too subtle for them: an hour's
explanation would doubtless put the matter right.

[1] Stanford is pilloried only because the examples are likely to be familiar to
everyone. Stanford's songs and secular choral works show few such defects;
his church music, however, exhibits a mixture of care and carelessness.
Perhaps he thought that false accentuation was part of the true church style
and tried to remedy it! One forgives these faults in him more readily than in
the less inspired composers who preceded him. See page 240.

28

CHOIR MUSIC

4. THE BETTER COMPOSERS

CROFT

Leaving inartistically the good wine till last, we pass to the more
effective work of the period, which is as good as the better work
of any other. William Croft[1] displays a convincing fusion of the
Restoration and the new styles used in the service of a lovable
personality. The Purcellian simplicity of the Burial Service looks
ordinary on paper, like Purcell's own *Thou knowest, Lord*, but
springs into beauty in its liturgical setting where it is very moving.
In a different mood the jubilant *God is gone up* has an honoured
and well-deserved place in the long line of cheerfully dignified
anthems; its middle section, though containing some long strings
of thirds in the Restoration manner, has a lovely transparence at
the words *sing praises* where the antiphonal appoggiatura chords
float and eddy from side to side of the choir—an unforgettable
moment.

Ex. 47

From a Verse in Croft's God is gone up

---

[1] William Croft (1678–1727). Child of the Chapel under Blow. 1700,
Gentleman and 1704 organist of the Chapel. 1708, organist at Westminster
and Master of the Children and Composer to the Chapel. Publications: 1724,
Musica Sacra or Select Anthems containing the Burial Service; the first
church work to be engraved on plates.

It has imaginative qualities of a higher sort than those in the more ordinary *We will rejoice* with its rather too ponderous 'chariots and horses' in what was later to be called the Handelian style. The larger works show some affinities with the larger tapestries of Blow.

GREENE

Maurice Greene[1] was born late enough to come under the influence of his friend Handel, but he had too strong a sense of the true English style to succumb entirely and withal he had a touch of genius. When his genius nods the result at its best is some charmingly wrought music like the smiling extract, *Thou visitest the earth*; the genius at work can weld together the English and Handelian styles into something fine and all his own. *Lord, let me know mine end*, a moving text, brings to birth one of the finest works of any period where the accompaniment plays an integral part—a rarity for its time—where the counterpoint sends the wondering questions from one voice to another, where the rests are used as movingly as the notes and where the slowly dying end, traditionally sung *morendo* for twenty bars or so, sounds like the coda of some great symphony. No less fine is *Lord, how long wilt thou be angry* in which the counterpoint is again used for expressive ends. But Greene is not a man of one mood: *God is our hope and strength* is a long verse-anthem which in spite of some Handelian touches and a little naïveté at the words *we will not fear though the earth tremble* has spaciousness and dignity and could not have been written by anybody else. The *O clap your hands* has a majestic joy and though in style very much of its period recaptures some of the spirit found in Tudor works of the Gibbons' *Hosanna* type as the following example will show.

[1] Maurice Greene (1695–1755). Chorister at St. Paul's under King. 1718, organist at St. Paul's, 1727, organist and Composer to the Chapel. 1730, Professor of Music at Cambridge. Publications: 1743, *Forty Select Anthems*. There are a few other anthems, some organ and much secular music.

Ex. 48

From Greene's O clap your hands

Given a sympathetic environment and possibly the capacity to take himself in hand, Greene might well have become the rallying standard of a generation of greater men; thus does history sometimes hang on the qualities of one man. Greene's little handful of masterworks is at any rate a bulwark of the true English style.

BOYCE

Boyce[1] was of different stuff: he had talent and used it. We can hardly accuse him of real genius or of the forcefulness which could create a school but in a time of much indifference he upheld the flag of care and competence and was moved enough by the words he set to make his music often thoughtful and sometimes stirring. His services are always constructed with an eye rather to usefulness but have a charm coupled with good workmanship in their varying rhythms and imaginative part-writing, and so admirably suit the purpose in hand. The verse parts of *O where shall wisdom be found* make a conversational and at times poetic commentary on the text though the choruses are more perfunctory work in the Handelian idiom. The old, expressively beautiful use of counterpoint drives home the point in *By the waters of Babylon* and *Turn thee unto me* and links his work with the best of his predecessors'. His more joyful work, seen for example in the extract *The Lord is king* (in its modern arrangement for men's voices it is electrical in effect), show a childlike happiness which is attractive and reveals the personality of the man behind the music. His standard in his church music was unvarying, no small feat for one who had plenty of success in the theatre and concert-hall.

BATTISHILL

We can be grateful to Battishill[2] for his *Call to remembrance* and *O Lord, look down from heaven*, both vital and expressive in spite

[1] William Boyce (1710–1779). Chorister at St. Paul's under King and later articled pupil of Greene. 1736, organist at St. Michael's, Cornhill, and Composer to the Chapel. 1755, Master of the king's band. 1758, organist at the Chapel. Publications: 1780, *Fifteen Anthems, Te Deum and Jubilate*, published by his widow. 1790, *Twelve Anthems and a Service*, edited by Philip Hayes. In all, five services and forty-six anthems.

[2] Jonathan Battishill (1736–1801). Chorister at St. Paul's. Worked much in the theatre. About 1764, organist at St. Clement, Eastcheap, and St. Martin, Ongar. Some anthems.

of their dignified reserve. To be remembered for two short works seems little enough title to fame, but they are lights in the surrounding twilight—1800 was perhaps the nadir of English music—and serve to bridge the gap between the best of Boyce and Wesley.

WESLEY

Samuel Sebastian Wesley[1] is perhaps the most remarkable man to appear after Blow and Purcell. If Greene showed genius it was only fitful, but Wesley produced a consistent flow of deserving works. They are seldom faultless but they all have the true spirit of church music about them and at times rise to heights of real beauty. His chief fault, to be laid perhaps at the door of his training, was lack of cohesion: he seems to think in terms of about sixteen bars rather than of the work as a whole. But not one man of his time was similarly fired to write passages of which one can say 'that is pure inspiration'. His music caught fire from the words which he was always at pains to set carefully; there are no false accents in Wesley who was the author of a pointed psalter showing ideas fifty years ahead of their time, and wrote recitative in tempo with the sure hand of a Purcell: see as an example the dramatic utterances in *Blessed be the God and Father*. His accompaniments are never more than a background to the imaginative vocal writing; his harmony is striking. The bold, felicitous modulations and chromaticisms are the outward sign of his intuitive vision of the text. Of all his output perhaps the serenest and purest gem is *Wash me throughly*, unsurpassed in expressive melody, a refreshing feeling for clean but chromatic harmony and above all its instinct for what suited his medium—a handful of singers, a small organ (he often notes the registration in his scores) and the acoustics of a cathedral. Here, too, the form is better managed than usual. In the otherwise lovely *Thou wilt keep him in perfect peace* this is not so: the section beginning *for thine is the kingdom* seems too short and undeveloped, while the return to the opening

---

[1] Samuel Sebastian Wesley (1810–1876). Chorister of the Chapel. 1832, organist at Hereford and the following year of Exeter. 1842, organist of Leeds Parish Church, where he wrote his psalter and the service in E. 1849, organist at Winchester, and 1865 of Gloucester. A brilliant organist and keen on the reform of cathedral music. Services in E, F and G chant services, and in F ('Cathedral'). About thirty anthems and some organ works. Two pamphlets on cathedral music reform.

theme is too sudden. But no one can forget the calm but moving sonority of the opening, the effective men's section which forms an inspired contrast, or the last three bars, matched only by the last page of *Cast me not away* and *Wash me throughly*. Of the bigger works the well-known *Ascribe unto the Lord* exhibits Wesley's power of finding broad lines of lyrical melody and contrasting them with passages of pure loveliness and majestic dignity. *Magnificat* of the service in E shows all these qualities, especially where the choir peals out the gorgeous, sweeping phrase *Abraham and his seed for ever* in eight parts.

Ex. 49

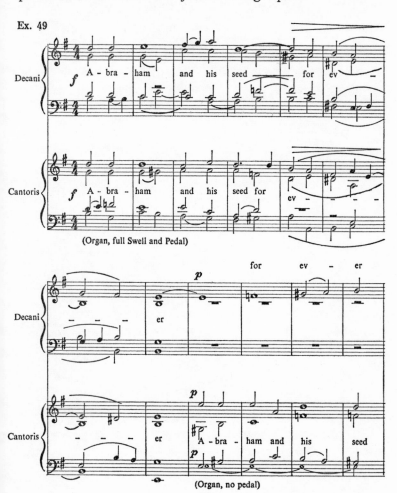

The 'Cathedral' service in F is, perhaps designedly, rather ordinary, but an interesting little chanting service in the same key (though it has a novel touch of modality about it) shows Wesley experimenting successfully along new lines. To a modern choirmaster Wesley's alto parts cause some trouble: they have a considerable range from E, even D, on the bass stave to treble C which only the Purcellian type of counter-tenor can accomplish. The general effect of his work is one of a real lyrical response to the text and a finely adjusted sense of his medium.

29

ORGANS AND ACCOMPANIMENT

SWELL ORGANS AND COUPLERS

In almost all particulars the organs of the eighteenth century showed no advance in tone or manageability on the Restoration instruments of Father Smith and Renatus Harris. Boyce's introductory symphonies and interludes, as for example in *I have surely built thee an house*, might have been written by Purcell as far as their performance is concerned; the technique is still one of contrast, in this anthem an opening trumpet passage playable by one hand being accompanied, perhaps on the Choir organ, by the other hand and followed by a figured bass passage on the Choir. The whole is playable without pedals, though it need not be played without sixteen-foot tone. Today it would be fitting to play the left-hand part of the opening symphony on the Pedal organ and fill in the implied chords with the left hand. Greene's basso continuo in *Lord, let me know mine end* shows the composer making a virtue of necessity, accompanying the bass with soft chords on another manual—or possibly on the same manual if it was a 'split' manual where the keys below middle or tenor C would act on a sixteen-foot stop for the rolling bass and those above on the eight-foot pipes for the accompanying chords. Though the technique is still one of contrast, Swell organs sporadically appeared throughout the century, the outcome of an original idea of the Jordans who in 1712 enclosed a few ranks of pipes in a sealed chamber in their organ at St. Magnus the Martyr, London Bridge, providing it with an opening door operated by a pedal. To keep the size of the swell chamber small, few if any of these enclosed ranks bore pipes speaking below tenor C so that it became the fashion to play with the left hand on the Choir and the other on the Swell; the effect is attractive even on a modern organ and is to be recommended as a method of accompaniment in work of the period. The only other advance in mechanism was inaugurated in 1762 when a sub-octave coupler was applied to the instrument in St. Mary Redcliffe, Bristol; provided the lower pipes were there this gave an effect of 'doubles' which in a large building is not bad if the eight-foot tone preponderates.

PEDAL ORGANS

It was not until 1790 or so that a few English organs were provided with a section played by the feet and containing the lower notes; Pedal organs had first appeared in Germany four hundred years before! They did not become a usual feature in England until thirty or forty years later though they were even then by no means complete in compass as today. The first pedalboards, like the board in St. James, Clerkenwell—erected by England in 1790—contained only an octave of notes which had no separate pipes but acted on the lower keys of the Great organ. During the ensuing five decades boards increased in compass (the 1834 instrument at York had a radiating board of two octaves up to C) and were provided with separate pipes in the larger organs. Even today, however, English Pedal organs have nothing like the complete provision of separate pipes found in continental organs, so that it is always necessary to couple them to the manual on which the hands are engaged, sometimes to the detriment of clarity, especially in Bach. Two evening services have an interest in connection with the introduction of Pedal organs. Benjamin Cooke's service in G is said to have been written to show off the newly erected Pedal organ in Westminster Abbey; it requires two octaves of pedals. In Walmisley's setting in D-minor the manual parts are so written that it would be impossible to play the work on an instrument without pedals; the pedal part presupposes a board of two octaves. The pedal-points of organ music are a distinctive feature whose exhilarating effect can be copied on no other instrument. Like the side-drum in the orchestra, however, the pedals sound most effective in their entries and exits, a fact noted well by Wesley in his accompaniments (see *Blessed be the God and Father* and *Thou wilt keep him in perfect peace*, where the pedal entries are carefully marked) and often forgotten by modern accompanists.

ADVANCE IN MECHANICAL CONTROL

The nineteenth century saw advances in construction and general ease of control equalled only by the progress shown in the fifteenth century. At the beginning of the century the increase in couplers, wind pressure and number of pipes made further mechanical improvement impossible if the touch was to remain light. By 1820 or so the player was almost incapable of playing loud and fast simultaneously—if that is desirable in a large building—and the nineteenth century shows many devices for gaining more ready control of this unwieldy elephant of an instrument. In 1809 Bishop effected an improvement in the composition pedals, the means whereby quick stop changes are made; still further progress was seen in Willis' organ shown at the 1851 Exhibition which placed finger pistons in the jambs between the manuals to operate a small bellows which in turn moved a prearranged group of sliders. These easily operated pistons and the now general Swell organs made the technique of organ accompaniments a technique of shading where a hundred years before it had been one of contrast, and brought many new effects into the tonal repertory of the organ. Contrast of a Boyce and Wesley accompaniment will show the difference clearly and unmistakably. The clear-cut Boyce accompaniment is replaced in Wesley by a less neat-looking, more romantic texture which shades off its tone colours like an impressionist picture. By means of the swell pedal and the finger piston it was possible to 'orchestrate' for the organ and Wesley sometimes gives subtle directions like the delightful claribel and Swell reed effect in *Blessed be the God and Father* or the magical touch of the reed with its carefully marked use of the Swell pedal to accompany the boy's solo in *Wash me throughly*. There is, indeed, a sure sense of organ registration in Wesley's work which uses for artistic ends all the new devices.

LIGHTER TOUCH

The Barker pneumatic lever, 1832, revolutionised the technique of writing for the organ by making the manuals' touch almost as light as that of a piano. It consists of a collapsed bellows into which air is admitted when the key is depressed; the bellows rises lifting with it the trackers and other mechanical rods between key and pallet. The player need no longer possess the strength of a horse and could play at the speed of a pianist; the effect on organ playing in general was of course far-reaching. Gauntlett, a pioneer and reformer, working as adviser to the builder Hill, gradually succeeded in making the compass of organs extend down to C on the manuals instead of G or F, so that by the time of Wesley's death in 1876 the organ was becoming an instrument which serious musicians could consider as a medium of expressive accompaniment. Just as the piano half a century before had in Schubert's songs become a partner with the voice by adding atmosphere, so now the organ, with Wesley at any rate, had stepped out of the background to contribute its own quota to the general effect; the figured bass had become the carefully written accompaniment and Wesley more than all the rest begins to litter his page with effective pedal notes, staccato, stabbing chords for the full swell, crescendos, diminuendos, a reed chord in close harmony or a flute solo, or some held chords for the chorus of diapasons. Romanticism had in fact begun to attack the organ loft.

BOOKS AND MUSIC RECOMMENDED
FOR FURTHER STUDY

HYMNS

Hymnody Past and Present, C. S. Phillips (*S.P.C.K.*, 1937)
Historical Edition of *Hymns A. & M.* for illustrations, anecdotes,
   etc. (*Clowes*)
A Dictionary of Hymnology, John Julian (*John Murray*, 1892–
   1925).
   The classical work of reference for notes on authors
and composers. 'Julian' is expensive for the average student
but its editor provides an invaluable reference book on most
hymns used in England. This is *Companion to Congregational
Praise*, actually most useful in conjunction with the hymnal
Congregational Praise; both are published by Independent
Press. Also recommended is Dr. Routley's stimulating and
provocative paperback, *Hymns Today and Tomorrow*
(*Libra Books*).

MUSIC AND COMPOSERS

English Cathedral Music, E. H. Fellowes (*Methuen*, 1941), which
   divides the period into Early Georgian, Later Georgian,
   Early Victorian, Mid-Victorian, and treats of the whole
   much more fully than here.
Mastersingers, Filson Young (*Grant Richards*, 1901), gives two
   charming and illuminating essays by an old cathedral articled
   pupil on 'The composer in England' and 'The old cathedral
   organists'.
The Old Church Gallery Minstrels, K. Macdermott (*S.P.C.K.*,
   1948)

MUSIC

TRADITIONAL AND USEFUL WORK

Boyce: Services in A and C.
B. Cooke: Evening Service in G.

Attwood: Turn thy face.
Goss: Service in E (Short type).
The wilderness (modern verse-anthem).
Barnby: See some excellent chants in the *New Cathedral* chant book.
Ouseley: How goodly. O saviour of the world (eight-part).

BETTER COMPOSERS

Croft: Burial Service, hymn-tunes. God is gone up.
Greene: Lord, let me know mine end. God is our hope and strength. O clap your hands together.
Boyce: O where shall wisdom. Turn thee unto me.
Battishill: O Lord, look down.
Wesley: Services in E and F (chant).
Ascribe unto the Lord. The wilderness (contrast with Goss' setting which it antedates). Wash me throughly. Thou wilt keep him.

The following composers have not been treated: Aldrich, Creyghton, Weldon, Stroud, Goldwin, S. Wesley, Clarke-Whitfeld, Elvey, Garrett, Steggall, Tours.

PART V

SINCE 1871

30

CHURCHMANSHIP AND THE PRAYER BOOK

THE TRACTARIANS

By the turn of the century the Tractarians had grown in influence and numbers and much care was being lavished on the sung eucharist which in many churches had become the only sung service on Sunday morning. Unfortunately, just as the first translators of the Latin breviaries had gone to corrupt modern French sources, so the 'Ritualists' followed and copied contemporary Roman furnishings and customs which are now considered even by the Romans as over-ornate and decadent. The present century saw the beginning of much research into the history and principles of the ancient liturgies and though the work is by no means ended the general plan is clear. By the unearthing of the simple beauties of the Sarum Use a national liturgy was given into the hands of those who wished to use it while a general pruning took place, at any rate theoretically, in the Roman Use; in liturgical change, however, movement is slow and prejudice tenacious, and those 'Catholics' who had become familiar with the ornate and corrupt Roman service were loth to turn to the simplicities either of Tridentine Rome or of pre-Reformation Sarum.[1]

THE PRESENT CENTURY

During the reigns of Edward VII and George V the 'Catholic' movement grew enormously and its ideas began to filter outside its own parishes. As ever, the majority of churchgoers were set against change, but many churches tried a compromise on Sunday morning, though a few ousted sung matins and lost their congregations; in some a sung eucharist was tried on great festivals, or

[1] The dignity of English Use has led many Roman Catholics, especially religious orders, to adopt many of its features; but if used in full it is more costly and elaborate than the Roman, however much it has the effect of 'simple dignity'. Availability and cheapness, as well as ignorance, explain Tractarian romanising.

once a month, or on alternate Sundays; in others both services were sung every Sunday with half the congregation at each, a tiring business of two and a half hours' continuous work for clergy, choir and organist, and calculated to drive growing choirboys from church for ever. More recently, especially in parishes where all social types are found, the experiment of a parish communion at an earlier hour, say 9.30, has been successfully attempted: the music is kept congregational, hymns are liberally inserted instead of the propers, a nave choir is formed to lead the singing–which gives the organist unrivalled opportunity to meet his critics–and the busy housewife is able to hurry back in time for cooking the equally important 'Sunday Dinner'.

EXTREMISTS

Such new departures were all made within the framework of the Prayer Book; both low and high extremists, however, were trying other experiments not to be found within its pages. Many churches retained the eighteenth- and early nineteenth-century practice of singing the eucharist as far as the Prayer for the Church Militant, when to the pointless accompaniment of a hymn the choir and people filed out leaving a scattered remnant to continue the service said; this arrangement could be preceded at discretion by matins, and it may be noted that Frere recommended that matins could be used as a preparation for the eucharist, *Benedictus* of matins being used as the mass introit and followed by Our Father. He never of course suggested that the people should leave before the canon. The idea is interesting, but besides making a very long service, especially if sung, it duplicates the section headed in the 1928 Book *The Ministry of the Word*, so that with the epistle and gospel there are four lessons. Other churches which might be characterised as 'low modernistic' made up their own services, shuffled the canticles into different places and sang their social service hymns from *Songs of Praise*. At the other end a handful–a growing handful in some dioceses–went more and more Roman by inserting lengthy passages of the Latin mass and omitting many portions of the English mass, so that the silent congregations got no help from their too protestant Books of Common Prayer. Little new bits of ritualistic refinement were added and devotional services, sung before the reserved Elements, were tacked on to evensong. The Book of Common Prayer was indeed becoming less and less useful in the very low and the very high services, but the trend of thought in both types of church showed that there was a growth in devotion to the church and a developing social awareness which were not met by the protestant and unenthusiastic Book of 1662.

31

THE 1928 REVISION

THE 1928 BOOK

The compilers of the 1928 Revision set themselves to make a book where the 'plain needs' of the modern man were 'plainly met', but recognising the mistrust of change in so many churchpeople they printed the 1662 Book side by side with their own. It is not our business here to discuss how well modern needs were plainly met by their book. Despite its obvious good sense in most matters, a few small but knotty points made the effect of its publication disastrous: it pleased neither high nor low churchmen and was not given parliamentary sanction. But no one could or would quarrel with nine-tenths of the book and it has had a tremendous sale and has been drawn upon in all kinds of unofficial ways: in certain cases it has been permitted to be used. It is a typically English, one might almost say Gilbertian, state of affairs; except by those with a strong sense of their legal duty the book is used by everyone. It is thus possible that the book may help to crystallise public opinion and so one day make an acceptable revision as possible as it is inevitable. Meanwhile, if we leave aside those controversial matters which prevented its legal acceptance, the book is from every other point of view admirable. The result of liturgical research, it does an important work in clearing away many untidy ends in our services and helping to give them a new reality. With the object of showing the psychological and artistic insight of the liturgical forms of our services we may here fitly summarise its contents.

THE CALENDAR, ETC.

In the preliminaries the 'Alternative Order how the Psalter is . . . to be read' gives proper psalms for every Sunday in the year and for other important occasions. The reading through in course of the psalter each month is rightly not interfered with, but the new Order avoids inappropriate psalms appearing on Sunday, the only day on which most people go to church. In the reprint of the psalms at the end of the book, where, fortunately for church musicians, still no change is made in the Coverdale translation, certain fiercer passages are recommended for excision. An 'Alternative Table of Lessons' is followed by an 'Alternative Calendar' which regularises many feasts customarily kept. A note gives the rules for referring feasts which fall at awkward times and many alternatives to the old collects, epistles and gospels are given in their place while the Appendix notes collects, epistles and gospels to be read on minor festivals.

OCCASIONAL SERVICES

The results of recent liturgical work are to be found in the new versions of the Occasional Services. Here the printed page shows clearly by careful selection of type-faces the structure of the service and the purpose of the ceremonial. The baptismal and confirmation services, already widely used, are models of good, clearly set out 'orders of the day', the headings showing to the uninitiated exactly what is being done and where a new section begins. The Catechism remains unaltered. In the Solemnisation of Matrimony the rather crude diction of 1662 is replaced by more pleasing phrases and some small concessions are made to the changed 'rights' of women. Liturgically this service is a mere prelude to the communion service and this is made clear by a new rubric noting that the psalm is the introit and the Our Father starts the communion which is provided with its proper collect, epistle and gospel. The arrangement of headings in the Visitation and Communion of the Sick is also excellently done. In the Burial of the Dead a clear distinction is drawn between the service in church and the committal at the graveside, the former alone being recommended for use at memorial services. The other occasional services, The Burial of a Child, The Churching of Women and The Commination, do not as a rule affect the church musician. An Appendix, besides supplying references for the collects, epistles and gospels of the lesser feasts, gives a translation of the medieval offices of prime and compline which as yet have no musical settings other than plainsong adaptations; it also contains An Exhortation which may take the place of the Commination and A Devotion which is really the ancient priest's and server's preparation for the communion service with the mutual confession omitted: it is directed to be said by priest and people in church and

in an audible voice, a direction which accords with the ideals of
the reformers but is not always followed.

THE DIVINE OFFICES

The Alternative Orders for the Divine Offices and the Holy
Communion are more interesting. Those of morning and evening
prayer begin at the versicle 'O Lord, open thou our lips', thus
omitting the preparation and so making the first versicle have
some real point. There is, indeed, little to be said in favour of the
practice of singing a hymn either during the entry of the choir or
before the preparation; it spoils the penitential character of the
opening and the meaning of the first versicle, especially if the
hymn is of the festal type, and makes the first versicle redundant.[1]
Processional and recessional hymns sung at the start and finish of
a service mar the ends of the service, the former ruining the
penitential opening and the latter forming an unnecessary anti-
climax after the ending provided– the psychologically just and
artistically perfect act of the blessing. The psychological and
liturgical point of a procession is that, as in the secular world, it is
an act of praise, witness or penitence in its own right. The liturgical procession, like a workers' May Day procession or the procession to the Whitehall Cenotaph on November 11th, sets out to
express something like witness, prayer or praise: it starts from the
chancel, may or may not make a 'station', e.g. at a memorial,
something to be dedicated or visited (e.g. crib, Easter Garden),
the font, the churchyard (All Souls' Day), the consecration crosses
(Patronal or Dedication Festival), and returns to the chancel for
the next bit of liturgical business. Well planned and not over-used
the festal *pompa* with no station until the return to the chancel can
witness to the church's joy in the occasion and her duty to go out
and proclaim it; though used *before* the eucharist (or at the
offertory) and *after* evensong, the procession should not be
muddled with those services but treated as a service in its own
right with preliminary responsory and concluding collect. Ritual
of litany type (e.g. with responses 'Thanks be to God') may be
included, and it is well for organists to prepare short versets and
not trust to long, noisy extemporisations in case 'lengthening' is

[1] Unless, of course, the psalmist's phrase 'open our lips' is meant to be
taken not only not literally but in a doubly Pickwickian sense, as it were.

needed. The normal orderly entry and leaving of clergy and choir should not be turned into 'singing walks'.

After the creed, the point as to who should sing which response is still left a little vague, but the printing of *Christ, have mercy upon us* in italics seems to indicate, as at the beginning of the communion, that the priest sings the first and last *Lord, have mercy upon us*, the method followed in the reprint of the responses issued by the School of English Church Music. It is made quite clear that matins and evensong end at the third collect; anything done after that is at the discretion of the minister.

THE LITANY

The structure of the Litany is made more clear. Ending essentially at the Our Father, the Litany proper is followed by a section headed 'A Supplication' consisting of a versicle and collect preceding an antiphon, here restored to its correct form, with further versicles and responses leading to the two ending prayers. In the performance of the Litany the use of the procession on special occasions adds much to the psychological effect. Cantors may be used instead of the minister for the first part before Our Father, the procession beginning to move at the words: 'Remember not, Lord, our offences.' A station or halt is best made at the Our Father, by which time the choir should have returned to the chancel steps. The collect at this point had no Amen in Cranmer; the Amen is better inserted here, as in the 1928 Book, so that the following antiphon and psalm-verse retain the true antiphon structure. According to tradition the cantors alone would intone *O Lord, arise*, the cantors and people continuing with *help us, and deliver us*, etc. *Gloria Patri* might also be sung the first part by the cantors alone, the cantors and people joining in at *As it was*. The last *O Lord, arise* would be sung like the first, or the whole might be sung by all as suggested by the printing in the 1928 Book. During the singing of the antiphon the clergy and choir return to their stalls so that the remaining responses and collect are sung in the chancel. The 1928 Book makes it clear that when the Litany is used, as it effectively can be, as the introduction to the communion, it ends before Our Father. Our Father is then said by the priest alone as usual and the communion has begun.

THE CANTICLES

Much is to be praised also in the printing of the canticles. *Venite*, which, it is suggested, should end at verse 7, the rest being deemed irrelevant when this psalm is used as an introduction to the psalms of the day, is provided with a set of seasonal invitatories to be sung as antiphons before and after. Their musical setting presents a small problem; they might be pointed and sung to the chant used for the psalm, or sung always to one special chant transposed to fit as in the adaptation issued by the Church Music Society to the music of Gibbons.[1] In *Te Deum*, always a problem when it has to be chanted, four sections are clearly indicated, the last of which is only a set of versicles and responses of a penitential type for the most part and might reasonably be omitted on occasions of special thanksgiving. Verses 5 and 6, and 11, 12 and 13 at the ends of sections 1 and 2, being indented on the printed page, need some special musical treatment like unisonal or unaccompanied singing. Four single chants would possibly bring out best this structure. *Benedicite* is similarly divided and should be treated musically in accordance. Psalm 51 is given as a further alternative to *Te Deum* and the seasonal use of all three has much to be said for it. In *Benedictus* a small refinement might be introduced, that of making verses 6 and 7 run thus, as in the New Testament version:

6. To perform the oath:
      which he sware to our forefather Abraham,
7. That he would give (=grant) us, that we being delivered out
            of the hand of our enemies:
      might serve him without fear;

The small alteration makes the meaning clear. In *Quicunque vult*, which is seldom sung as directed in the 1662 Book on account of its supposedly intransigent attitude,[2] some improvement is effected by a revised translation set out in four sections and the suggestion that the offending verses may be omitted; it may also be shortened by singing only two sections at a time. No musical

---

[1] *A setting of the Invitatories adapted from Orlando Gibbons* (S.P.C.K., for the Church Music Society).

[2] Perhaps we are a little squeamish nowadays. *Quicunque vult* may be speaking sober facts, and we are imparting the wrong meaning to the word *saved* which occurs so frequently. The laws of the universe operate whether we like them or not.

The Village Choir
Thomas Webster 1847

May Morning on Magdalen Tower
Holman Hunt

May Morning on Magdalen Tower
A modern press photograph

setting, aside from a simple chant in the *Cathedral Prayer Book*, has ever been forthcoming for this 'creed'; it is perhaps unsuitable for singing, being rather a dissertation than a lyrical outpouring, and would possibly gain by being read by the minister as the rubric suggests.

THE HOLY COMMUNION

Of all the improvements made to the setting out of the services in the 1928 Revision, the Alternative Order for the Holy Communion is the most interesting. The service is divided into sections as follows:

The Introduction	– containing the matter as far as the collect for the day.
The Ministry of the Word	– epistle, gospel and creed.
The Offertory	– of the Elements, with 'alms and oblations'.
The Intercession	– Prayer for the Church.
The Preparation	– confession, comfortable words and Prayer of Humble Access.
The Consecration	– restored to its ancient length.
The Communion	– as before.
The Thanksgiving	– a thanksgiving prayer, *Gloria in excelsis* and blessing.

This crystal-clear arrangement is an obvious improvement in clarity of intention, not congenial perhaps to the conservative mind but actually a return to earlier use. The Anaphora, which in the 1662 Book is purposely split up, is tidied by placing the Prayer of Humble Access in another place—where psychologically it clearly belongs—thus restoring the great eucharistic Prayer of Consecration to its original imposing length[1] and following it immediately by a communal recitation of the Our Father. If a clear break is made before the canon as suggested, during which the celebrant can arrange the Elements on the altar, the general tidying-up process will be made plain. By splitting up the Anaphora as it did, the 1662 Book fused the two ideas of consecration and communion, which in the present revision are separated. The actual Prayer of Consecration, by containing the invocation clause to the Holy Spirit, ceases to identify the actual

---

[1] And much superior structure, though not strictly to its original wording.

act of consecration solely with the words of institution, the whole prayer becoming an act of consecration, built up like a legal document according to the following outline:

ALL GLORY BE TO THEE, Almighty God . . .
>for that thou didst give thine only Son . . .
>who . . . took bread . . .
WHEREFORE . . . we . . . do celebrate . . .
HEAR US . . . and . . . vouchsafe to bless . . . us and these thy gifts . . .
AND WE DESIRE thy . . . goodness to accept this . . . sacrifice . . .
>and here we offer . . . ourselves . . .
>and . . . beseech thee to accept this our . . . duty through Jesus Christ.

Amen and Our Father are then said by all the people. The canon is thus treated as one continuous act starting with praise at *Sursum corda*, passing to the actual consecration and ending with Our Father.

THE DETAILS OF THE MASS

For the *Kyries* there are many alternatives; a shortened version of the Mosaic Decalogue with the customary responses, the New Testament summary of the law with the response *Lord, have mercy upon us, and incline our hearts to keep this law* (for some reason one often hears this done with the wrong response) and the ninefold of threefold *Kyrie* in Greek or English, which may also be said or sung on Sundays after the decalogue or summary. The creed may be omitted on ferial weekdays, the exhortations following being now placed at the end so that they do not interfere with the setting out of the liturgy, while the next rubric announces that the offertory sentences may be sung by the priest or clerks. They are, of course, usually said followed by a hymn or motet—a necessity at this part of the service which in the Orthodox Liturgy is made much of but is very short in our own Use. It might be a welcome change for the choir to sing an offertory sentence in place of or as well as the hymn, though none of the sentences has any well-known setting as yet. Improvement is effected in the Prayer for the Church: the section dealing with the king is preceded by a clause 'We beseech thee also to lead all nations in the way of righteousness and peace', and two later sections are inserted, one a prayer for work in the mission field and the other a thanksgiving for the work of the saints. A shortened version of the confession for use on ferial weekdays precedes the comfortable words which are aptly followed by the Prayer of Humble Access. After the communion of the priest and people the thanksgiving starts with a short explanatory exhortation, much in the Lutheran manner, which makes a suitable beginning to the end of the service.

THE END OF THE MASS

It is thus made clear that the service ends on a note of gratitude and giving of thanks which some churches spoil by chanting a sentimental *Nunc dimittis* as the choir file out—surely a liturgical *faux pas*; any hymn and any organ voluntary at this point should stress the note of thanksgiving on which the service ends. At the end of the service the 1928 Revision prints *Benedictus qui venit* as an 'Anthem' to be sung after *Sanctus* with its Amen; its musical setting when used with this alternative order should not be less subdued than that of the preceding setting of *Sanctus*,[1] especially as it is not followed by the Prayer of Humble Access. Anyone who has assisted at a good musical or said service on the lines here laid down will need no convincing of its efficacy and psychological tidiness.

NEED FOR A MODERN 'BOOK OF COMMON PRAYER NOTED'

It is surprising that the bishops of the Church of England have presumably never once thought it worth while to compile or order a musical counterpart to the Prayer Book. Two private ventures have been put forward in the three hundred years since 1549: Merbecke's book, which became unusable within two years, and Stainer's well-meaning *Cathedral Prayer Book* of 1891, with its barred, four-part version of Merbecke's service, its harmonised Lord's Prayer and its accompanied comfortable words. What is badly needed is an authoritative book which would give simply and clearly the following particulars for the use of the clergy and

[1] If *Benedictus* is used it should immediately follow *Sanctus*, which should then have an Amen.

choirs in village and town churches, with suggestions as to alternatives which might be used in cathedrals and similar establishments:

Morning and Evening Prayer

1. Clear directions as to what should be said and what sung at different types of service, remembering that not all the clergy sing.

2. An agreed pointing of the psalms and canticles with recommended chants whose reciting note is never higher than C. (Perhaps an agreed pointing is an unattainable ideal.)

3. The psalms and canticles paragraphed with suggestions as to how musically to bring out their structure and make their meaning clear.

4. The various alternatives for singing the responses, Sarum ferial and festal, harmonised and unison; for the latter a simple organ accompaniment to be used *ad lib.*

5. Full directions to the clergy of the Sarum and Roman inflexions for collects, with perhaps some simple explanation to the unmusical of the music type. The appropriate Amens for the choir.

6. Tables of recommended hymns for all places in the service at all seasons of the year.

7. Settings, or suggestions for settings, of the new invitatories to *Venite.*

8. Suggestions for the performance of *Quicunque vult* in both translations.

The Litany

Three settings might be given, the Sarum with and without accompaniment, a simple harmonised version[1] and some slightly more ornate setting with directions as to the procession and station. It may be well to state here that Cranmer's adaptation was not always sung in unison, even in the sixteenth century. Many harmonised versions were made, simple and more complex, like the magnificent five-part setting by Byrd;[2] they are available in the

---

[1] The first, for example, in the Fellowes-Nicholson edition—*Four Settings of the Litany* (*S.P.C.K.*) – which is somewhat more interesting and beautiful than the bald setting found in the *Cathedral Prayer Book.*

[2] Which loses much of its majesty when sung in any four-part adaptation. The same may be said of the Tallis 'festal' responses.

Fellowes-Nicholson edition. In sheer beauty the Sarum Litany, now published in English, perhaps outtops them all.

The Communion

1. Principles and suggestions of what is to be said and what sung in the various types of service—sung eucharist, mass with music, parish communion, etc.

2. Merbecke's setting with *ad lib.* accompaniment and possibly one simple modern setting, or suggestions of three or four. The responses to the commandments, the threefold *Kyrie* in Greek and English and *Benedictus qui venit* should be included.

3. Clear indications of the possible ways of reading or intoning collects, epistles and gospels.

4. The Sarum and Roman *Sursum corda* with accompaniments for the people's part to be used *ad lib.* The proper prefaces would also be given in their Sarum and Roman versions.

5. A table of recommended psalms for introits and hymns for all places in the service at all seasons of the year. As at morning and evening prayer it would be necessary to recommend hymns from all the usual hymn-books in use. The Sundays after Trinity could all be dealt with, for example, by giving a list of something like half a dozen as graduals, etc. Suitable hymns might also be recommended for baptisms, confirmations, weddings and funerals – a much needed help to the uninitiated who wish nevertheless to choose their own hymns at these 'family' services. The musical settings of these might well be published as a separate book which would concern itself chiefly with weddings and funerals.

Such a modern 'Prayer Book Noted' might well include a set of gramophone recordings. The production of such a book would be hard only in one or two controversial matters like the pointing of the psalms. The rest of the matter is already in print but is awkwardly dispersed among many different books. Unlike the *Cathedral Prayer Book* this modern 'Prayer Book Noted' would not seek to suggest cathedral customs for village churches or parish church idioms in cathedrals; each type will obviously solve its own problems in its own way. But the 'Prayer Book Noted' would at least show the principles underlying choice of intonations, responses, hymns and psalms, which musical parts of the service can be tackled by the congregation, what are the functions of the choir in a given church, or how and when to use the organ. Then clergy, organists, even church councils will at least have some helpful authority to consult when problems and differences arise.

Yet we may be glad that the Church of England, unlike the Episcopal Church of America, has no 'official' music book. (The American one contains not only hymns but other material, including Communion settings.) The danger would be lack of enterprise; already there is too much rigidity concerning what should be sung and how it should be sung, with defence by appeal to history or non-existent authority. The R.S.C.M. is very careful not to 'prescribe', but to recommend what seems suited to particular conditions. In most churches unison and unaccompanied responses and the saying of the Nicene Creed (as well as much else) would be preferable to the present belief that other treatments are 'official'. When the priest says a versicle or prayers it is incongruous to sing the response or Amen. These matters are considered further in the next chapter.

The principles discussed in this chapter and elsewhere are not affected by the new, post-1928 liturgies now being used for a trial period in cathedrals and parish churches. Since none of these new services are statutory, it has not been thought expedient to examine it here.

32

PRIEST'S AND PEOPLE'S MUSIC

PRIEST'S MUSIC

We may here fitly bring together what is to be told of that corpus of music which is to be sung by the priest or antiphonally by priest and people. These simple melodies are perhaps the oldest music of any that is still performed, and as they have undergone little or no change they are doubly interesting: they were a thousand years old at least when the oldest of our folk-songs were first composed. They were older still if, as we may suppose, they were taken over from the synagogue services. Throughout the middle ages these priestly melodies remained without any fundamental alterations and on the appearance of the 1549 Prayer Book we may suppose that the new English versicles, responses and other melodies were fitted experimentally to the old Latin tunes.

AFTER THE RESTORATION

It has been shown[1] that Merbecke's *Book of Common Prayer Noted*, 1550, Lowe's *A Short Direction*, 1661, and Clifford's *Brief Directions*, 1664, prove that an effort was made to preserve the continuity of the music for priest and people.[2] At the Restoration, even in the royal chapels where many innovations were made in the music performed by the choir, no hand was laid on the old responses. No doubt the same was true of those parish churches throughout the country which had any sort of musical establishment. During the following two hundred years the traditional versicles and responses were not altered in any way, though from time to time various composers thought fit to write versions of their own in many cases not founded on the plainsong melody. Such, for example, was the nineteenth-century compilation called the 'Ely Use' which is still sung in some churches. There is obviously much to be said in these days of diocesan choir festivals and similar co-operative efforts for a standardising of the details of

---

[1] See page 120.
[2] The 1662 preces differed slightly from those in the two previous books.

response settings, and the publications of the Church Music Society and the School of English Church Music might well form a simple model. Recently the Sarum plainsong version, much less plain than the usual responses, has been Englished and is useful where a four-part choir is not available. The same applies to the Sarum *Sursum corda* and proper prefaces for the mass. The Mutual Salutation (℣. The Lord be with you. ℟. And with thy spirit.) whether used sporadically throughout the mass or merely before the *Sursum corda* is sung usually to the plainsong versions. As its use ordinarily denotes the start of a new section of the service some care should be taken to make a pause before it is sung.

METHOD OF SINGING

The method of singing the responses has varied from a deliberate 'chanting', the usual plan up to the end of the last century, to a talking speed as commonly used today. The old cathedral tradition accompanied the so-called Festal Responses of Tallis with a fairly full organ and a liberal use of the preliminary 'door-knocker' pedal note before each response; modern usage tends towards the disuse of the organ where speech-rhythm – singing as near slow speech as possible, with regard paid to word-accent – is practised. Sung unaccompanied at a slow speech-speed and in speech-rhythm the responses (and the versicles) are made to keep their true place in the service, that of introductory matter to something else. At matins and evensong, for example, the opening set leads to the act of praise of *Venite* or the psalms; the second set leads to the collects. There is therefore every reason for not singing the last response before the collects any more slowly than those preceding: to do so gives the impression that the last response ends a section of the service. We should rather press eagerly forward to the climax which is the collect for the day. Apart from spoiling the structure of the service – which is really spoiling the psychological efficacy of it – to drawl out *And take not thy holy Spirit from us* suggests rather a pagan slave groaning under the heel of some cruel god than a hopeful, rejoicing Christian. Responses are in general best sincerely 'spoken on a note' rather than 'sung'; they are sometimes given too much emphasis or sung like an anthem. The inflexions in the singing of collects are in general giving way to a plain intoning on a note: some ending inflexion is, however, possibly desirable to prevent the occasional premature Amen.

THE SPOKEN VOICE

There is a growing practice of saying in the natural voice the creed, Lord's Prayer and General Confession. Such a practice, where unanimity of utterance is rehearsed and achieved, makes for artistic relief from uninterrupted singing and enables everyone, even those shy of singing, to join in these important acts. At the start of matins and evensong it helps, too, to make the structure of the opening clear—penitence followed by praise. Massed speaking, which can be achieved with an experienced leader, is in fact as impressive as massed singing; but its pace must be well suited to the building. The sorry and blasphemous gabble, still heard from some thoughtless congregations (though it is often the direct result of thoughtless and inexperienced leadership), might well be cured by a course of singing instead of speaking. The larger the building the more difficult it is, of course, to achieve good massed speaking; for that reason much more speaking on a note is advisable in large churches and cathedrals, especially when a numerous congregation is present. Even in cathedrals and when singing is good, constant recourse to four-part harmony and the organ becomes wearisome. The speaking voice, unaccompanied unison and, above all, *silence* at such moments as the end of the Consecration Prayer (with no intrusion of the organ) are much to be desired in our services.

33

CONGREGATIONAL MUSIC

1. THE PSALMS

CHANTING BEFORE 1900

With the establishment at the Restoration of the anglican chant as the sole solution for providing music for the psalms a long period of stagnation set in: from 1660 to 1900 there is little or no development or change of method, Wesley alone betraying some dissatisfaction, though his work bore little fruit. During the eighteenth century the methods of singing the metrical psalm and the chanted prose psalm had become much alike. It is quite as easy to sing the prose psalm to a psalm-tune (by using the first note of each line as the reciting note) as it is to sing the metrical version of a psalm to an anglican chant. The latter method was certainly tried as the following extract from a nineteenth-century manuscript choir-book copied by the writer at Wheddon Cross on Exmoor will show; the chant is the familiar one by R. Langdon, the text by Charles Wesley:

Ex. 50

O for a thousand tongues to sing   My   great Re - deemer's   praise,

The glories of our God and   King,   The   tri - umphs of His   grace

Compare also the tune 'Troyte's Chant'—a specially written short chant of a type used later for some special psalms in *The Parish Psalter*—found in *Hymns A. & M.* to *Abide with me*, which, like Example 50 above, is quite a successful, if dull, method of singing the hymn; it might also, of course, be sung to an ordinary double chant repeated.

There are no certain means of knowing how the chanting of the prose psalms was done; in many books the only pointing given was the Prayer Book colon halfway through each verse, and presumably the choirmaster pointed the difficult verses in ink or pencil and left the others to luck and custom. Wesley's psalter, produced for his choir at Leeds Parish Church, inserts marks to correspond with the bar-lines of the chant, which by his time was almost invariably barred as it is normally today. The chanting by his day had possibly become formal and stiff but there is reason to suppose that though it was done at a deliberate pace it was more elastic than the sort of chanting heard everywhere in 1900. It is, indeed, true to say that the extremely stiff chanting still sometimes heard in churches is no older than Stainer's *Cathedral Prayer Book*.[1] The new parish church choirs formed as a result of the Oxford Movement were often composed of persons with very little literary feeling; indeed, one may suppose that before the advent of compulsory education in 1876 many of them had received only elementary instruction in the art of reading the printed word. In his book, therefore, Stainer, who took much interest in these new choirs, felt obliged to give them all the help he could and provided the psalter with plenty of marking based on the musical notation of the chant. To such unliterary choirs the appeal of the music was stronger than that of the text which was made to fit willy-nilly into a preconceived chant-rhythm. Absurdities of sense, 'church' pronunciations, false quantities, queer accentuations of words and phrases began to abound. By 1900 the educated man could listen to the psalms sung in church only by leaving his common sense in the porch with his umbrella.

REACTION

Inevitable reaction followed. The feeling after freer rhythms in chanting was but one of the many signs that the clear-cut, four-square rhythmic outlines of the Victorians were slowly being replaced. As early as 1870 or so Wagner was writing his music dramas in a kind of free recitative which caused consternation among his aria-loving prime donne. Research into folk-music and plainsong, each in its own way rhythmically unfettered, quickened the minds of composers into new notions of rhythmic balance where two-plus-two did not always bring the inevitable four.

[1] Which used the pointing and methods of the old *Cathedral Psalter*.

Men of liberal education, men with a love and understanding of language, were being attracted to the cloth and organ loft: Robert Bridges, who did much research into the more unusual poetic metres, proved himself as interested in religious verse as he was in secular. It is thus no wonder that in the matter of chanting—with which Bridges also concerned himself—dissatisfaction grew and experiments were made. A spate of newly pointed psalters followed and much study was undertaken on the principles involved in good chanting.

PRINCIPLES: THE WORDS

It soon became clear that the laws underlying true speech had to be reinstated: the ideal must be rather to fit chant to words than words to chant. The norm of good speech was that heard in good reading, not that in casual conversation. The details began to be clear: words must have their correct tonic accent (*our* FORE*fathers*, not as hitherto, OUR *fore*FATH*ers*) and vowels should have their true length (no long or double notes on short vowels like *yet*, *spirit*, *thanksgiving*). In the sentence words must take their stress from the sense (*for* THIS *God is* OUR *God for* EV*er and* EV*er*: in the old pointing the second *God* took length and stress in defiance of vowel length and sense accent.) Certain difficulties soon became apparent, notably the very short verses in some psalms. In *Thou art the king of glory: O Christ*, the *O* in the second half is long but unstressed and *Christ* is long but stressed, and the whole phrase which contains but one accent has to be fitted to a musical phrase of four accents.

THE CHANT

Not only the words presented problems. Attention was directed to the chant which up to now had been thought of as a melody with seven accents in *alla breve* (two-two) time. Research, however, showed that it was possible to think of the chant in other rhythms: in the chant books of the eighteenth and early nineteenth centuries the chants were set out in many different forms. It was noticed, too, that by barring the chant in the Sapphic rhythm (that of Monk's well-known tune to *Abide with me* which makes a simple quadruple chant when thought of in this way) more even results were got for certain verses of the psalms. Here, then, are the two versions of the anglican chant which seem to suit most verses of the psalms:[1]

Ex. 51
Chant by Doctor William Turner
(a) Barred alla breve

(b) Barred as a Sapphic

As for the last two hundred years all chants have been composed on the *alla breve* system it is not always possible to convert them satisfactorily to Sapphics; where it is possible the accents are reduced from seven to four, an obvious advantage for verses whose words contain fewer accents than seven.[2] Both the above methods treat the chant as a hymn-tune, i.e. a melody with fixed accents. It has, however, been suggested that the chant can be thought of as containing only two fixed accents—the final note of each half[3]—the other notes taking accent or not at will as in a plainsong tone. This is a questionable procedure as there is no doubt that harmony tends to create its own accents (the less notes two consecutive chords have in common the stronger the accent), but it works for some difficult verses as will be shown.

WORD-FITTING

We have, then, two systems, the first which we may call the hymn-tune method giving the chant a fixed number of stresses (seven in *alla breve*, four in Sapphic) and the other, the free-chant method presupposing only two fixed accents. In both systems the final word-stress is taken normally on the last musical accent. To

[1] See *Collected Essays, XXI–XXVI* by Robert Bridges, *O.U.P.*, 1935, where by repeating the reciting note after the first bar-line or repeating melody notes of the chant interesting rhythmic variants are suggested. The book also gives examples of the various barrings used in early chant books.

[2] Examples are given later (page 222) of fitting the words to the two schemes.

[3] That is in a single chant. For the purpose of this exposé the double chant is considered as merely two single chants.

find the principles involved in fitting the words to the chant we
may take a few verses and fit them to the chant in various ways. In
the verse:

> Let us come before his PREsence with THANKSgiving:
> and shew ourselves GLAD in him with PSALMS.

we have (neglecting the recited portion which presents no difficulties because there is no melody) four word-accents and shall
get the best result by treating the chant as a Sapphic:

Ex. 52

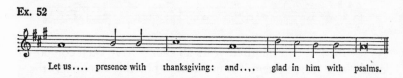

The notation used does not, of course, mean that the beat is strictly
regular: unstressed words, especially those with short vowels,
should be sung quickly and lightly exactly as a good reader would
speak them. The example is sung, as far as notation can render it,
somewhat as follows:

Ex. 53

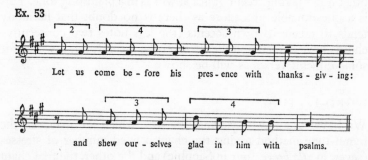

The Sapphic structure of the chant is felt under the ordinary
reading stresses like a theme hidden in a variation; the effect, in
fact, is something different from reading pure and simple. Treating this verse with the *alla breve* chant we get:

Ex. 54

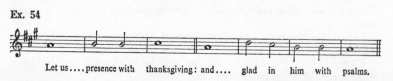

The result is not so good, with its unnecessary stress on *and* and *him*. The *New Cathedral Psalter*[1] points the first half of the verse thus:

Ex. 55

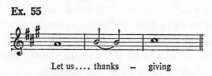

Let us.... thanks — giving

showing the poor effect of not making final accents coincide. In The *English Psalter*[2] which, like the *New Cathedral*, works with the seven-accent chant, the pointing always manages to get the word-stresses to coincide with the musical accents. The pointing of the second half of another verse taken from some modern psalters is instructive; the verse chosen could hardly be called a controversial one, yet there are many variants. They are all successful and any choice would be entirely personal:

Ex. 56

(a) Pointing from New Cathedral Psalter

and we are the.... sheep —— of his hand

(b) Pointed to the Sapphic Chant

and we are the.... sheep —— of his hand

(c) Pointing from English and Oxford Psalter

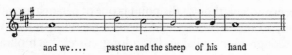

and we.... pasture and the sheep of his hand

(d) Pointing from Parish Psalter

and we are the.... sheep of his—— hand

[1] *The New Cathedral Psalter*, ed. Lang, Scott Holland, Lloyd and Martin, Published by Novello.

[2] *The English Psalter*, ed. Macpherson, Bairstow and Buck. Novello, 1925.

Further study would show that modern pointed psalters tend to use each of the rhythmic systems of barring chants as occasion dictates, awkward verses usually requiring a departure from the norm: the *New Cathedral* and *English Psalters,* however, use the *alla breve* chant more or less exclusively, the latter relying on other methods to ease difficult situations, as will be shown. The *Parish Psalter*[1] uses the *alla breve* or the Sapphic freely alternating, while the *Oxford Psalter*[2] is freer still, the pointing often presupposing the free chant, more often the Sapphic and seldom the *alla breve.* Pointing can be judged only in performance. The mere possession of a well-pointed psalter will not ensure a good rendering: one choir will attain excellent results from a psalter which in the hands of another produces nonsense. Choirs who are fortunate enough to contain members with a sense of literary values can soon be made keen on solving the fascinating problems of pointing; with other choirs ideals must be restricted, though much can be done with the use at rehearsals of gramophone recordings.[3]

SHORT VERSES

The numerous short half-verses in the psalms cause much difficulty and it is interesting to note the various solutions offered by modern pointings. In Psalm 115 which abounds in such verses we find:

> *eyes have they and see   not.*
> *noses have they and smell not.*

Both phrases occur in the second half of the verse where the chant in *alla breve* has four accents. In reading there are but two accents, on *eyes*, *see*, and *noses*, *smell* with a subsidiary stress (rhetorical, not a sense accent, though the point is one of personal predilection) on *have*, so that *have they and* forms a dactyl or musical triplet. *Eyes*, though monosyllabic, has a long vowel. Each phrase contains two (or three) accents only. Such are the data of the problem. The *New Cathedral* pointing cannot be considered a very satisfactory solution:

---

[1] *The Parish Psalter*, ed. Nicholson (Faith Press).

[2] *The Oxford Psalter (O.U.P.)*.

[3] Those interested would do well to apply the principles described above to the other published psalters not mentioned here.

Choristers at work in the crypt of Canterbury Cathedral

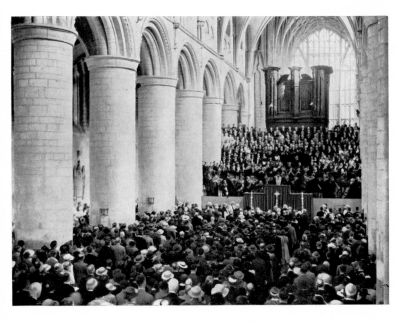

Opening service of the Three Choirs Festival

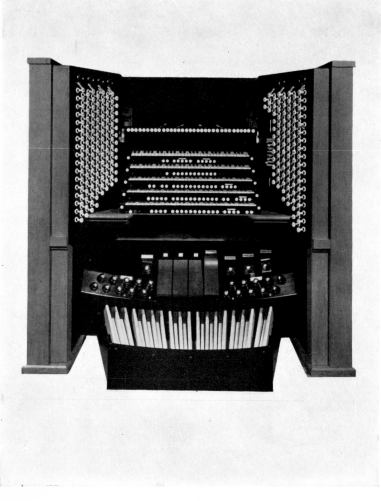

The nave console in Liverpool Cathedral

Ex. 57

Pointing from New Cathedral Psalter

It lengthens the short vowel of *have* and gives unwarrantable stress to *they*. A slightly better result is got in *The Psalter Newly Pointed* by treating the chant as a Sapphic thus:

Ex. 58

Pointing from Newly Pointed Psalter

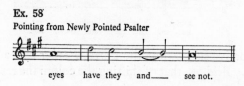

This gives two notes to the word *and* (short vowel) though, sung lightly and quickly, the two notes on the short vowel are not distressing. By clamping verses together and thus hiding the parallel structure of the text—very obvious and dramatic here—the *English Psalter* achieves with the *alla breve* chant an otherwise good result by neglecting the reciting note (it is made to carry the first half of the verse) from the first phrase and by taking the second phrase on the first half of the chant, thus:

Ex. 59

The Psalter Newly Pointed (S.P.C.K. 1925.)

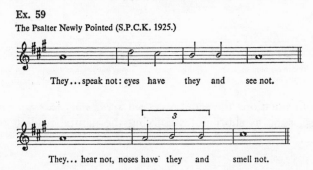

Here the second phrase also uses a device suggested by Bridges, that of repeating the reciting note after the first bar-line, making at that place a bar of three-two time. The result is quite good.[1] The

---

[1] There is much to be said for using chants of varying structure, chiefly for psalms of special difficulty. Little has been done in this direction. See *Free Chant Canticles* by S. H. Nicholson (Faith Press) for the method applied to the canticles which in these particular settings come off remarkably

Parish Psalter cuts the Gordian knot by singing the whole psalm to a shortened chant having only three accents in the second half instead of the usual four—a successful solution. In the *Oxford* psalter still another solution is found by presupposing a free chant with only two final accents. Written out as sung it goes thus:

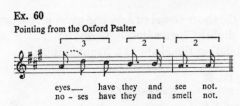

As an alternative suggestion, the *Parish Psalter* uses a device also suggested by Bridges, that of shifting the colon: the result is novel and interesting:

Or perhaps it is better noted as a Sapphic:

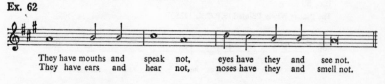

In both notations the semibreves on *speak not, hear not* are, of course, sung as short notes copying the natural reading of the words.

UNANIMITY

In chanting the pointing of the text is only one of the difficulties. The psalms sung solo would present few problems. The actual

well in performance. It is also possible that the notation used in this book (the words are placed under the chant in their correct positions) would solve many singers' problems if applied in pointed psalters to difficult psalms.

result at performance is as much the choirmaster's problem as that of the editor. Cathedral choirs, because of their daily singing, can quickly achieve excellent results. In parish church choirs the problem is harder since they sing together only two or three times a week. There is an easy solution to their difficulties which requires only courage and patience on the part of the clergy and congregation: it is that of restricting the psalm repertory until the psalms sung are known by heart. A start can be made with the canticles and about six psalms. When they are working well gradual additions can be made. It is difficult to define the congregation's part in chanting the psalms–either its actual part or its ideal part. History shows that the congregation has seldom been able to tackle the psalms except in metrical translations. Experience shows, however, that the congregation can, in the course of a year or two, get to know the pointing by heart when the repertory of psalms is temporarily restricted. By long familiarity they learnt–some of them –the old pointings: by similar means they will learn the new. But if it takes a choir many months of hard but fascinating labour to achieve a good result in chanting, a congregation of sensible and enthusiastic people will not expect to acquire proficiency without a similar expenditure of effort and patience.

POINTED PSALTERS

Modern psalters can be judged at the bar of the principles mentioned above. If it is ever produced, the ideal psalter will not restrict itself to any one method; the psalms vary too much for that. Some psalms will need specially written chants, short verses will need their own treatment–which need not be uniform– alternate 'proper' chants should undoubtedly be provided which suit their own psalm, and the chants themselves should have most of their passing-notes eliminated. As for the text of the psalms, it is high time that it was paragraphed and expurgated of pre-Christian cursings. It is a pity that the short verses cannot be retranslated; it would be easy to do but impossible to popularise. Without a good choir, psalms are best said or sung in unison, perhaps antiphonally (at the *half* verse) between priest or leaders and people, or used in metrical versions.

34

CONGREGATIONAL MUSIC

2. HYMNS AND HYMN-BOOKS

'HYMNS A. & M.'

On its first appearance in 1861 *Hymns Ancient and Modern* was looked upon as a high-church, 'ritualistic' book.[1] It contained translations of medieval office hymns, arranged its matter seasonally, and its proprietors identified themselves with the Tractarians by issuing further publications giving translations, set to the original plainsong, of such things as the propers of the mass. In 1868 the book was furnished with an appendix and in 1875 under the musical editorship of Monk the book acquired a larger proportion of contemporary tunes. Steggall, in 1889, edited a supplement (called in the present book 'First Supplement' and consisting of hymns 474–638) and this Old Edition is the book which came in for so much criticism at the beginning of the present century. Three lesser-used books had meanwhile been published mainly as protestant counterblasts to *A. & M.*: they were *Hymnal Companion*, 1870, *Church Hymns*, 1874, and the *Oxford Hymnal*, 1898.

THE 'YATTENDON HYMNAL'

Robert Bridges, working with a village choir at Yattendon, near Oxford, and feeling outraged by current hymns, issued in 1899 his *Yattendon Hymnal*, an important book for many reasons though it never became popular. By its printing, paper and format it showed that a hymnal could be produced to look well (its general get-up certainly shamed the ugly pages of all the other hymnals) and sent editors to new sources, especially to the unknown melodies of Bourgeois and Goudimel, Gibbons and Henry Lawes, Croft and Jeremiah Clarke. As many of their tunes were written in unusual metres, Bridges wrote for them some excellent verses. Bridges

---

[1] This misnomer came from confusing ceremonial, what is done, with ritual, what is said or sung.

rightly argued that for hymns this method of suiting text to tune is excellent, for it assures correct mechanical details in matters of accent and quantity; there are no lines in the *Yattendon Hymnal* to rival the reformers' doggerel of the metrical psalms or that unbelievable and unsingable line of Charles Wesley:

With inextinguishable blaʒe.

In an illuminating preface the author defends the practice of writing words to existing melodies, champions Clarke as the inventor of the modern English hymn-tune, treats at length of the gathering-notes and finals of the psalm-tunes and gives much information about Bourgeois and his interesting metres. The book contains eight tunes by Tallis, fifteen by Bourgeois, eight by Gibbons, seven by Clarke and four by Croft; it henceforth became a source-book for future compilers. It was not a popular book, for like their eighteenth-century forebears who 'quavered and semi-quavered care away' the nineteenth-century hymn-singers, even in Yattendon, were very tenacious for their favourite hymns. But its influence on scholarly research and future compilation was important.

THE 'ENGLISH HYMNAL'

At the turn of the century, thanks to the work of Bridges, the compilers of hymnals and church musicians in general began to develop a conscience about hymns. In 1904 two new-style hymn-books were issued: *Songs of Syon* and a root and branch revision of *Hymns A. & M.* The first was the work of a fervent disciple of Neale, a medievalist with Neale's cast of mind and similar love of quaint, humourless[1] symbolism, the Rev. G. R. Woodward. His uncompromising book of 431 hymns gave plainsong melodies unharmonised, psalm-tunes, Lutheran chorales in their bald, early settings and in their ornate Bach versions, providing them with words where such no longer existed. Here again the get-up of the book was beautiful. The New Edition of *A. & M.* was virtually a new book. It incorporated the results of research and scholarship, cast out most of the poorer contemporary tunes and went to original sources of words where these had hitherto been tampered

---

[1] What choir dare ever sing his carol containing the line, '*The alto of yon ass*'?

with; the whole was set out in a most presentable manner. As far as practical use was concerned both books were failures; they were born before their time. *Songs of Syon* was too good musically, in texts too precious to become popular, while the 1904 edition of *A. & M.* was killed by a headline in the cheaper press which shows the hold that hymns and *Hymns A. & M.* had over the hymn-singing public. It was literally laughed out of existence because of its renumbering and the fact that it gave Wesley's original:

> *Hark how all the welkin rings,*
> *Glory to the King of kings.*

The welkin became a screaming headline backed up by the awful truth that *Abide with me* was no longer number twenty-seven. Hardly a parish in England ordered the book. The time was ripe for the appearance of a rival: *The English Hymnal* first showed its head in 1906 and became the standard and banner of the high-church party. The ritualistic *A. & M.* had become a protestant book. The bright green cover of *The English Hymnal* and its well set-up pages could be seen in all churches which boasted a set of vestments: their aisles were soon echoing to the sounds of hymns in praise of the Blessed Virgin, to jiggy, rediscovered folk-tunes now for the first time pressed into the service of public worship, and to the attractive, modal French three-fours of modern times. Party feeling was high and it was soon a point of honour to deride *A. & M.* if you sang *E.H.* and to be horrified at *E.H.* if your protestant sympathies led you to sing from *A. & M.* Eventually the two books have come to be admired, *The English Hymnal* contributing a few new and popular hymns like Bunyan's *He who would valiant be*, whose altered text was set to a vigorous old English melody, or the stirring 'Sine Nomine' to the hymn *For all the saints*, which were not to be found in *A. & M.* In 1916, under the editorship of S. H. Nicholson, a second supplement was added to the Old Edition of *Hymns A. & M.*, the 1904 book being written off as an unfortunate failure. It consisted of 140 hymns drawn from all sources, the tunes containing some good specimens by Wise, Clarke and Boyce and some new melodies of which many were inserted in the old part of the book, like Stanford's fine tune to *Love divine, all loves excelling.* The 1916 Supplement contained little dross and made the complete book into a good representative collection; but at that time the temperature of hymn-singers still ran high and while those who disliked *A. & M.*

refused to admit the excellence of this new edition, those who used the book refused to examine the contents of the second supplement in case some new hymn should supplant an old favourite. The book was indeed still stuffed out with much poor and unused work, but its 779 hymns contained nearly all that was best in hymnody; despite the popularity of its rival its sales remained astronomical. In the *Shortened Music Edition*, 1939, the unused portions were cleared away, the get-up improved—it is now the most elegant of all practical hymnals—and a few new tunes added. The awkward general arrangement, like three hymnals bound together, remains, for *A. & M.* would not, presumably, risk another renumbering.[1]

'SONGS OF PRAISE'

Someone has called hymns modern folk-songs, and it is true that the 'man in the street' knows and loves certain hymns better than any other music. They are indeed the only music in which he ever takes part. In 1925 *Songs of Praise* marked a new departure in hymnals. It took the hymn from the church to the market square. There are many occasions, it argued, when men who meet together need to sing together, for nothing equals a hymn for summing up the prevailing tone of a meeting and firing its audience with a common enthusiasm. *Songs of Praise* set out to cater not so much for the liturgical services of the church as for 'certain kinds of services in church as well as for schools, lecture meetings, and other public gatherings. *Songs of Praise* is intended to be national, in the sense of including a full expression of that faith which is common to English-speaking peoples today. . . .' This common faith to which it is so difficult to set limits has often led the compilers into a drastic bowdlerisation of Christian texts, so that it can hardly be called a church hymnal and thus comes outside the scope of enquiry of this book. But the book is used in church and serves useful purposes even though the Stabat Mater is wrenched into a loose paraphrase which never once mentions the subject of its title—the paraphrase is merely signed A.F.—while the editor appends his name to a watered-down 'suggestion' of Neale's *Christian, dost thou see them* taken from a Greek original of some vividness and power. Some of the modern texts are little more

[1] A risky prophecy! The revised *A. & M.* appeared only five years after Dr. Phillips' book.

than competent work while more poetic pens supply verses perhaps too lovely and fanciful to stand the test of being sung by a
large audience (yet what more unsuitable for that purpose than
Abide with me which is popular enough: the taste of the crowd is
ever unaccountable). But such 'spiritual lyrics' might well be sung
by a small band of *literati*, those people so badly treated by most
hymnals, if they boasted the voices to sing them. The music is
almost without exception good and several modern tunes are
included. Like the *Yattendon Hymnal*, it provides many glorious
melodies which everyone is the better for knowing and it is to be
hoped that as the book is used in so many schools generations to
come will possess a store of worthy tunes which they will value as
new 'old favourites'. Such a book is invaluable to parish choirs in
providing interesting little pieces to be sung in place of the anthem:
sung thus by a good choir some of the more fanciful lyrics may be
introduced to congregations as something to listen to rather than
to sing. Mention may finally be made of two hymn-books appealing to special congregations. The *Plainsong Hymn Book*, published by the proprietors of *Hymns Ancient and Modern* in 1932,
has collected together the best plainsong tunes and provided them
with first-class English versions.

The *Anglican Hymnal*, 1960, represents the churchmanship of
former *Church Hymns*, the opponent of *A. & M.* This is chiefly
noticeable in the alterations to words, 'We love thine altar, Lord'
becoming 'We love the Father's board'. The *English Hymnal
Service Book*, 1962, is intended for small churches, schools, clubs,
the forces, etc.: it gives 300 hymns from the parent book (chosen
by enquiry about demand) with a supplement of 35 which had
proved popular between 1906 and 1960. These include a selection
of carols for Christmas and Easter. By providing the *R.S.C.M.*
versicles and responses, a pointing of canticles and Merbecke's
Communion setting this publication seeks to provide within two
covers all that its patrons need for all services: it does not seek to
supplant *E.H.*, A.M.R. or any larger book where the scope of
worship needs a wide selection. The latest hymn collection, the
Cambridge Hymnal, 1967, caused raised eyebrows because of what
is included under 'hymn' and because of liberties of harmony and
arrangement to familiar tunes: but it is in no sense a church book
by editors with ecclesiastical loyalties. It is a compilation of 139
pieces for school assembly.

35

CONGREGATIONAL MUSIC

3. PRINCIPLES OF THE HYMN

SUBJECT

The nature of a hymn, one supposes, is to sum up, in language which evokes a response in the human personality, the idea which is moving a congregation to worship. Crowds normally react to simple ideas and hymns must therefore treat simply of some single theme like the best of Ambrose, Watts or Wesley. That theme varies from generation to generation, from congregation to congregation; in the missionary time of Ambrose the emphasis was laid on the fundamentals of religion, the nature of the Trinity, the attitude of God to man and man to God, the purpose of the Incarnation and so forth. As one would expect, later hymns dealt more with details like the mass, the saints, the incidents of the Incarnation, commemorations. The Wesleys wrote enough hymns to treat all these subjects and to add a number of exhortation hymns calling men to a change of motives or to faith and thanksgiving. During the nineteenth century hymns were preoccupied with the aspirations and difficulties, the weaknesses and strength of men and only occasionally, as in *Holy, Holy, Holy,* did they deal with basic concepts. In our own time the most popular hymns seem to sing of service to one's fellow men: national, social service has become the watchword of the shopkeeper both in his shop and his church. It is good that trading and hymn-singing are thus linked but such service hymns are dealing with the results rather than with the first causes of Christianity. Each generation, including our own, has provided in addition a number of mystical, symbolic hymns which have an appeal limited in scope but strong in feeling.

TECHNIQUE

Mere adequacy of subject-matter is not enough.

> *O for a man-*
> *O for a man-*
> *O for a mansion in the sky*

expresses clearly the aspiration of a man who seeks the closer presence of his maker but its technique lacks poetic decorum.

> *Jerusalem on high*
> *My song and city is*

voices the same theme with a better technique and so is more moving. Many hymns foisted on congregations express great ideas and worthy sentiments in dull, prosaic language and so lack driving power. As an example we may quote the verse of a hymn popular in some quarters:

> *Was there ever kindest shepherd*
> *Half so gentle, half so sweet*
> *As the Saviour who would have us*
> *Come and gather round his feet?*

When read without music it has no more moving power than a popular love-song emanating from Charing Cross Road. It is partly a mere statement, partly absurd sentiment. It could please only those whose conception of religion is a set of intellectual propositions backed up by cheap sentiment. A mind imbued with a vital and working faith would find it hard to reawaken or retain the emotion born of such a worthy idea when it is expressed in such a mundane and cheap-jack manner. How much more moving the similar phrase:

> *He shall feed his flock like a shepherd and gather the lambs*
> *in his arms.*

To the principles of decorum and power we must add that of apt word-rhythm: the words must fit the tune. *How sweet the name of Jesus sounds* and *Jesus, my shepherd, husband, friend* can fit the same tune only if it is the right tune (it could, for example, be made more easily to fit 'St. Anne' than its usual tune because of the lie of the melody). These particular words also lack the power of:

> *Jesu, the very thought is sweet,*
> *In that dear name all heart-joys meet.*

If we set beside these weak lines some of the finer phrases from English hymnody we see clearly the importance of word association and get consequent power:

> *O God, our help in ages past*[1]

[1] Watts' original first word is 'Our' not 'O'.

where *ages* evokes a strong association; or

> *He plants his footsteps in the sea*
> *And rides upon the storm*

which gives a startling picture; or the familiar

> *Jesu, lover of my soul*

which gets an immediate response; or Watts'

> *When I survey the wondrous cross*
> *On which the prince of glory died*

where *survey* gives a picture, *wondrous cross* calls the inert mind to attention by its oxymoron, *prince* calls up some radiant figure of childhood days and its association with *glory* contrasts with *cross* in the previous line. But word association must not be too imaginative for congregational singing, and for this reason Myers' magical lines:

> *Hark, what a sound, and too divine for hearing*
> *Stirs on the earth, and trembles in the air!*
> *Is it the thunder of the Lord's appearing?*
> *Is it the music of his people's prayer?*

are successful where the extract from Masefield's beautiful lyric:

> *O Christ, who holds the open gate,*
> *O Christ who drives the furrow straight,*
> *O Christ, the plough, O Christ the laughter*
> *Of holy white birds flying after.*

is too intimate and truly poetic to be so. Blake's 'Jerusalem', however, gives the lie to our thesis: the symbolism of the words is obscure but the hymn has become popular possibly because, as often, a fine tune has made the uncomprehended text acceptable.[1]

THE MUSIC AND ITS POWER

The example of 'Jerusalem' shows that the tune has a power of its own, enough here to rob the singer of his critical faculty. Music may exert that power for good or evil, strength or weakness, banality or poetry, and people ordinarily judge their hymns by the

---

[1] Possibly the words are misunderstood. With his 'Satanic mills' Blake is almost undoubtedly tilting at organised religion. At any rate he certainly does not mean the cotton mills of Lancashire.

pleasure they give rather than by the quality of the feeling evoked. Stainer's highly emotional, almost self-pitying tune to *The saints of God, their conflict past* wrenches the strong meaning of the words into something less strong, just as Barnby's tune to *For all the saints* weakens the force of the text while 'Sine Nomine' by its vigour gives it a bracing feeling which it would not have if recited. The words have strength in their own right but Vaughan Williams' tune gives them exultation. The banal words and tune of *While shepherds watched* have yet become popular; here, however, the Christmas story exerts its perennial appeal so that the hymn resembles a folk-song ballad where plot overrides tune and words. In *Hark, the herald angels sing* the unadorned theology would perhaps, like 'Jerusalem', never have been popularised without its jubilant tune. The power of music should in fact teach a lesson to those whose business it is to choose hymns.

THE MUSIC: ITS TECHNIQUE

To be sung by the unskilled music must naturally keep its difficulties of performance within limits. Of these limits that of compass and tessitura come first in importance: a compass of a tenth and a tessitura centring round G, A, B suit all voices. Unskilled singers who have quite a tenor-quality speaking voice find notes above C beyond them, except occasionally, without a trained choir to lead them. Congregations should seldom be expected to sing above E-flat, even D in villages where the number of singers is small and the organ often a semitone above normal pitch. As for the melodic shape, no criterion can be set. Conjunct melodies always give easy results but the 'stilt tunes' of the eighteenth century show that conjunct motion can become unutterably dull. The large number of popular stilt tunes shows that leaps are no bar to success as we see in *O God, our help*, the seventh drop in 'Richmond' or *God moves in a mysterious way*. Too much rhythmic parallelism sounds dull to a musician but often delights the simple collective mind of a congregation; rhythmic sutblety, in fact, is out of place with a large body of singers though it can often be effective where the congregation is small or fairly skilled. By lengthening the notes at certain places in 'Old Hundredth' many think to improve the tune, but it is questionable whether the new parallelism attained is any better than the other obtained when the tune is sung in equal notes and words are not

distorted (short vowels on long notes).[1] Melodies are indeed
sometimes more subtle in rhythm when the gathering-note is
abandoned but the metric beat of the hymn is eased on the initial
note of each line. No doubt the best system is to vary the length of
the gathering-note as one varies the reciting-note of the chant in
psalm-singing; but perhaps time and experience alone would
induce congregations to think so intensely during their hymn-
singing.

THE OFFERTORY HYMN

Queer and presumably unalterable is the custom of taking up the
collection during the singing of an act of praise to the Almighty.[2]
It requires much practice and experience in members of the
congregation—and even choir—who must at some place in the
hymn hold a hymn-book with one hand and with the other take
the bag, release their mite and pass the bag besides keeping the
act of praise going. There are obvious solutions, but few churches
seem to adopt them. One day, perhaps, every church will print
and distribute its music lists; the calling out of arithmetical numbers during divine service is as unseemly as it is unnecessary,
especially at Holy Communion.

[1] The advantage of unequal notes in the 'Old Hundredth' is that they prevent a dragging pace. It should not be supposed that either version is 'authentic', the gathering notes being merely customary in early printings, as were the
fermata on German chorales. Common sense decides for or against initial
long notes in such a tune as 'Dundee'; they are obtrusive if most lines begin
with 'the', 'to', 'for', etc.

[2] In Scotland, America, and several other countries it is widely customary
for an organ piece or an anthem to cover a collection!

36

CHOIR MUSIC

1. RECOVERY

GERMAN INSTRUMENTAL MUSIC

Since 1700 or so music composed in England had become a mere black and white copy, as it were, of the highly coloured work produced in the Teutonic countries, which for two hundred years had been travelling along a purely instrumental path. Taking their cue from the suites of Bach and Handel, composers like Haydn, Mozart, Beethoven had evolved their sonatas and symphonies; after Waterloo the romantic spirit had been patent in the work of Chopin, Schumann, some of Mendelssohn, Liszt, Brahms, Wagner and Strauss. All this music was based fundamentally on the playing of instruments; writing for voices had had to fit a preconceived instrumental scheme in the cantatas of Bach, the oratorios of Handel, the songs of Schubert, Schumann, Brahms, and even the music dramas of Wagner for the most part. Accompaniment was no longer a background as with Ford, Campion, Dowland, Lawes and Purcell but an equal partner as in German songs and Wagner. In Russia, France and England few at first could be found of sufficient genius and personality to withstand the influence of this steady stream of masterpieces. But in Russia a national school, amateur but efficient admirers of Glinka, was working in St. Petersburg chiefly during the sixties and seventies; their music, which owed little to Teutonic influences, was not known in England until 1914 or so. Debussy in France tried with courage, fervour and a rather restricted genius to establish a school of truly French music founded on the French tradition of Couperin and Rameau and equal in vitality to the contemporary literature and painting of France: that he was successful is shown by the work of Ravel and 'Les Six'.

MUSIC IN ENGLAND

Secular music in England had, after the death of Purcell, come

238

under many successive influences. Handel, the hordes of Italian
opera singers and instrumentalists who followed him, the more
drawing-room side of Mendelssohn (he had other, better styles
like those of the enchanting *Midsummer Night's Dream* music,
the *Hebrides* overture and the organ sonatas) and later still
Gounod (but only the Gounod of the maudlin-sweet church
music) and the chromatic harmonies of Spohr. No genius appeared
in England of a calibre to produce 'English' music of any real
staying power against the charmed onslaught of the invaders. Not
that there was no music in England. More music was being produced than ever by Englishmen, but much had charm without
vitality: so it was with the operas of Boyce and Arne, the symphonies of Boyce, the pleasant pieces of Shield, the countless
imitations of *Cherry ripe* or *Lo, here the gentle lark*, the slight,
well-wrought glees, and most of the later works of Sterndale
Bennett.

MUSICAL RECOVERY IN ENGLAND

The recovery came late. It is often dated from two works, *Trial
by Jury* of Sullivan, 1875, and *Prometheus Unbound* of Parry,
1880. These were certainly more alive than most of the work
being produced in England at the time, and to them the church
musician likes to add the service in B-flat of Stanford. The new
and creative vitality behind these works is hard for us to seize
today as we look at them across the later and better achievements
of their authors; they tend to pale before such works as 'The
Mikado', 'Blest Pair of Sirens' and Stanford's service in C. But the
creative force behind the earlier works is plain enough compared
with the milk and water compositions of twenty years before,
though it is not until after 1900 that a recovery of English music
can really be said to have taken place. Without mentioning
living composers we may signalise Elgar and Holst to show that
English music is no longer the colourless thing it was in 1850.
Living composers have no less a share of creative power than
these men and that in spite of the fact that secular music in England
enjoys no patronage save that of the concert-going public and so
dooms composers of promise to a drudgery of uncreative work.
Even with these disadvantages England has already retaken her
place beside the other musical nations of Europe in the realms of
chamber music and orchestral and choral works.

37

CHOIR MUSIC

2. CHURCH MUSIC AND COMPOSERS

CHURCH MUSIC

In church music the story is also an encouraging one. Wesley was
no doubt a genius who relaid, as it were, the track along which
cathedral music was to travel; but, his work and perhaps the best
of Walmisley apart, the music of the nineteenth century had been
either nondescript but competent or else frankly dramatic and
emotional. All of it was what might be called 'easy' music; it was
easy to write, easy to sing, easy to play. And its worst fault was
usually that it did not derive from the text to which it was set;
it could be complacently pretty when the text was charged with a
strange beauty or competently dull when the words were afire with
some tremendous thought. It was Stanford who followed Wesley
in setting his face against writing any of this easy music. He
brought to his work a competence of a much higher creative order
and one which was influenced by other styles besides that of
church music. His own influence and that of Charles Wood are
such that these two might justly be called in an Elizabethan phrase
'the fathers of modern English church music'.

STANFORD

Stanford[1] tried his hand at every known form of composition;
although it is still early to judge it is certain that he has left his
mark on two branches of composition—the solo song and church
music. Because he was not primarily a church musician Stanford
brought to his work for the church new springs of inspiration and
technique. It is a trick of history that his chief fount of technical

---

[1] Charles Villiers Stanford (1852–1924). 1873, organist at Trinity
College, Cambridge (till 1892). 1874, degree in Classical Honours. 1874–6,
studied in Leipzig and Berlin. 1887, Professor of Music at Cambridge and
later at the Royal College of Music, London. Publications: Services in A,
B-flat, C, D, F and G and many anthems.

inspiration was the Teutonic instrumental school which in lesser men had been their undoing. But Stanford had talent and personality and so was not swamped entirely by the influence of Beethoven and Brahms.

THE SERVICE IN B-FLAT

His service in B-flat has many faults but they are the faults to be found in most of the church music of the time. He could be careless still—he was quite a young man—about his setting of words, giving sometimes the impression that he thought of a tune first and made the words fit afterwards, or, what is more usual, that he set one phrase of words whose tune, owing to the exigencies of form founded on instrumental principles, had to do duty for another phrase which would not fit. He can also, notably in the settings of *Magnificat* and the Nicene Creed, become too symphonic in structure, repeating the same music to words differing in sentiment and giving an instrumental bias to music intended for a church service; he sets his service, in fact, too much like a movement of a symphony. But the composer more than compensated for these faults—which he was later to correct—by many good points which put fresh blood into the music of the eighties. The rhythms are no longer always square: *Magnificat* opens with a three-plus-four phrase but follows at *for he hath regarded* with a lapse into four-plus-four which brings a false stress on *lowli*NESS and forces a pointless word repetition on *of his*. The formal structure is clear—too clear, perhaps, in *Magnificat*, but admirable in *Benedictus*—and although it sometimes springs from that of instrumental forms rather than from the text, it was a fault on the right side when so many contemporary works were either amorphous or built in dull sections. Stanford's use in *Te Deum* and creed of the plainsong intonations (made, however, to fit his harmonic and rhythmic scheme) and of the Dresden Amen as themes on which to build re-established a long-forgotten device of the sixteenth century and before, to the lasting good of the church music which was to follow; such old themes are full of association and inspire a man in the right vein. In both the harmony and the vocal writing new and fertile ideas appear; Wesley apart, no one had for a long time written such a vivid harmonic passage as that at the words *is now and ever shall be* in the *Gloria* to *Magnificat*. The dominant—and diminished—sevenths are relegated to a true, subordinate position more fitting their emotional nature and minor triads begin to be more frequent. His basses move with vigour, a happy correction of the usual static basses of his contemporaries. Good tunes abound which are never trivial or sentimental but move beautifully to their goal like those which open *Benedictus* and *Nunc dimittis*. The accompaniments, as well as using all the resources of the modern organ (the passage at the words *is now* mentioned above is marked *crescendo* and could be thus performed only on an organ with pistons), have an unmistakably new and more musical interest. The writing in short shows signs of a more stringent training than his contemporaries seem to have had, and coupled with Stanford's ready invention produced music which needs a corresponding effort on the part of the listener.

THE OTHER SERVICES

From the musical seed sown in his B-flat service Stanford reaped a plentiful harvest. In the true tradition of English composers he was moved into utterance by his literary feeling for the texts he set. It is refreshing to see what he makes of the old familiar liturgical texts. The Nicene Creeds of the B-flat and C services avoid the obvious dramatic possibilities of the words—a field too well tilled by his contemporaries—and stress instead what is surely more fundamental, a flaming belief in the B-flat service and a solid, happy assurance in the C. *Benedictus* in the B-flat, possibly the finest number, makes all contemporary settings seem dull and unimaginative while that in C has a seraphic quality which was easily Stanford's best vein, recaptured in the G *Magnificat*, the little *Benedictus qui venit* and *Agnus Dei* in F, and the opening pages of *The Lord is my shepherd* and *How beauteous*. The setting in F was Stanford's only venture into the old cathedral, *a cappella* type of short service and is work of good solid worth. His versatility is shown by a completely different type of service, the early work in A with orchestral accompaniments, a work of many fine moments laid out on festival lines; that he could be lyrical in the best sense is shown beautifully enough in the setting of *Magnificat* in the G service. The service in C captures some quality which is found nowhere else, a kind of spacious beauty highly charged emotionally, seraphic at times and always restrained which makes it perhaps the best of all his services.

THE ANTHEMS

The anthems show the same principles applied to purely choir pieces. Stanford always chooses his text with care and is always obviously fired with the words he sets. Here again his best mood is the seraphic: the happy, pastoral contentment of the opening to *The Lord is my shepherd* has already been mentioned; it is matched by the opening to *How beauteous* where the inspiration of the key-word *beauteous* is transmuted into some lovely music. There is, indeed, never any gloom in Stanford: one can hardly imagine his choosing *Lord, let me know mine end as* a text. He is always positive though sometimes thoughtful as in *O for a closer walk*, a model for the anthem of the hymn-tune prelude type, and excels best in cheerful texts like *Ye choirs of new Jerusalem* which well catches the spirit of Easter. His one dramatic experiment—*When God of old*—is anything but successful, but even here, as always, the harmony breaks down the old tonic-dominant-tonic rut of most nineteenth-century music, which makes its music sound like a series of perfect cadences. His part-writing is unique, Stanfordian, always founded on true contrapuntal principles, admirably suited to the voices and always obeying the dictates of the text he is setting. In his evident singableness he beat his contemporaries at their own game, for no one could charge them with writing ineffectively for voices; Stanford writes more imaginatively, more musically and is still just as effective. He has a pleasing trick in the later work, used to perfection in the service in C, of making the organ pedal the real bass while the vocal basses hover above giving an effect of great freedom and lightness. Rhythmically he becomes less and less four-square as he grows to maturity (see, for example, the lovely opening of the C *Magnificat* which goes four-plus-three-plus-six) but is still led at times by his melodic invention into cruel misaccentuations, as in *which kings and prophets waited* FOR in *How beauteous*. But on the whole with his lyrical gift, his well of melody, his refreshing harmony and rhythm, Stanford released many needed draughts of fresh air into the stuffy or quasi-dramatic work of his contemporaries. By the time he had passed his sixtieth year Stanford indeed found himself the doyen and teacher of all serious-minded church composers; church music could not have wished for a better master. He is never dull and always emotionally clean; if his work is sometimes more lyrical than ecclesiastical that was all to the good: church music is all the better for an occasional breeze from such work as the spiritual part-song *Glorious and powerful God*. As an inspiration to his pupils his work has a historic importance.

WOOD

Stanford remained for the most part untouched by the ecclesiastical temper of his age. His cheerful protestantism had nothing to do with the birettas and cottas of the Tractarians or the researches into liturgiology, plainsong and, later, the sixteenth century. By discovering and delighting in the prose-like rhythms and elusive harmonies suggested by plainsong, or the subtler rhythmic and contrapuntal technique of the Tudors, men like Charles Wood[1] managed to add to their technical resources an abundance of new or at least rediscovered devices. In the hands of Wood these technical discoveries were put at the behest of a real feeling for the beauty of the liturgy and the Christian message as opposed to mere theism. With lesser men the result has sometimes been, as ever, a mere copying of the work of the Tudors or of the plainsong idiom, but Wood had a knack of transmuting these things to something his own. He harks back to the early days of the sixteenth century in his love of contrapuntal devices ('Canon to right of them, canon to left of them', as some wag has put it) but in his best work he manages his canons with suavity and unobtrusiveness; they merely serve to give the work a subtle unity. The early and pleasant sounding 'Mass mainly in the Phrygian Mode' shows Wood writing in this vein and giving a model for many similar *a cappella* masses by other men. The C-minor mass is not so felicitously wrought and struggles for expression through the quasi-modal texture but in *Glory and honour* he achieves a convincing blend of ancient and modern which sums up the significance of Palm Sunday and can take a worthy place by the side of two famous Tudor works written for the same occasion. But there are two Woods: the other works entirely in a modern harmonic idiom and is best represented by the glorious intricacies of *O thou, the central orb*, where the rich harmonies delight in his beloved sevenths and ninths, and the deeply felt miniature *Expectans expectavi*, an English anthem whose tenuous lines create a hushed

[1] Charles Wood (1866–1926). Studied with Stanford. Organ scholar of Gonville and Caius College, Cambridge, 1889. 1897, University lecturer in harmony and counterpoint. 1924, Professor. Much secular work.

beauty seldom achieved by anyone in English church music. Both works are thoroughly 'Christian' in feeling. If Stanford's *Glorious and powerful God* is theistic, *O thou, the central orb* shows us God the Father seen athwart the humanity of God the Son. *Expectans expectavi* sets another musical standard in Christian feeling; it exhales a strange suggestion of the New Testament and instinctively recalls the spirit of the first Christian martyr. It has become the forerunner of many more recent works which capture the human side of Christianity without losing any of the strange 'Easter' freshness of light and joy found in the gospels.

RECENT WORK

Of more recent work it is pointless to say much if living composers are not to be mentioned. It is of course easy to find the influence of Stanford and Wood, of Tudor music and plainsong in all of it. The weakest work is merely derivative without the composer adding any new vistas. The best work is derivative too, as it should be, but there are many workers who show individual style and catch their inspiration in a wide but always good choice of texts—the seventeenth-century English mystics are popular—and who show how the wide cleft once to be seen between secular and church styles can be bridged. More and more music is being written for the parish choirs and less for the cathedral service. That is perhaps inevitable until the cathedrals recapture an enthusiasm for their basic function of daily choral worship (it is certainly not the organists' fault that some of them have lost it). Of this growing corpus of simpler music, most of it is cleanly written and at its best has vitality and good feeling for its medium. A fault in some work of this kind has been an austerity which too easily develops into harmonic and rhythmic angularity or unvocal writing. Such work may well learn from the Victorians—if it will so humble itself—the secret of writing effectively for the voices and of not being afraid of a good tune. But there are signs that the stark period has passed. It was the result of over-correction of Victorian sweetnesses, no doubt, and gave a queer, primitive kind of conception of the Christian ethic which had more of Calvin in it than of Christ. Many composers are turning to the more warmly courageous and lyrical moods of their religion, and there is reason for just rejoicing that New Testament texts are easily more popular than those from the Old. But the lyricism of the modern composer is not the romantic, unreal, even sentimental lyricism of his grandfathers; his feet are firmly planted on the ground of realism without his head being turned by the prospect of a wicked world. The result is music whose beauty is more than skin deep and which often achieves the noble joy which once the Elizabethans succeeded in expressing—a joy which does not forget the sorrows and hardnesses of life, a restrained Christian joy.

MUSIC OUTSIDE THE ENGLISH TRADITION

A word may be said about music used in the English Church service which was not composed for it. Of this the greater part comes from the Bach cantatas and the oratorios of Handel and Mendelssohn. In *Jesu, joy of man's desiring, All glory, laud and honour* and *Awake us, Lord, and hasten* and other similar work Bach is drawn upon for some unambitious movements suitable for the average church choir; he provides more exacting fare for those who can tackle the longer movements from the cantatas. 'Messiah' supplies plenty of seasonal music for Christmas and Good Friday for choirs who boast tenors to whom top A is no bugbear, and the appendix chorus *Let all the angels of God* gives a joyous anthem in honour of the angels. 'Elijah' is drawn upon chiefly for the lovely eight-part *For he shall give his angels charge over thee*, while *He that shall endure* and *Cast thy burden* are not too hard to be tackled by most choirs in parish churches. From 'St. Paul' comes *See what love hath the father* and an anthem which can be used in honour of the Conversion, *And as he journeyed.* For Epiphany, many choirs give the pretty *Lo, star-led chiefs* from Crotch's 'Palestine'.[1] Increasing use is being made of the music written for other rites of the Christian church; some of the work of Palestrina and Victoria (Vittoria) have been given English translations, and two worthy favourites are Eccard's *When to the temple Mary went* for the feast of the Presentation of Christ, a sonorous six-part work of much beauty, and the highly emotional but very effective *Faithful Cross* by King John IV of Portugal for Passiontide.

[1] More virile and interesting is *There shall a star come forth* (usually entitled *Say, where is he born*) from Mendelssohn's unfinished *Christus.* Excellent, too, for boys' voices is the S-S-A *Lift thine eyes* from *Elijah.*

CAROLS

One of the features of the recent recovery of old music has been the attention devoted to medieval folk-music dealing with the incidents of the Incarnation, originally used in connection with the mystery plays. These carols may be classed according to subjects: the lullaby, Virgin and Child type is popular and familiar enough, while the theme of the Magi supplies a good number, others dealing with the Shepherds, the Annunciation, Easter and Corpus Christi. 'Good cheer' carols like *The boar's head in hand bear I* cannot of course be used in church. Apart from these folk-products there is an increasing number of modern settings, all loosely called carols, which partake of the nature of the true carol, treating some aspect of the Christmas story in a human way, though some are over-precious. Byrd and Lawes have left such 'carols' and there was a spate of Christmas part-songs at the end of the last century. Pearsall's fine setting of *In dulci jubilo* might almost be called an anachronism, so well has the composer caught the spirit of this lovely tune. But at the end of the century some fine tunes of this kind have been vulgarised by being given poor texts: *Good Christian men, rejoice* is unsuitably matched with the beauty of *In dulci jubilo* and *Good King Wenceslas*, a text in folk-ballad style, seems to be the poor relations of the *Piae Cantiones* melody to which it is usually sung. Christmas hymns like *Hark, the herald angels sing* or *Angels, from the realms of glory* are of course not carols in any sense of the word.

Standard collections of carols, as well as books like *Songs of Syon* which draw heavily on *Piae Cantiones* and German sources, reveal much attractive material that is far from hackneyed—not only for Christmas and Epiphany. It is a pity that we rarely hear more than the same two or three Easter carols.

Note added 1968:

To avoid mentioning a few of the many musicians who were his personal friends, Dr. Phillips wisely excluded comment upon living composers—even of that galaxy which had received early training from Stanford. A supplementary 'Since 1947' need not and should not apply that policy to composers aged over fifty. None of the famous Stanford pupils was permanently employed by the church and only two wrote church music of any value.

Their styles were so admired among their countrymen between
1920 and 1940 that they notably suffered from the reaction of
taste between 1940 and 1960, when the younger musicians and
critics complained of insularity and the unawareness in our
teaching institutions of the advances made by continental composers from *c.* 1920. Yet modish disparagement has been dis-
armed by the suitability of 'Englishry' for worship, especially as
seen in the work of Herbert Howells, b. 1892.

The doyen of the 'Stanford-trained' group (with Holst the most
unlike Stanford as a composer) was Vaughan Williams. Charac-
teristically he wrote little for cathedrals that does not sound just
as convincing when performed by enthusiastic amateurs in
villages or schools, yet the mention of his few liturgical settings,
along with two by John Ireland which are more recognisably in
cathedral tradition, in the R.S.C.M. 'recommended' list suggests
that they will remain in the repertory. Both these men provided a
few organ pieces for which parish musicians are grateful and both
left hymn-tunes which secure a wide appeal and yet elicit the
admiration of musicians—a feat much more rare than might be
supposed.

Howells, happily still composing, was the youngest of this
group and the only one whose experience as a cathedral chorister
gave him enviable insight into church music. He richly compen-
sates us for the paucity of church music by his contemporaries,
and posterity is unlikely to reproach him for not giving more time
to music for the theatre and concert hall which might forfeit much
in his unforcedly restrained muse, though he becomes rapturous
and colourful at points of climax. Indeed it is possible that the
fascination of liturgical composition brought a breadth, both of
total conception and of phrase and paragraph, to music which, if
allied with the action and changing atmosphere of opera, would
have been admirably nervous (in the best sense), colourful and
impassioned, but have served chiefly to show the effect upon a
scholarly English mind of Strauss, Debussy and other composers
of the early decades of our century. We can see this by comparing
some of the first 'Psalm Preludes' for organ with another early
work, the Evening Service in G major (surely one of the finest in
the whole repertory) and note the broad sweep of the phrasing in
the latter, even at the magnificent 'lead in' to *Gloria*; it certainly
does not lose by shunning some of the harmonic and rhythmic
intricacies which are essential to the organ pieces, and yet it is

thoroughly of this century and thoroughly unlike any setting by Stanford. Space does not allow comment upon Howells' many canticle settings dedicated to different anglican cathedrals and choral foundations, nor upon his longer choral and choral-orchestral settings of mystical verse from the popular *Here is the little door* to the difficult and ambitious *Hymnus Paradisi*; time must tell if those most in favour will remain so, but it is in no disparagement of British composers younger than Howells—Rubbra, Joubert, Britten and others—that one feels their settings of religious words, even if very strictly liturgical, to be very much more 'special' and 'occasional' than his. Scarcely any choral foundation or good parish choir is without at least some of Howells' music in its regular repertory.

Since 1947 many a cathedral organist or church musician who, unlike Howells, cannot claim to be wholly dedicated to composition has contributed securely to the repertory a number of settings and anthems which survive because they have something more than usefulness to commend them although their style of harmony is traditional. Among them may be mentioned Bullock, Darke, Harris, Lang, Ley, Macpherson, Oldroyd, Statham, Sumsion and Willan. The last named, who left England to serve notably in Canada, as well as the fact that music by others mentioned (for instance one of Oldroyd's settings of the communion office) is widely used overseas, brings to mind the importance since the last war of the exchanges of choirs, and of the mutual visits of church musicians between Great Britain and other countries that have been brought about chiefly by the ever-widening activities of the R.S.C.M.

Yet perhaps the fact that has most affected the actual music heard in churches has been the growth of communication by gramophone and radio, even television, and the consequent spread of musical knowledge—*what* is available as much as the standards possible with different resources. Copying and photographic processes, where breaches of copyright are not involved, have also played their part in widespread fertilisation, and should play an even bigger one. English church musicians who explore the riches of Schütz, Sweelinck, Bach, even Bruckner, for their choirs as well as their organs are those most likely to do justice to the English treasury.

38

MODERN ORGANS

TONAL ENSEMBLE

Most improvements in the organ have been made with a view to rendering the instrument easier to handle. In every generation there are, as one would expect, voicers who by general consent obtain results which defy analysis, and our own age is no different from others in this matter. Tone-creations by modern builders are worthy to rank beside those of Harris and Smith, or 'Father' Willis. Tonally, however, the best builders have been preoccupied in producing timbres which are not only good in themselves but which make for a pleasant ensemble. Gauntlett, a pioneer, working in collaboration with the builder Hill, did important work in extending the manual compass down to C and adding doubles and mixtures, about which there is still much controversy; this collaboration of player and builder has always been a useful feature of English organ building. Henry Willis (genius enough to be called by the church musicians' favourite term of approbation 'Father Willis') was pre-eminently successful in securing balance between the tone colour of individual ranks and the requirements of the ensemble. Both in Europe and America the last two decades have witnessed the building and rebuilding of organs to suit the performance of Bach and other baroque composers and realise, both in 'continuo' accompaniment and solo pieces, the effect they had in mind. The influence of this movement upon small church organs, making for good chorus work at all levels of dynamics, has been decidedly beneficial.

MANAGEABILITY

On the recommendation of the Royal College of Organists, London, standard measurements were adopted by all reputable firms for the console so that knees no longer knocked against the under edge of the manuals and one was no longer called upon to pedal underneath oneself, as it were. Foot pistons were made to reduplicate and supplement the finger pistons, the pistons themselves were made readily adjustable with regard to the stops drawn; balanced swell-pedals which would stay in any desired position and which were placed centrally over the pedalboard soon became standard on all important instruments.

PEDAL ORGANS

The most far-reaching improvement, which has had much effect on the technique of pedalling, was the making of radiating-concave boards with keys of standard width, their edges smooth and their surface with the right degree of 'slide' in them. Pedal playing was revolutionised; from being a rough and ready, uncertain toe and toe business which made for bustling work in scale passages it has become a matter of each foot providing six points of contact with the key—right, left and centre of toe and heel. Organists are, however, slow to adopt new methods and not only has no 'fingering' notation been devised for the new system but every existing tutor starts off by teaching the old toe and toe method first and relearning the new later.[1] Some continental organists still use the old system because their instruments have the old straight boards; for the same reason an assistant to manage their stops is a necessity at the consoles of French organs where the jambs are quite out of reach. But if English organs have improved their pedalboards, the pedal organs themselves, except in very large instruments, still lag far behind those of the continent in the variety of stops provided, so that the pedal couplers have almost always to be drawn.

EXTENSION AND BORROWING

Increasing costs and the prevalent poverty of many churches have forced builders to experiment, chiefly on smaller organs, with 'extension' and 'borrowing'. By 'borrowing' the same stop is made available on more than one manual so that on small instruments the player of soft voluntaries can, for example, get more simultaneous tone colours. It is hardly necessary on an organ of more than, say, twenty stops, though even here it enables one to use

---

[1] See *Systematic Organ Pedal Technique*, R. Goss Custard (*Stainer and Bell*) for an outline of one modern method, and *The Science of Organ Pedalling*, H. F. Ellingford and E. G. Meers (*Office of Musical Opinion*, 1928) for a full exposition of the subject. Dr. Phillips' own book on the subject is one of the most useful.

two stops on the Great in simultaneous contrast, supposing one is 'borrowed' on to the Choir. By 'extension' one rank of pipes is made to provide sixteen-, eight-, four-, and two-foot tone played from the same key, thus saving space and expense. It has many advocates for and against, but the question of expense usually overrides acoustical considerations. It should be noted that for accompanying the congregations in hymn-singing a good full-bodied diapason running right down to the bottom note is indispensable; if the provision of such a stop costs a large proportion of the available outlay, then borrowing with or without extension will provide the means of satisfying the second *raison d'être* of an organ—the player's voluntaries. Naturally, in a borrowed or extension organ the full organ cannot give the rich chorus tone of a straight instrument. The enclosure of the whole organ in swell boxes would of course supply additional variety but take the 'bite' off the *fortissimo*.

THE APPLICATION OF ELECTRICITY

As far back as the middle of last century Gauntlett was advocating the use of electrical contact between key and pallet. By this means, he argued, the console could be placed in any convenient position. A scheme which came to nothing was suggested whereby eight different organs placed in various parts of the Crystal Palace could be played from manuals set up in the central nave. Organists, as instrumentalists have ever done, set their faces against such new-fangled ideas, though Barker in 1868 took out a patent for an electric system and Bryceson managed to apply it to a few instruments. The real objection then was that electric power was not easy to come by. Willis, taking advantage perhaps of this, fitted to St. Paul's organ in 1874 a device which achieved much the same result, tubular-pneumatic action; this enabled him to transmit wind-pressure through flexible tubing over appreciable distances. His scheme has since been adopted in all large organs and in many smaller instruments. It was reliable and not only enabled the builder to place his pipes where he wanted them but allowed the player clearly to hear the result of his efforts by removing the console from the pipes.

Now that electric power is almost universally available the organ is rapidly becoming electrified. The advantages are many, the most useful of which is remote control, though full use is not always made of it. An octave or two of keys set in the choir of cathedrals for giving the chord when the anthem is unaccompanied has yet to appear; all large churches might with advantage have two consoles placed at different ends of the building for nave services, accompanied processions and so forth. The electric organ can be built on the spare-part principle where broken and worn parts are easily replaceable, the action can be accessible and visible under glass dust-covers, and takes up incredibly little space. Hope-Jones' invention of double touch has been little exploited in church organs, yet its advantages are obvious. Stop-tabs arranged as a keyboard above the manuals (they might well be reduplicated at the sides and between the manuals) have divided loyalty from players. Electric systems of blowing more and more supplant the old hand-, water-, and gas-driven methods, the most efficient being the rotary fan which maintains a constant wind-pressure. A minor difficulty has been the electrical transmission over long distances of a graduated crescendo, but the problem bids fair to have been successfully solved. The application of electric power to the organ has in fact transformed the mechanism and made the instrument less unwieldy, less extravagant of space, less costly in repair bills. It must always be remembered that an 'organ' is not just the mechanism and pipes; the building in which it is erected is acoustically part of it and the player is playing the building as much as the pipes.

'ELECTROPHONES'

Experiments in radio resulted in the invention of the 'electronic' organ, the various types of which may be classed together as 'electrophones'. In all these instruments the tone emanates from a loud-speaker diaphragm. By various means, which need not be described, an electric current is made and broken at a given frequency per second: these electrical impulses set up a vibration of equal frequency in the loud-speaker diaphragm (after being amplified) which gives off a pure note with few or no harmonics. Different timbres are then built up artificially to resemble the various types of organ stop, though it has not been found possible as yet to use enough artificial harmonics—which produce the different tone colours—to copy exactly a given pipe. Even if it becomes an economic possibility to do so, no diaphragm has yet been used which will vibrate in a wide enough range of frequencies;

no doubt the making of such a diaphragm (or set of diaphragms) will be merely a matter of time and experiment. These new instruments are as yet imperfect, and their distinctive tone has not been too favourably received. Its chief characteristics are an unusual suddenness or click in the 'coming on' of the tone and a kind of colourless purity with no 'edge' or 'drive', resembling the faded notes of a tuning fork. With the use of more harmonics this pure but dull tone should disappear, but history shows that instruments best improve when they cease to ape other instruments and develop their own characteristics. In fact, electrophones will claim serious attention when they stop imitating or claiming to be organs and boldly become themselves.

THEIR FUTURE

It is unlikely that they will replace organs. Like the piano and harmonium—and the regals before them—they may become useful substitutes with a character all their own. In other words a future in some musical milieu for the electrophone is no doubt assured, but its place in church is as yet a matter of experiment. All that dare be said is that, like the piano and harmonium, the electrophone is portable, cheap (though not cheap enough) to buy and run; it needs no tuning, but it might need replacement of burnt-out or broken valves. Its tone is pleasant enough up to the *mezzo forte* but at the *fortissimo* it seldom pleases the musician. It is, in fact, in the form we have it today, essentially a quiet instrument: the present size of its sound producer ensures that. It has solved many problems including the accompaniment of nave services and processions in cathedrals, portability and the utilisation of restricted space; one may even hope that a cheap practising model with earphones may one day become a useful part of the equipment of every organist. The technique of writing for it as a solo instrument has scarcely yet been tackled. Given half a century of development it may yet prove useful in church; one must always remember that Bach had little good to say of the pianos at Potsdam.

PART VI

AN ESSAY ON PRINCIPLES AND PRACTICE

1. PUBLIC WORSHIP

If worship may be described as the human response to the love of God, then any man who is aware of God's love is already in a worshipping attitude. But that is only the first step. Such a man may then envisage the myriad worshippers living, dead or unborn, the Communion of Saints. Only then can he seize the *raison d'être* of public worship, that pale reflection of the worshipping 'saints'. Our incarnate worship uses the things of this world—personalities, talents, churches, language, music, robes, incense; with those materials and a few models given us by the fathers of old and by our incarnate Lord we have constructed our own liturgies. Because man is not perfect, because his mind does not easily attain unsullied concentration, forms and patterns are as necessary in public as in private worship.

Worship demands more than will and thought; it demands imagination or 'heart'. The material setting of worship is thus important. Springing arches, stained glass, sacerdotal robes, music—all these quicken the vision of the worshipping man. By surrendering his own beloved personality to a bigger whole the individual is raised to higher efficacy; and that surrender in a public service is a picture of what must happen in his own life. Public worship, in fact, has repercussions in the human soul. The experience, faith and thanksgiving which are the bone and sinew of worship are given back, as it were, revitalised at a higher voltage. Worship thus becomes not only the natural reaction to God's love but an important factor in the psychological development of the worshipper. That development becomes stronger as the worship is more real: the worship is stronger as the attention of the whole man—body, emotions, mind, imagination—is centred on the idea of God.

It is with the object of securing and holding this all-important attention that liturgies and set forms of prayer are used. Set prayers, set acts bring back old associations and so serve to 'tune in' the mind and secure the attention.[1] The ceremonial acts of kneeling, processing, reading from different parts of the church and so forth help to hold the secured attention by change and variety. To worship God alone or 'in a field' or in an ugly church demands immense imagination; the well-ordered service helps the unimaginative back into his worshipping attitude. The worshipping attitude should ultimately become part of the warp and woof of daily life and the church 'service' is a kind of burning-glass focusing the 'life-service' into a communal act. Is it fanciful to suppose that a church which makes much of the social act of public worship will carry that social consciousness into the world outside to redress wrongs and succour the needy?

In the church service a man sinks his own self and becomes one of the myriads of beings who consciously and socially worship God—all the living, dead and yet to live, the saints 'above', the angels and archangels. He identifies himself with humanity and the angels and his consciousness is thereby raised to a higher level. But merely being present at a public service will not attain this end; to assure that he is making a given act of worship he must take part with his body and mind. He must actually say the creed, feel its emotional and intellectual import and rise to the meaning and vision of the lessons. The experienced worshipper can sometimes dispense with these acts because he has built up strong worshipping associations; thus he may listen to a musical setting of the creed and still identify himself with its intention. Congregations, like the men of whom they are composed, are at different points on the road to perfect worship—attainable only, presumably, in heaven. There the 'accidents' of worship are no doubt reduced to a minimum, but here on earth such worship is to most impossible. One congregation—as, for example, a 'Children's Church' or a street-corner meeting—will need to take an active part in almost every act of the service; a congregation of specialists, as for instance a monastery at its office, will need fewer stimuli.

The dangers inherent in public worship are many and obvious. It is indeed easy and natural to become enamoured of the means and so fail to proceed to the end in view. The musician will sense the musical beauty and lose the purpose; the actor will love the

---

[1] The old associations *may* be those of boredom and inattention; it is the worshipper's task to see that they are not. Hence the reformers of every century.

dressing-up, the sonorous language, the ceremonial movements and miss their import; the slothful will allow the sheer sonority of the prayers to drug him into an intellectual sleep; the ungodly will thrill to the service on Sunday and swindle his neighbour on Monday. Imagination alone can pierce the veil of sound and action and so enter the true temple where God is worshipped 'in spirit and in truth'. Those who plan public services must use every effort to help their congregations through the veil, and to see that they themselves when they have ministered to others fail not.

2. MUSIC AND THE APPARATUS OF WORSHIP

From experience men have found that music not only kindles the imagination but serves as the most practical vehicle of corporate utterance. No effort is needed to see how the imagination is lighted by music: we sense it in the cinema 'trailer', in the organ recital before the political meeting, in the band playing by the seaside. It is as easy to see how music makes a unique contribution to corporate expression. Few congregations can make a said *Pater Noster* sound inspired (it needs very little rehearsal really) but nearly all can attain unanimity in a response or a hymn. We may, in fact, state that as a general rule music, like all the other accidents of worship, is a necessity with congregations whose churchmanship is at the beginner's stage—for they need its kindling power. From the strictly practical point of view music becomes more of a necessity the larger the building and congregation, as it alone can ensure unanimity (the more frequent use of loud-speakers may, however, nullify this statement). At the 'low mass' alone music seems an intruder, for here the central acts of the service themselves provide stimulation. At the 'high mass' or 'sung eucharist' of the high churches, where the communion aspect of the service has given way to the sacrificial and worshipping side, music has an honoured and indeed necessary function.

That the church has always regarded music as an important part of its worship 'here below' is shown first by the work of Ambrose, Bishop of Milan, and Pope Gregory, and by the very nature of plainsong,[1] the music of the medieval church. These two men busied themselves with making musical collections and revisions and founding a musical tradition. Gregory's musical

[1] See pages 36–7.

counterpart of his liturgical work was not an afterthought. He recognised that the sung text was something potent; music then as now could alter the meaning and effect of the text to which it was set.[1] Gregory saw to it that the text was enhanced. The Genevan reformers sought also to regularise the sort of music sung as well as doctrines and forms, and as their reaction to the methods of worship in their day was dour and unimaginative so the music they allowed followed suit in the strait-laced metrical psalm-tunes; but it did not dawn on even the strict Calvin to ban music from the services. The Tridentine reformers at the end of the sixteenth century called the musicians to book for over-elaborating their contribution to the worship, but again had no thought of ousting choirs and organists. During the Restoration period in England the social aspect of public worship became, at the Chapel Royal at any rate, stronger than the God-fearing attitude essential to true worship, and the less worthy music followed suit: its joy deteriorated to joyfulness, its sorrows to operatic sentimentality, and the anthem became an item in a 'sacred' concert. But works like *Salvator mundi* of Blow, *Hear, O heavens* of Wise or *Thou knowest, Lord* of Purcell are great Christian works which add a deeper meaning to their texts and vindicate music; they show, too, a self-effacing sobriety which puts music into its true place in the service as a quickener of the spirit. And if further vindication were necessary one has but to think how much the spiritual experience of Christians would suffer from the lack of musical settings of the psalms and the finest hymns. Music is, indeed, part and parcel of the apparatus of earthly worship; without it our approach to the things of the Spirit would inevitably suffer.

Because of the power of music, especially on the uninitiated, the choosing and rendering of music are important matters. Performance of music, like the reading of lessons, must be within the competence of the performer. Though most people could read a parable well, it is not everyone who can read the finer lines of Isaiah, Paul or The Revelation. It is thus with psalms, hymns, anthems. Psalm 23 is easy and clear where Psalm 139 is deep in meaning. *While shepherds watched* tells a simple story where Myers' *Hark what a sound* is more highly imaginative, subtle and beautiful. Stanford's setting in B-flat of *Magnificat* is easy and

[1] Music gets 'under the skin', affects the subconscious and deeper or higher levels of a man more readily, perhaps, than any other art.

obvious while *Thou knowest, Lord* is a subtle commentary on a profound text. It will be seen that this has nothing to do with musical difficulty. A thousand choirs can sing the Stanford to one which can deliver the weighty words of the Purcell; it may be added that a thousand congregations can listen with understanding to the former to one which will seize the essence of the other. The choice itself—really an integral part of the worship—must be a matter of mutual aid and discussion between parson and musician; wise selection will be made only when each agrees to learn something of the other's outlook and when both set aside ample time each month to go fully into the points involved. Progress there must be, but more harm than good is done by casting pearls before swine.

Sincerity in the services will be achieved by thought and example, by teaching and by a care for the unity of theme in each service. But much can be done in the general planning which will at least remove some of the obstacles to reality. The treatment of latecomers, the orderly giving-out and collecting of books, the taking up of the alms, ringing of bells, playing of organs, the organisation of servers which does not deplete the small choir at important moments, the audibility of those who sing and read are all matters which have easy solutions. More difficult but as important are the community recitation and singing which can be dealt with by instruction, exhortation and rehearsal. Even lethargic congregations respond to enthusiasm in these matters. Small points like the unanimous utterance of Amens must be tackled, and the organist's voluntaries, like the music in general, can do much to make or mar; to prove that they are chosen with care they should find a place on the music list. It is hardly necessary to insist that the arrangements in the vestry must be clear and orderly and should not be the concern of the man at the organ who needs preparation for his important job: it is still less the job of the parson who should also be allowed freedom from petty worries in the moments before the service. Numbers of village churches, town churches, cathedrals have managed to make their organisation run so smoothly that the 'works' are never noticed, and if smooth running in itself is not worship at any rate it ensures that the atmosphere is one of freedom and lack of tension. An analogy may be found in amateur theatricals: if the lighting, scene-shifting and curtain are well managed that is half the battle. Poor acting may only mean that the play was badly chosen for the material to hand.

In church the stage-managing can be always good; a wise choice of music is of much help in attaining an adequate performance.

It has often been proved that given efficient and enthusiastic leaders even the remotest village choirs will produce excellent results. The fault of poor services lies more frequently in the handling than in the material. Organists and clergy alike must receive adequate training; the resultant zeal and mission-sense will overcome what look like insurmountable difficulties. But for choirs, organists and clergy adequate means must be forthcoming. In the business world the text 'cast thy bread upon the waters' is well understood: you risk one talent in advertising to gain ten talents in profit. Is it too much to suggest that the children of this world can instruct the children of light? Too often the choir is shoddily equipped with ugly, uncomfortable stalls, torn books, unmendable garments; the organ has long been out of date, the organist is paid a pittance. The result is shoddy worship, and so bad business. A church where these things are not so is seldom empty for, rightly or wrongly, bad music keeps people away or drives them elsewhere. Often the attitude to such conditions is that of the bad businessman: How can I improve without the means? The cart has been put before the horse; these things must somehow be improved before the means come, as come they will. A bold policy of this sort seldom errs. It is possible that by regrouping parishes, or establishing a central fund for repayable loans, or supplying a travelling musical leader in charge of a group of country or town churches and run perhaps by the diocese a solution will be found. A church which cares for its children must find a way of providing the means of worship.

3. PARSON AND MUSICIAN

A parson (I suppose) has two main tasks: that of saving souls and that of directing public worship. As director of worship he must perforce—it would seem—use music and must therefore be interested in music. He cannot normally be skilled in music and thus will have to trust those who have made church music their special job.

The artist who directs the music has first to recognise that his parson is not primarily interested in music. Music is merely one aspect of his direction of the worship. Too often in the eighteenth and early nineteenth centuries the cathedral organist strode the organ loft like a captain on his quarter-deck, regarding the church as his ship to use as he would and the parsons as so many nuisances: there are a hundred anecdotes to prove it. His artistry was often fine but his vision of Christian worship extremely limited. His colourful personality is still apt to make us approve of him. The modern cathedral organist is better fitted to his important job and if he has shed the anecdotal radiance he has at least a sincere appreciation of his work. But his task is easy compared with that of the parish church organist who cannot command cathedral resources and whose congregation must be considered as a vital element in the worshipping life of the church. Here is a job demanding certainly musical skill and artistry, but also a flair for public ceremonies, a knowledge of liturgical matters, a dynamic personality and careful social tact combined with teaching power.

It is as hard for a good parson to 'understand' a good artist as for a good artist to be able to share the point of view of a good parish priest. But if each has made some bid to study the other's job they can make a dynamic and invincible combination. Their common work includes first deciding on a liturgical and musical policy, having in view the type and level of the congregation and the resources at their command. For arriving at the right plan they will both need the experience not only of many types of church but also of liturgical and musical history. Thus the reforms of Gregory can teach them to have a clear policy, the sixteenth century will open to them the problems of congregational singing and show them the snares of over-elaborate music, while the Restoration will show them that the music must not create a purely 'social' service with music as the *bonne bouche*.

With a clear plan in their heads they can go ahead to map out their future progress, their teaching, the music of their ferials and festivals, the highlights of the year and of each service. They will no doubt adopt a monthly routine of meeting to work out the services so that each achieves a unity and the choir and congregation shall have both progressive and fallow, consolidating periods. They may plan choirless Sundays, congregational rehearsals, oratorio performances by an enlarged choir, times for teaching new principles, new hymns, new psalms, holiday arrangements, and so forth. They may even at times co-opt some discriminating member of the congregation and would certainly have the master of ceremonies at meetings where he was concerned. They would come to an agreement (not necessarily a lasting one) about the varied performance of hymns, about the thorny question of who shall sing the psalms—it need not always be the congregation or always the choir—and go through past achievements with a view to seeing what the next step is to be.

It is foolish to legislate for the future of congregational and choir music in our English churches. If the principles are clear and the leaders are creative the future of English church music is assured. A mistake in a church where congregations vary not only socially but in liturgical- and worship-sense would be uniformity. There will be a place for the unison choir, the choir which is unrobed and sits as part of the congregation, the normal surpliced choir. Central training schools will certainly be necessary for musicians and the system of providing peripatetic choirmasters may help to solve the difficulties in country districts. Perhaps from such a centre sections of a resident boys' choir would visit and help at the churches most in need, while interest would be stimulated and teaching given as at present in many dioceses by means of choir 'festival' services in the cathedrals and bigger churches and visiting services by sections of the cathedral choirs.[1] Future conditions may show that it is better to work by groups the size of a deanery than by isolated parishes, and it may be that such groups would best be formed not by one central authority but rather by diocesan organisation; a central authority, however, would find useful work to do in the shape of co-ordination, courses for choirmasters and general propaganda work. The gramophone and the piano will no doubt continue to be useful for teaching purposes or in isolated churches where there is no competent instructor, and new uses will doubtless be found for the radio and the cinema. There is, indeed, no end to the suggestions which might be made, for worship, if it is to be part of life here on earth, must always strive to be vital by using the everyday things which God has given and which the wit of man has devised.

Since the days a hundred years ago when surpliced choirs began to appear in every parish church and ape the cathedral choir, churchpeople have come to see that uniformity in worship is to be eschewed. Many now hope to see unity of doctrine and principles rather than uniformity of types and details. Uniformity with the past is no more attractive; in a world which is rapidly

---

[1] Since Dr. Phillips wrote this the R.S.C.M. may claim to have gone as far towards these desiderata as to setting high musical standards at its headquarters.

changing its basic ideas the living church will be keen to use the new creations of man in the service of God. New accompanying instruments, new shifts of population, new transport facilities, the radio, the television will foster new departures in public worship. There will be no danger of pollution if the first principles of worship are kept clear and the purpose of music is understood. If changed economics make us revise the details of our services let us trust that the new details will be painted in on a background of great ideas, not regretfully but joyfully in a creative way.

GENERAL BIBLIOGRAPHY

LITURGY

An Outline of Christian Worship, Maxwell (*O.U.P.*, 1936)
Worship and Theology in England (2 vols. No. 1 up to 1700),
    Davies (*Princeton*, 1965)
The Parson's Handbook, Dearmer (*O.U.P.*, 1965 edition revised
    by C. E. Pocknee)
Dictionary of the Christian Church, Cross (*O.U.P.*, 1965)
Liturgy and Worship, Hardman (*London Univ. Press*, 1957)
The Principles of Religious Ceremonial, Frere (*Mowbray*, 1928)

ENGLISH CHURCH HISTORY

Penguin History of the Church. The following two books already
    available:
    The Age of Reason, Cross
    The Age of Revolution, Vidler
Anglicanism in History and Today, Wand (*Weidenfeld & Nicolson*,
    1961)
History of the Modern Church, Wand (*O.U.P.*, 1947)
Anglicanism, Neill (*Penguin Books*, 1960)

PRAYER BOOK

The Story of the Prayer Book, Dearmer (*O.U.P.*, 1921)
A New History of the Book of Common Prayer, Procter and Frere
    (*Macmillan*, 1932)
The Book of Common Prayer, Harrison (*S.P.C.K.*, 1959)

THE PSALMS

The Psalms in Christian Worship, Lamb (*Faith Press*, 1967)
English and Scottish Psalm Tunes, Frost (*S.P.C.K.*, 1953)
The Revised Psalter (*S.P.C.K.*, 1963)
The Psalms in New Translation (*Fontana Books*, 1963)

HYMNS

Hymns Today and Tomorrow, Routley (*Libra Books*, 1966)
The Music of Christian Hymnody, Routley (*Independent Press*, 1957)
Historical Edition (1904) of *Hymns Ancient & Modern* (*Clowes*)
Songs of Syon (esp. Preface), Woodward (*Schott*)
(Refce.) *A Dictionary of Hymnology*, Julian (*Murray*, 1925)

MUSIC HISTORY

English Cathedral Music, Fellowes (*O.U.P.*, 1924)
A History of Music in England, Walker, revised Westrup (*O.U.P.*)
Voice and Verse, Colles (*O.U.P.*, 1928)
Music in the Baroque Era, Bukofzer (*Dent*, 1947)
Music and the Reformation in England, le Huray (*Jenkins*, 1964)
Church Music in the Nineteenth Century, Hutchings (*Jenkins*, 1967)
Twentieth Century Church Music, Routley (*Jenkins*, 1965)

PRACTICAL BOOKS

Masterpieces of Music before 1750 (Anthology), Parrish and Ohl (*Faber*, 1952)
Sixteenth Century Polyphony, Merritt (*O.U.P.*, 1948)
The Interpretation of Early Music, Donington (*Faber*, 1962)
The Training of Boys' Voices, Vale (*Faith Press*, 1952)
Choirs in Little Churches, Morgan (*Faith Press*, 1951)
Music in Village Churches, Morgan (*S.P.C.K.*, 1959)
The Parish Church Organ, Sumner (*R.S.C.M. Study Notes*)
One of the following is of the utmost importance for the church musician unless he possesses a complete set of *Grove*:
Harvard Dictionary of Music, Apel (*Foyle*, 1946)
Collins's Music Encyclopedia, Westrup and Harrison (*Collins*, 1960)

HISTORY CHART. I. PRE-REFORMATION

	CHURCH MUSIC HISTORY		SECULAR HISTORY
		27	Augustus Emperor
		54	
	60 Epistles and gospels—primitive service		
100		100	
	150 Justin Martyr—communion formalised		
200	Hippolytus—further formalisation of canon	200	
			Romans in Britain
300	Eastern influence—*cantus antiphonarius*, monasteries, hymns	300	
	313 Edict of Milan—Christianity the official religion of the Empire		
400	Ambrose of Milan—music collected, metrical hymns popularised	400	
			407
			449 English invasion
500		500	
			560 Ethelbert, king of Britain
	597 Augustine brought music to England		570 (Mahomet born)
600	Gregory—Schola Cantorum, liturgy and music codified	600	
			627 Edwin, king of Northumbria, a Christian
700		700	Christianity everywhere in Britain
			735 Venerable Bede died
			Beginnings of Feudal System
			793 Northmen's invasion
800	Organs at Aachen	800	Charlemagne Emperor
	852 Notker—proses and sequences		
			871 Alfred, king of Wessex (till 900)
900		900	
			911 Northmen to Normandy
	950 First experiments in organum		994 Danish invasion
1000	Beginnings of stave notation	1000	
	1030 Wipo—*Victimae Paschali*, leading to mystery plays		1003 Danish invasion
			1016 Canute
			1042 Edward the Confessor
	1050 Great Schism		1066 Norman invasion
			1095 First Crusade
1100		1100	
	1150 Adam de S. Victor—metrical sequence		
1200	Faux-bourdon, conductus	1200	1170 Thomas à Becket
	1215 'Sumer is i-cumen in'		1215 Magna Carta
1300	Musica Ficta, development of	1300	
1400	modern notation	1400	
			1415 Agincourt
	1450 Dunstable		1455 Wars of Roses
			1485 Bosworth—the Tudors
1500	Organs with keyboards	1500	

HISTORY CHART. II. SIXTEENTH CENTURY

SECULAR HISTORY

1509	Henry VIII (Tudor)
1534	King head of the church
1536	Spoliation of lesser monasteries (Greater, 1538, 1539)
1547	Edward VI (Protectorate)
1553	Mary (Catholic)
1558	Elizabeth
1588	Defeat of the Armada
1603	James I (Stuart)
1604	Millenary Petition and Hampton Court Conference
1625	Charles I

Date axis: 1500 · 1510 · 1520 · 1530 · 1540 · 1550 · 1560 · 1570 · 1580 · 1590 · 1600 · 1610 · 1620 · 1630

COMPOSERS

Composer	Span
Redford	1485?–1545
Tye	1500?–1573
R. Farrant	?–1580
Tallis	1505–1585
Byrd	1543–1623
Weelkes	1575–1623
Gibbons	1583–1625

CHURCH MUSIC HISTORY

1538	Chained bibles in English
1541	Bourgeois in Geneva (till 1557)
1542	Clément Marot's first Psalms
1544	Cranmer's litany
1548	Order of Communion
1549	First English Prayer Book
	Merbecke's *Booke of Common Praier Noted*
1552	Second Prayer Book
1559	Elizabeth's Prayer Book
	Day's *Certaine Notes*
1562	Sternhold and Hopkins' *Standard Edition* (Old Version)
	Marot and Béza Whole Psalter
1575	*Cantiones Sacrae* (Tallis and Byrd)
1592	Este's *Whole Book of Psalms*
1597	Morley's *Plaine and Easie Introduction*
1605 1607	Byrd's Latin *Gradualia*
1623	Wither-Gibbons' *Hymns of the Church*

HISTORY CHART. III. SEVENTEENTH CENTURY

CHURCH MUSIC HISTORY		COMPOSERS		SECULAR HISTORY
Verse-anthems and accompanied music	1600		1600	
			1603	James I (Stuart)
			1604	Millenary Petition and Hampton Court Conference
			1605	Guy Fawkes
	1610		1610	
	1620		1620	
Byrd and Weelkes died	1623			
Gibbons died	1625		1625	Charles I
Figured bass accompaniments	1630		1630	
Scottish Prayer Book	1637			
	1640		1640	
Barnard's Collection	1641		1642	Civil War began
Westminster Assembly overthrows the church	1643			
Directory of Public Worship	1645		1649	Commonwealth
	1650		1650	
			1653	Cromwell Protector
				Charles II. Bunyan in prison
Anglican chant	1661		1660	
Cooke's Chapel Royal choir				
Lowe's *A Short Direction*				
Prayer Book	1662			
Clifford's Collection of anthem words	1663			
Clifford's *Brief Directions*	1664		1666	Fire of London
Harris and Father Smith organs				
	1670		1670	
Playford's *Psalms and Hymns*	1671			
Playford's *Whole Book of Psalms*	1677		1680	
	1680		1685	James II. Huguenots in England
Church of Scotland disestablished	1688		1689	William and Mary
	1690		1690	
New Version—Tate and Brady	1696		1697	New St. Paul's
	1700		1700	
Playford's *David's Harp New Tun'd*	1701		1702	Anne
Handel comes to England				
	1710		1710	
	1720		1714	George I (Hanover)
			1720	

Composers (date ranges):

- H. Lawes: 1595–1662
- Child: 1606–1697
- Rogers: 1614–1698
- Locke: 1630–1677
- Humfrey: 1647–1674
- Blow: 1648–1708
- Wise: 1648–1687
- Purcell: 1659–1695

HISTORY CHART. IV. CROFT TO WESLEY

CHURCH MUSIC HISTORY

1700	Gallery choirs and orchestras
1710	Handel comes to England
1731	Scottish Prayer Book adopted
1739	Wesleys' 'Foundery' established at Moorfields
1748	Death of Watts (born 1674)
1761	Boyce's *Cathedral Music*
1788	Charles Wesley died (born 1707)
1789	American Liturgy
	Arnold's Collection
1791	John Wesley died (born 1703)
1833	Hymn legally established
	Keble's sermon (Oxford Movement)
1841	*Sacred Hymns from the German*
1847	Rimbault
1852	Convocation reformed
1856	S. Michael's, Tenbury
	Organs and surpliced choirs in parish churches
1861	*Hymns Ancient and Modern*
1863	*Chorale Book for England*
1866	Neale died (born 1818)
1871	Minor revisions to the Prayer Book

COMPOSERS

Composer	Dates
Croft	1678–1727
Greene	1695–1755
Boyce	1710–1779
Battishill	1738–1801
Attwood	1765–1838
Goss	1800–1880
Wesley	1810–1876
Walmisley	1814–1856
Ouseley	1825–1889
Stainer	1840–1901

SECULAR HISTORY

1702	Anne
1714	George I (Hanover)
1727	George II
1742	Handel's 'Messiah'
	Bach died
1760	George III
1761	Canals constructed
1769	Watt, Hargreaves, Arkwright
1783	First Sunday School
1789	French Revolution
	Mozart, Haydn
	Beethoven
1815	Waterloo
1819	Atlantic crossed by steam
1820	George IV
1830	William IV
1833	First railway passenger line
1837	Victoria
1847	Mendelssohn died
1876	Liszt, Wagner
	Compulsory education

HISTORY CHART. V. SINCE 1871

CHURCH MUSIC HISTORY		COMPOSERS	SECULAR HISTORY	
1850		1850		1850
1852	Convocation reformed			
1856	S. Michael's, Tenbury	Stanford 1852 —		
1860		1860		1860
1861	Organs and surpliced choirs in parish churches			
1863	*Hymns Ancient and Modern* / *Chorale Book for England*			
1870		1870	Liszt, Wagner	1870
1871	Minor revisions to the Prayer Book	Wood 1866 —		
1880		1880	'Trial by Jury' (Sullivan)	1875
			Compulsory education / 'Prometheus Unbound' (Parry)	1876
1890		1890		1880 / 1890
1891	*Cathedral Prayer Book*			
1899	*Yattendon Hymnal*			
1900		1900	Board schools—free education	1896
1904	*A. & M.* revision / *Songs of Syon*		Gramophones / Edward VII / National music	1901
1906	*English Hymnal*			1900
1910		1910		1910
1916	*A. & M.* second supplement		George V / World War I	1914
1919	Volume I of *Tudor Church Music* / Church in Wales disestablished			
1920		1920 (Stanford 1924)	Radio telephony	1920
1922	Report of Archbishops' Committee *Music in Worship*		Broadcasting	
1925	*Songs of Praise* (enlarged edition 1931)			
1927	School of English Church Music (renamed Royal School of Church Music 1945)	Wood 1926		
1928	Revision of Prayer Book (not sanctioned by parliament), *Oxford Book of Carols*			
1929	School of English Church Music / Electrophones			
1930		1930	Edward VIII	1937
			George VI	1938
			World War II	1939
1940		1940		1940
1951	*Musica Britannica* founded (still being issued)		Elizabeth II	1953

HISTORY CHART. VI. GENERAL

		CHURCH MUSIC HISTORY			SECULAR HISTORY
100			100		Romans in Britain
	150	Formalisation of Communion			
200			200		
300		Influence of east: *Cantus Antiphonarius,* hymns, monasteries, hours of prayer	300		
	313	Edict of Milan—Christianity the established religion			
400		Ambrose—metrical hymns	400		
				407	Romans leave Britain
					Invasions of England begin
500			500		
	597	Augustine came to England			
600		Gregory—liturgy and music codified	600		
700		Christianity everywhere in England	700		
800		Organs at Aachen	800		Charlemagne
	852	Notker—proses and sequences			Feudal System
900			900		
	950	Organum: first experiments			
1000		Stave notation	1000		
	1050	Great Schism		1066	Norman invasion
1100		End of best plainsong	1100		
	1150	Adam de S. Victor: metrical sequences			
1200		Faux-bourdon, conductus	1200		
				1215	Magna Carta
1300		Musica Ficta	1300		Mystery plays
1400		Improvements in organs	1400		Carols and folk-music
	1450	Dunstable			
				1492	Columbus
1500			1500		
	1549	First English Prayer Book		1536	Monasteries disestablished
					End of feudalism
1600		Polyphonic school: psalm-tunes	1600		
	1649	Commonwealth: no services			
	1660	Anglican chant: Restoration school			
1700		English hymn: gallery choirs	1700		Bach, Handel
1800			1800		Viennese composers
	1850	Parish church surpliced choirs			
				1876	Compulsory education
					National music
1900		Musical recovery in England	1900		
		Electricity applied to the organ			

GENERAL INDEX

INDEX TO MUSIC EXAMPLES